Forces and Energy

interactive SCIENCE

PEARSON

Boston, Massachusetts
Chandler, Arizona
Glenview, Illinois
Upper Saddle River, New Jersey

You're an author!

As you write in this science book, your answers and personal discoveries will be recorded for you to keep, making this book unique to you. That is why you are one of the primary authors of this book.

✏️ **In the space below, print your name, school, town, and state. Then write a short autobiography that includes your interests and accomplishments.**

YOUR NAME _____

SCHOOL _____

TOWN, STATE _____

AUTOBIOGRAPHY _____

_____

_____

_____

_____

_____

_____

Your Photo

Acknowledgments appear on pages 246–247, which constitutes an extension of this copyright page.

ISBN-13: 978-0-13-368480-3
ISBN-10: 0-13-368480-6
1 2 3 4 5 6 7 8 9 10 V063 13 12 11 10 09

ON THE COVER
Causing Motion
Did you know that you use the principles of physics whenever you play a sport? To control the motion of an object, you have to apply force. Force allows you to change the speed or direction of an object, like this soccer ball, so that it goes where you need it to go.

Program Authors

DON BUCKLEY, M.Sc.
Information and Communications Technology Director, The School at Columbia University, New York, New York
Mr. Buckley has been at the forefront of K–12 educational technology for nearly two decades. A founder of New York City Independent School Technologists (NYCIST) and long-time chair of New York Association of Independent Schools' annual IT conference, he has taught students on two continents and created multimedia and Internet-based instructional systems for schools worldwide.

ZIPPORAH MILLER, M.A.Ed.
Associate Executive Director for Professional Programs and Conferences, National Science Teachers Association, Arlington, Virginia
Associate executive director for professional programs and conferences at NSTA, Ms. Zipporah Miller is a former K–12 science supervisor and STEM coordinator for the Prince George's County Public School District in Maryland. She is a science education consultant who has overseen curriculum development and staff training for more than 150 district science coordinators.

MICHAEL J. PADILLA, Ph.D.
Associate Dean and Director, Eugene P. Moore School of Education, Clemson University, Clemson, South Carolina
A former middle school teacher and a leader in middle school science education, Dr. Michael Padilla has served as president of the National Science Teachers Association and as a writer of the National Science Education Standards. He is professor of science education at Clemson University. As lead author of the *Science Explorer* series, Dr. Padilla has inspired the team in developing a program that promotes student inquiry and meets the needs of today's students.

KATHRYN THORNTON, Ph.D.
Professor and Associate Dean, School of Engineering and Applied Science, University of Virginia, Charlottesville, Virginia
Selected by NASA in May 1984, Dr. Kathryn Thornton is a veteran of four space flights. She has logged over 975 hours in space, including more than 21 hours of extravehicular activity. As an author on the *Scott Foresman Science* series, Dr. Thornton's enthusiasm for science has inspired teachers around the globe.

MICHAEL E. WYSESSION, Ph.D.
Associate Professor of Earth and Planetary Science, Washington University, St. Louis, Missouri
An author on more than 50 scientific publications, Dr. Wysession was awarded the prestigious Packard Foundation Fellowship and Presidential Faculty Fellowship for his research in geophysics. Dr. Wysession is an expert on Earth's inner structure and has mapped various regions of Earth using seismic tomography. He is known internationally for his work in geoscience education and outreach.

Understanding by Design Author

GRANT WIGGINS, Ed.D.
President, Authentic Education, Hopewell, New Jersey
Dr. Wiggins is coauthor of *Understanding by Design®* (UbD), a philosophy of instructional design. UbD is a disciplined way of thinking about curriculum design, assessment, and instruction that moves teaching from covering the content to ensuring understanding. Dr. Wiggins is one of today's most influential educational reformers, and consults with schools, districts, and state education departments.

Planet Diary Author

JACK HANKIN
Science/Mathematics Teacher, The Hilldale School, Daly City, California Founder, Planet Diary Web site
Mr. Hankin is the creator and writer of Planet Diary, a science current events Web site. Mr. Hankin is passionate about bringing science news and environmental awareness into classrooms. He's offered numerous Planet Diary workshops at NSTA and other events to train middle school and high school teachers.

ELL Consultant

JIM CUMMINS, Ph.D.
Professor and Canada Research Chair, Curriculum, Teaching and Learning department at the University of Toronto
Dr. Cummins's research focuses on literacy development in multilingual schools and the role of technology in promoting student learning across the curriculum. The *Interactive Science* program incorporates essential research-based principles for integrating language with the teaching of academic content based on Dr. Cummins's instructional framework.

Reading Consultant

HARVEY DANIELS, Ph.D.
Professor of Secondary Education, University of New Mexico, Albuquerque, New Mexico
Dr. Daniels serves as an international consultant to schools, districts, and educational agencies. Dr. Daniels has authored or coauthored 13 books on language, literacy, and education. His most recent works include *Comprehension and Collaboration: Inquiry Circles in Action* and *Subjects Matter: Every Teacher's Guide to Content-Area Reading*.

Contributing Writers

Edward Aguado, Ph.D.
Professor, Department of Geography
San Diego State University
San Diego, California

Elizabeth Coolidge-Stolz, M.D.
Medical Writer
North Reading, Massachusetts

Donald L. Cronkite, Ph.D.
Professor of Biology
Hope College
Holland, Michigan

Jan Jenner, Ph.D.
Science Writer
Talladega, Alabama

Linda Cronin Jones, Ph.D.
Associate Professor of Science and Environmental Education
University of Florida
Gainesville, Florida

T. Griffith Jones, Ph.D.
Clinical Associate Professor of Science Education
College of Education
University of Florida
Gainesville, Florida

Andrew C. Kemp, Ph.D.
Teacher
Jefferson County Public Schools
Louisville, Kentucky

Matthew Stoneking, Ph.D.
Associate Professor of Physics
Lawrence University
Appleton, Wisconsin

R. Bruce Ward, Ed.D.
Senior Research Associate
Science Education Department
Harvard-Smithsonian Center for Astrophysics
Cambridge, Massachusetts

Content Reviewers

Paul D. Beale, Ph.D.
Department of Physics
University of Colorado at Boulder
Boulder, Colorado

Jeff R. Bodart, Ph.D.
Professor of Physical Sciences
Chipola College
Marianna, Florida

Joy Branlund, Ph.D.
Department of Earth Science
Southwestern Illinois College
Granite City, Illinois

Marguerite Brickman, Ph.D.
Division of Biological Sciences
University of Georgia
Athens, Georgia

Bonnie J. Brunkhorst, Ph.D.
Science Education and Geological Sciences
California State University
San Bernardino, California

Michael Castellani, Ph.D.
Department of Chemistry
Marshall University
Huntington, West Virginia

Charles C. Curtis, Ph.D.
Research Associate Professor of Physics
University of Arizona
Tucson, Arizona

Diane I. Doser, Ph.D.
Department of Geological Sciences
University of Texas
El Paso, Texas

Rick Duhrkopf, Ph.D.
Department of Biology
Baylor University
Waco, Texas

Alice K. Hankla, Ph.D.
The Galloway School
Atlanta, Georgia

Mark Henriksen, Ph.D.
Physics Department
University of Maryland
Baltimore, Maryland

Chad Hershock, Ph.D.
Center for Research on Learning and Teaching
University of Michigan
Ann Arbor, Michigan

Jeremiah N. Jarrett, Ph.D.
Department of Biology
Central Connecticut State University
New Britain, Connecticut

Scott L. Kight, Ph.D.
Department of Biology
Montclair State University
Montclair, New Jersey

Jennifer O. Liang, Ph.D.
Department of Biology
University of Minnesota–Duluth
Duluth, Minnesota

Candace Lutzow-Felling, Ph.D.
Director of Education
The State Arboretum of Virginia
University of Virginia
Boyce, Virginia

Cortney V. Martin, Ph.D.
Virginia Polytechnic Institute
Blacksburg, Virginia

Joseph F. McCullough, Ph.D.
Physics Program Chair
Cabrillo College
Aptos, California

Heather Mernitz, Ph.D.
Department of Physical Science
Alverno College
Milwaukee, Wisconsin

Sadredin C. Moosavi, Ph.D.
Department of Earth and Environmental Sciences
Tulane University
New Orleans, Louisiana

David L. Reid, Ph.D.
Department of Biology
Blackburn College
Carlinville, Illinois

Scott M. Rochette, Ph.D.
Department of the Earth Sciences
SUNY College at Brockport
Brockport, New York

Karyn L. Rogers, Ph.D.
Department of Geological Sciences
University of Missouri
Columbia, Missouri

Laurence Rosenhein, Ph.D.
Department of Chemistry
Indiana State University
Terre Haute, Indiana

Sara Seager, Ph.D.
Department of Planetary Sciences and Physics
Massachusetts Institute of Technology
Cambridge, Massachusetts

Tom Shoberg, Ph.D.
Missouri University of Science and Technology
Rolla, Missouri

Patricia Simmons, Ph.D.
North Carolina State University
Raleigh, North Carolina

William H. Steinecker, Ph.D.
Research Scholar
Miami University
Oxford, Ohio

Paul R. Stoddard, Ph.D.
Department of Geology and Environmental Geosciences
Northern Illinois University
DeKalb, Illinois

John R. Villarreal, Ph.D.
Department of Chemistry
The University of Texas–Pan American
Edinburg, Texas

John R. Wagner, Ph.D.
Department of Geology
Clemson University
Clemson, South Carolina

Jerry Waldvogel, Ph.D.
Department of Biological Sciences
Clemson University
Clemson, South Carolina

Donna L. Witter, Ph.D.
Department of Geology
Kent State University
Kent, Ohio

Edward J. Zalisko, Ph.D.
Department of Biology
Blackburn College
Carlinville, Illinois

Museum of Science.

Special thanks to the Museum of Science, Boston, Massachusetts, and Ioannis Miaoulis, the Museum's president and director, for serving as content advisors for the technology and design strand in this program.

v

 Enter the Lab zone for hands-on inquiry.

△ **Chapter Lab Investigation:**
  • Directed Inquiry: Stopping on a Dime
  • Open Inquiry: Stopping on a Dime

△ **Inquiry Warm-Ups:** • What Is Motion?
  • How Fast and How Far? • Will You Hurry Up?

△ **Quick Labs:** • Identifying Motion • Velocity
  • Motion Graphs • Describing Acceleration
  • Graphing Acceleration

my science online.com

Go to MyScienceOnline.com to interact with this chapter's content. Keyword: Motion

> **UNTAMED SCIENCE**
• The Adventures of Velocity Girl

> **PLANET DIARY**
• Motion

> **INTERACTIVE ART**
• Speed and Acceleration

> **INTERACTIVE ART**
• Graphing Motion

> **ART IN MOTION**
• Relative Motion

> **VIRTUAL LAB**
• How Can You Measure Acceleration?

Lab zone® Enter the Lab zone for hands-on inquiry.

Chapter Lab Investigation:
• Directed Inquiry: Sticky Sneakers
• Open Inquiry: Sticky Sneakers

Inquiry Warm-Ups: • Is the Force With You?
• Observing Friction • What Changes Motion?
• How Pushy Is a Straw? • What Makes an
Object Move in a Circle?

Quick Labs: • What Is Force? • Modeling
Unbalanced Forces • Calculating • Around and
Around • Newton's Second Law • Interpreting
Illustrations • Colliding Cars • Which Lands
First? • Orbiting Earth

my science online.com

Go to MyScienceOnline.com to
interact with this chapter's content.
Keyword: **Forces**

> **UNTAMED SCIENCE**
• Sir Isaac Visits the Circus

> **PLANET DIARY**
• Forces

> **INTERACTIVE ART**
• Balanced and Unbalanced Forces
• Conservation of Momentum

> **ART IN MOTION**
• Types of Friction

> **VIRTUAL LAB**
• Investigating Newton's Laws of Motion

Enter the Lab zone for hands-on inquiry.

Chapter Lab Investigation:
• Directed Inquiry: Angling for Access
• Open Inquiry: Angling for Access

Inquiry Warm-Ups: • Pulling at an Angle
• Is It a Machine? • Inclined Planes and Levers
• Machines That Turn

Quick Labs: • What Is Work? • Investigating
Power • Going Up • Mechanical Advantage
• Friction and Efficiency • Modeling Levers
• Building Pulleys • Machines in the Kitchen

my science online.com

Go to MyScienceOnline.com to
interact with this chapter's content.
Keyword: Work and Machines

> **UNTAMED SCIENCE**
• Remodeling Stonehenge

> **PLANET DIARY**
• Work and Machines

> **INTERACTIVE ART**
• Types of Pulleys • Work

> **ART IN MOTION**
• Levers

> **REAL-WORLD INQUIRY**
• Bicycle Racing and Efficiency

Enter the Lab zone for hands-on inquiry.

Chapter Lab Investigation:
• Directed Inquiry: Can You Feel the Power?
• Open Inquiry: Can You Feel the Power?

Inquiry Warm-Ups: • How High Does a Ball Bounce? • What Makes a Flashlight Shine? • What Would Make a Card Jump?

Quick Labs: • Mass, Velocity, and Kinetic Energy • Determining Mechanical Energy • Sources of Energy • Soaring Straws • Law of Conservation of Energy

my science online.com

Go to MyScienceOnline.com to interact with this chapter's content.
Keyword: Energy

> **UNTAMED SCIENCE**
• The Potential for Fun

> **PLANET DIARY**
• Energy

> **ART IN MOTION**
• Kinetic and Potential Energy

> **INTERACTIVE ART**
• Types of Energy

> **INTERACTIVE ART**
• Energy Transformations

> **VIRTUAL LAB**
• Exploring Potential and Kinetic Energy

CHAPTER 5

Thermal Energy and Heat

 The Big Question **132**
How does heat flow from one object to another?

Vocabulary Skill: Identify Multiple Meanings 134
Reading Skills 135

Lab® zone Enter the Lab zone for hands-on inquiry.

△ **Chapter Lab Investigation:**
• Directed Inquiry: Build Your Own Thermometer
• Open Inquiry: Build Your Own Thermometer

△ **Inquiry Warm-Ups:** • How Cold Is the Water? • What Does It Mean to Heat Up?
• Thermal Properties

△ **Quick Labs:** • Temperature and Thermal Energy • Visualizing Convection Currents
• Frosty Balloons

my science online.com

Go to MyScienceOnline.com to interact with this chapter's content.
Keyword: Thermal Energy and Heat

> **UNTAMED SCIENCE**
• Why Is This Inner Tube So Hot?

> **PLANET DIARY**
• Thermal Energy and Heat

> **INTERACTIVE ART**
• Heat Transfer

> **ART IN MOTION**
• Temperature and Thermal Energy
• Conductors and Insulators

> **VIRTUAL LAB**
• Temperature or Heat? What's the Difference?

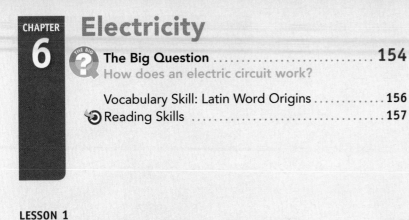

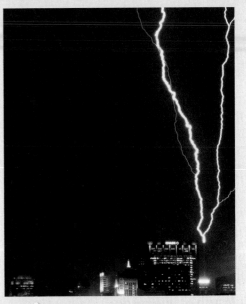

Lab zone® Enter the Lab zone for hands-on inquiry.

Chapter Lab Investigation:
• Directed Inquiry: Build a Flashlight
• Open Inquiry: Build a Flashlight

Inquiry Warm-Ups: • Can You Move a Can Without Touching It? • How Can Current Be Measured? • Do the Lights Keep Shining? • How Can You Make a Bulb Burn More Brightly?

Quick Labs: • Drawing Conclusions • Sparks Are Flying • Producing Electric Current • Conductors and Insulators • Modeling Potential Difference • Ohm's Law • Calculating Electric Power and Energy Use • Electric Shock and Short Circuit Safety

my science online.com

Go to MyScienceOnline.com to interact with this chapter's content. Keyword: **Electricity**

▶ PLANET DIARY
• Electricity

▶ INTERACTIVE ART
• Series and Parallel Circuits • Current Flow

▶ ART IN MOTION
• Static Charge

▶ VIRTUAL LAB
• Discovering Ohm's Law

▶ REAL-WORLD INQUIRY
• Energy Conservation

 Enter the Lab zone for hands-on inquiry.

Chapter Lab Investigation:
• Directed Inquiry: Detecting Fake Coins
• Open Inquiry: Detecting Fake Coins

Inquiry Warm-Ups: • Natural Magnets
• Predict the Field • Electromagnetism • How
Are Electricity, Magnets, and Motion Related?
• Electric Current Without a Battery

Quick Labs: • Magnetic Poles • Spinning
in Circles • Earth's Magnetic Field • Electric
Current and Magnetism • Magnetic Fields
From Electric Current • Electromagnet • Can a
Magnet Move a Wire? • How Galvanometers
Work • Parts of an Electric Motor • Inducing
an Electric Current • How Generators Work
• How Transformers Work

my science online.com

Go to MyScienceOnline.com to
interact with this chapter's content.
Keyword: Magnetism and
Electromagnetism

> **PLANET DIARY**
• Magnetism and Electromagnetism

> **INTERACTIVE ART**
• Magnetic Fields • Motors and Generators

> **ART IN MOTION**
• Maglev Train

> **REAL-WORLD INQUIRY**
• Exploring Electromagnetism

Video Series: Chapter Adventures

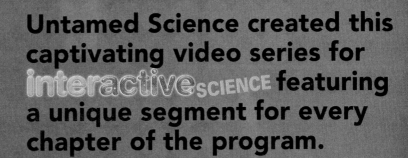

Untamed Science created this captivating video series for *interactive* SCIENCE featuring a unique segment for every chapter of the program.

Featuring videos such as

The Adventures of Velocity Girl
Chapter 1 The Untamed Science crew explains how a roller coaster demonstrates the concepts of motion.

Sir Isaac Visits the Circus
Chapter 2 The crew meets circus troupers who *flip* for the basic laws of motion.

Remodeling Stonehenge
Chapter 3 Join the crew and one big lever as they do some heavy lifting.

The Potential for Fun
Chapter 4 The crew explores the energy transformations in snowboarding.

Why Is This Inner Tube So Hot?
Chapter 5 The crew learns how to heat things up and how to keep things cool!

Shining Some Light on Lightning
Chapter 6 A physicist teaches the crew about lightning and electricity.

Magnetism: What's the Attraction?
Chapter 7 Learn how to levitate by riding a maglev train.

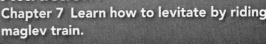

interactive SCIENCE

This is your book. You can write in it!

Get Engaged!

At the start of each chapter, you will see two questions: an Engaging Question and the Big Question. Each chapter's Big Question will help you start thinking about the Big Ideas of Science. Look for the Big Q symbol throughout the chapter!

HOW CAN WIND KEEP YOUR LIGHTS ON?

THE BIG ? What are some of Earth's energy sources?

This man is repairing a wind turbine at a wind farm in Texas. Most wind turbines are at least 30 meters off the ground where the winds are fast. Wind speed and blade length help determine the best way to capture the wind and turn it into power. Develop Hypotheses Why do you think people are working to increase the amount of power we get from wind?

Wind energy collected by the turbine does not cause air pollution.

▶ UNTAMED SCIENCE Watch the Untamed Science video to learn more about energy resources.

174 Energy Resources

my scie

Untamed Science™

Follow the Untamed Science video crew as they travel the globe exploring the Big Ideas of Science.

Interact with your textbook.   **Interact with inquiry.**   **Interact online.**

Build Reading, Inquiry, and Vocabulary Skills

In every lesson you will learn new ↻ Reading and ▲ Inquiry skills. These skills will help you read and think like a scientist. Vocabulary skills will help you communicate effectively and uncover the meaning of words.

Go Online!

Look for the MyScienceOnline.com technology options. At MyScienceOnline.com you can immerse yourself in amazing virtual environments, get extra practice, and even blog about current events in science.

Explore the Key Concepts.

Each lesson begins with a series of Key Concept questions. The interactivities in each lesson will help you understand these concepts and Unlock the Big Question.

my planet Diary

At the start of each lesson, My Planet Diary will introduce you to amazing events, significant people, and important discoveries in science or help you to overcome common misconceptions about science concepts.

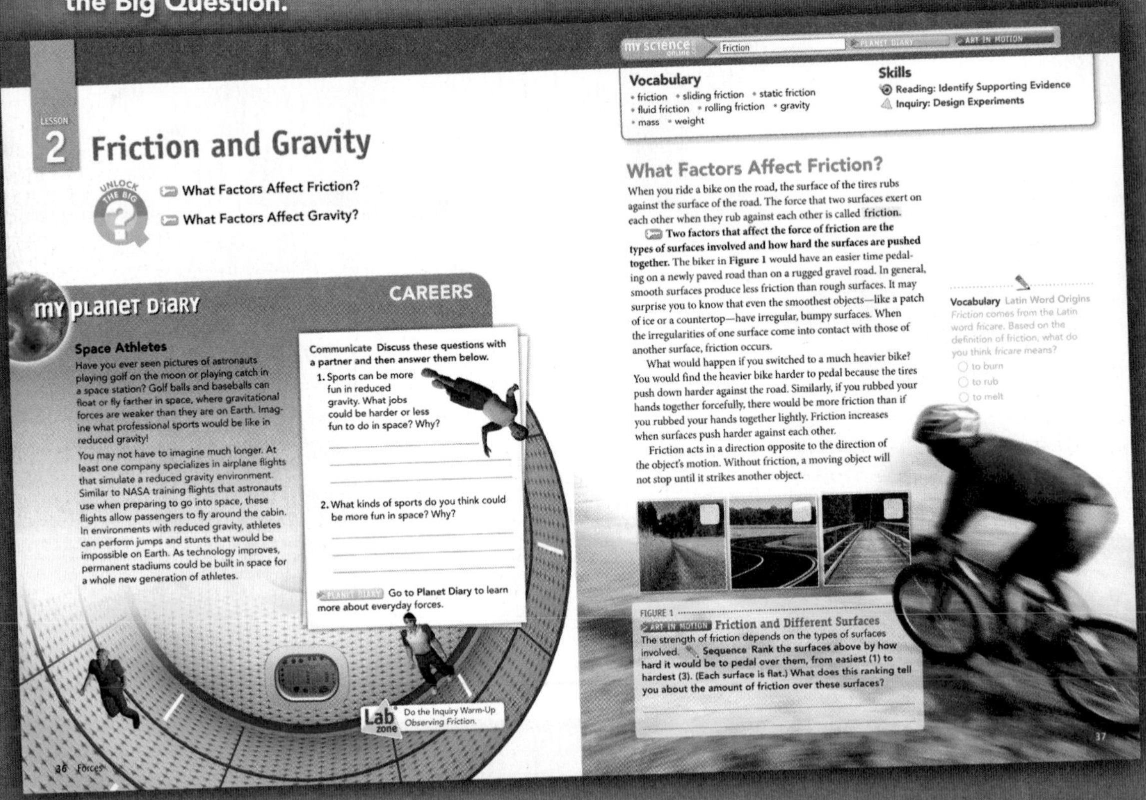

Desertification If the soil in a of moisture and nutrients, the are advance of desertlike conditions i fertile is called **desertification** (d

One cause of desertification is is a period when less rain than no droughts, crops fail. Without plan blows away. Overgrazing of grassl cutting down trees for firewood c

Desertification is a serious pro and graze livestock where desertif people may face famine and starv central Africa. Millions of rural pe cities because they can no longer

LESSON 2 — Friction and Gravity

- What Factors Affect Friction?
- What Factors Affect Gravity?

my planet Diary — CAREERS

Space Athletes

Have you ever seen pictures of astronauts playing golf on the moon or playing catch in a space station? Golf balls and baseballs can float or fly farther in space, where gravitational forces are weaker than they are on Earth. Imagine what professional sports would be like in reduced gravity!

You may not have to imagine much longer. At least one company specializes in airplane flights that simulate a reduced gravity environment. Similar to NASA training flights that astronauts use when preparing to go into space, these flights allow passengers to fly around the cabin. In environments with reduced gravity, athletes can perform jumps and stunts that would be impossible on Earth. As technology improves, permanent stadiums could be built in space for a whole new generation of athletes.

Communicate Discuss these questions with a partner and then answer them below.

1. Sports can be more fun in reduced gravity. What jobs could be harder or less fun to do in space? Why?

2. What kinds of sports do you think could be more fun in space? Why?

> PLANET DIARY Go to Planet Diary to learn more about everyday forces.

Lab zone Do the Inquiry Warm-Up Observing Friction.

46 Forces

my science — Friction — PLANET DIARY — ART IN MOTION

Vocabulary
- friction • sliding friction • static friction
- fluid friction • rolling friction • gravity
- mass • weight

Skills
- Reading: Identify Supporting Evidence
- Inquiry: Design Experiments

What Factors Affect Friction?

When you ride a bike on the road, the surface of the tires rubs against the surface of the road. The force that two surfaces exert on each other when they rub against each other is called **friction**.

Two factors that affect the force of friction are the types of surfaces involved and how hard the surfaces are pushed together. The biker in **Figure 1** would have an easier time pedaling on a newly paved road than on a rugged gravel road. In general, smooth surfaces produce less friction than rough surfaces. It may surprise you to know that even the smoothest objects—like a patch of ice or a countertop—have irregular, bumpy surfaces. When the irregularities of one surface come into contact with those of another surface, friction occurs.

What would happen if you switched to a much heavier bike? You would find the heavier bike harder to pedal because the tires push down harder against the road. Similarly, if you rubbed your hands together forcefully, there would be more friction than if you rubbed your hands together lightly. Friction increases when surfaces push harder against each other.

Friction acts in a direction opposite to the direction of the object's motion. Without friction, a moving object will not stop until it strikes another object.

Vocabulary Latin Word Origins Friction comes from the Latin word fricare. Based on the definition of friction, what do you think fricare means?
○ to burn
○ to rub
○ to melt

FIGURE 1
ART IN MOTION **Friction and Different Surfaces**
The strength of friction depends on the types of surfaces involved. Sequence Rank the surfaces above by how hard it would be to pedal over them, from easiest (1) to hardest (3). (Each surface is flat.) What does this ranking tell you about the amount of friction over these surfaces?

37

apply it!

Desertification affects many areas around the world.

1 **Name** Which continent has the most existing desert?

2 **Interpret Maps** Where in the United States is the greatest risk of desertification?

3 **Infer** Is desertification a threat is existing desert? Explain. Circle a your answer.

4 CHALLENGE If an area is facing things people could do to possibly

132 Land, Air, and Water Resourc

Explain what you know.

Look for the pencil. When you see it, it's time to interact with your book and demonstrate what you have learned.

apply it

Elaborate further with the Apply It activities. This is your opportunity to take what you've learned and apply those skills to new situations.

WITH INQUIRY ... ONLINE ...
Interact with your world.

Lab Zone

Look for the Lab zone triangle. This means it's time to do a hands-on inquiry lab. In every lesson, you'll have the opportunity to do a hands-on inquiry activity that will help reinforce your understanding of the lesson topic.

...fertile area becomes depleted
...become a desert. The
...reas that previously were
...rt uh fih KAY shun).
...ate. For example, a **drought**
...falls in an area. During
...er, the exposed soil easily
...by cattle and sheep and
...ause desertification, too.
... People cannot grow crops
...on has occurred. As a result,
...a. Desertification is severe in
...there are moving to the
...ort themselves on the land.

...y in areas where there
...ea on the map to support

...ertification, what are some
...t its effects?

Land Reclamation Fortunately, it is possible to replace land damaged by erosion or mining. The process of restoring an area of land to a more productive state is called **land reclamation**. In addition to restoring land for agriculture, land reclamation can restore habitats for wildlife. Many different types of land reclamation projects are currently underway all over the world. But it is generally more difficult and expensive to restore damaged land and soil than it is to protect those resources in the first place. In some cases, the land may not return to its original state.

FIGURE 4 ....
Land Reclamation
These pictures show land before and after it was mined.

✎ **Communicate** Below the pictures, write a story about what happened to the land.

⬚ Assess Your Understanding

1a. Review Subsoil has (less/more) plant and animal matter than topsoil.

b. Explain What can happen to soil if plants are removed?

c. Apply Concepts ...
that could prev...
land reclama...

Do the Quick Lab
Modeling Soil

got it?

O I get it! Now I know that soil management is important beca...

O I need extra help with ....
Go to MY SCIENCE 🟤 COACH online for help with this subject.

got it?

Evaluate Your Progress.

After answering the Got It question, think about how you're doing. Did you get it or do you need a little help? Remember, MY SCIENCE 🟤 COACH is there for you if you need extra help.

xvii

Explore the Big Question.

At one point in the chapter, you'll have the opportunity to take all that you've learned to further explore the Big Question.

Pollution and Solutions

EXPLORE THE BIG ?

What can people do to use resources wisely?

FIGURE 4 ....

REAL-WORLD INQUIRY All living things depend on land, air, and water. Conserving these resources for the future is important. Part of resource conservation is identifying and limiting sources of pollution.

Interpret Photos On the photograph, write the letter from the key into the circle that best identifies the source of pollution.

Land
Describe at least one thing your community could do to reduce pollution on land.

Air
Describe at least one thing your community could do to reduce air pollution.

Water
Describe at least one thing your community could do to reduce water pollution.

Pollution Sources
A. Sediments
B. Municipal solid waste
C. Runoff from development

Lab zone Do t Get

Assess Your Under

1a. Define What are sediments?

b. Explain How can bacteria hel spill in the ocean?

c. ANSWER What can people do t resources wisely?

d. CHALLENGE Why might a cor to recycle the waste they pre would reduce water pollutio

got it? ....

○ I get it! Now I know that w can be reduced by _____

○ I need extra help with _____

Go to MY SCIENCE coac with this subject.

ANSWER THE BIG ?

Answer the Big Question.

Now it's time to show what you know and answer the Big Question.

Review What You've Learned.

Use the Chapter Study Guide to review the Big Question and prepare for the test.

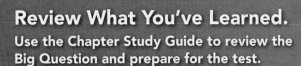

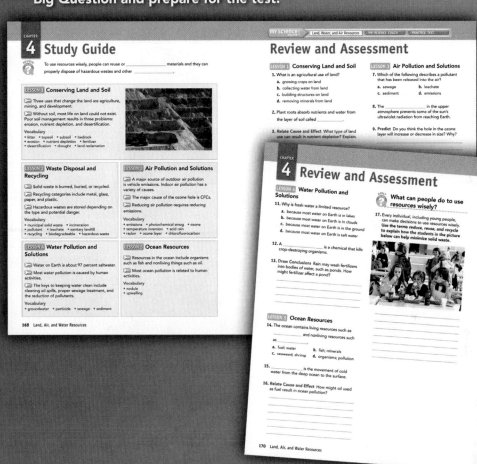

Practice Taking Tests.

Apply the Big Question and take a practice test in standardized test format.

Go to **MyScienceOnline.com** and immerse yourself in amazing virtual environments.

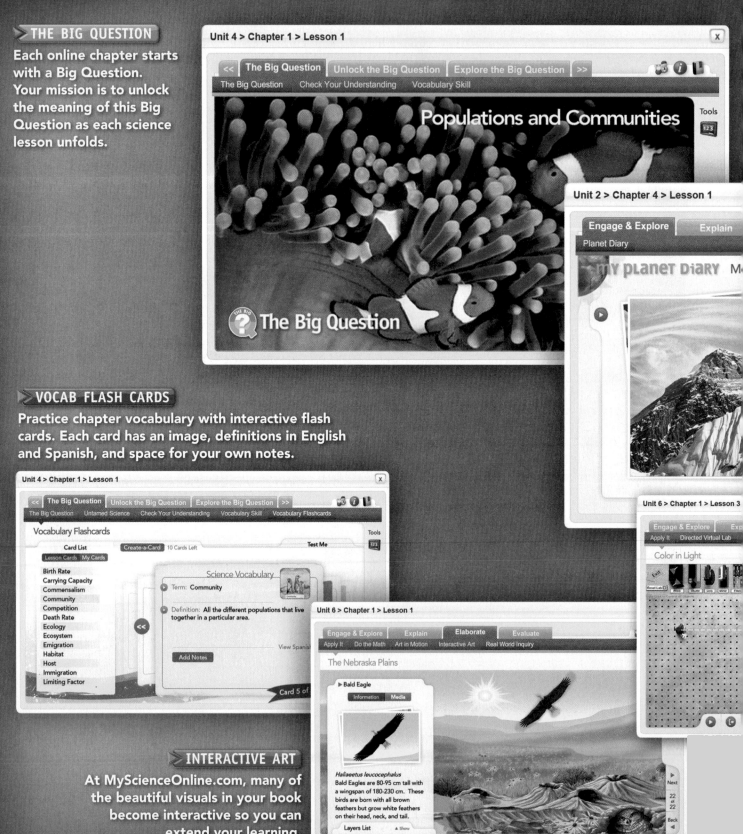

▷ THE BIG QUESTION

Each online chapter starts with a Big Question. Your mission is to unlock the meaning of this Big Question as each science lesson unfolds.

▷ VOCAB FLASH CARDS

Practice chapter vocabulary with interactive flash cards. Each card has an image, definitions in English and Spanish, and space for your own notes.

▷ INTERACTIVE ART

At MyScienceOnline.com, many of the beautiful visuals in your book become interactive so you can extend your learning.

Unit 4 > Chapter 1 > Lesson 1

The Big Question | Unlock the Big Question | Explore the Big Question | >>
The Big Question   Check Your Understanding   Vocabulary Skill

Populations and Communities

Tools

The Big Question

Unit 2 > Chapter 4 > Lesson 1

Engage & Explore | Explain
Planet Diary

my planet Diary   M

Unit 6 > Chapter 1 > Lesson 3

Engage & Explore | Exp
Apply It   Directed Virtual Lab

Color in Light

Exit
Reset Lab

Unit 4 > Chapter 1 > Lesson 1

The Big Question | Unlock the Big Question | Explore the Big Question | >>
The Big Question   Untamed Science   Check Your Understanding   Vocabulary Skill   Vocabulary Flashcards

Vocabulary Flashcards

Tools

Card List   Create-a-Card   10 Cards Left   Test Me
Lesson Cards | My Cards

Birth Rate
Carrying Capacity
Commensalism
Community   Science Vocabulary
Competition
Death Rate   ● Term: **Community**
Ecology
Ecosystem   ● Definition: **All the different populations that live
Emigration   together in a particular area.**
Habitat
Host   View Spanis
Immigration   Add Notes
Limiting Factor
                                                             Card 5 of

Unit 6 > Chapter 1 > Lesson 1

Engage & Explore | Explain | **Elaborate** | Evaluate
Apply It   Do the Math   Art in Motion   Interactive Art   Real World Inquiry

The Nebraska Plains

▶ Bald Eagle
    Information   Media

Haliaeetus leucocephalus
Bald Eagles are 80-95 cm tall with a wingspan of 180-230 cm. These birds are born with all brown feathers but grow white feathers on their head, neck, and tail.

Layers List   ▲ Show

Next
22
of
22
Back

GO ONLINE

my science online.com > Populations and Communities > PLANET DIARY > LAB ZONE > VIRTUAL LAB

C + 🌐 http://www.myscienceonline.com/

> PLANET DIARY

My Planet Diary online is the place to find more information and activities related to the topic in the lesson.

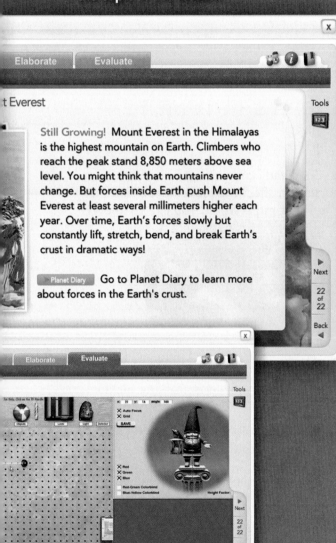

Elaborate Evaluate

t Everest

Tools

Still Growing! Mount Everest in the Himalayas is the highest mountain on Earth. Climbers who reach the peak stand 8,850 meters above sea level. You might think that mountains never change. But forces inside Earth push Mount Everest at least several millimeters higher each year. Over time, Earth's forces slowly but constantly lift, stretch, bend, and break Earth's crust in dramatic ways!

Planet Diary Go to Planet Diary to learn more about forces in the Earth's crust.

Next

22 of 22

Back

> VIRTUAL LAB

Get more practice with realistic virtual labs. Manipulate the variables on-screen and test your hypothesis.

Find Your Chapter

1 Go to www.myscienceonline.com.

2 Log in with username and password.

3 Click on your program and select your chapter.

Keyword Search

1 Go to www.myscienceonline.com.

2 Log in with username and password.

3 Click on your program and select Search.

4 Enter the keyword (from your book) in the search box.

Other Content Available Online

> **UNTAMED SCIENCE** Follow these young scientists through their amazing online video blogs as they travel the globe in search of answers to the Big Questions of Science.

> **MY SCIENCE COACH** Need extra help? My Science Coach is your personal online study partner. My Science Coach is a chance for you to get more practice on key science concepts. There you can choose from a variety of tools that will help guide you through each science lesson.

> **MY READING WEB** Need extra reading help on a particular science topic? At My Reading Web you will find a choice of reading selections targeted to your specific reading level.

? BIG IDEAS OF SCIENCE

Have you ever worked on a jigsaw puzzle? Usually a puzzle has a theme that leads you to group the pieces by what they have in common. But until you put all the pieces together you can't solve the puzzle. Studying science is similar to solving a puzzle. The big ideas of science are like puzzle themes. To understand big ideas, scientists ask questions. The answers to those questions are like pieces of a puzzle. Each chapter in this book asks a big question to help you think about a big idea of science. By answering the big questions, you will get closer to understanding the big idea.

✎ **Before you read each chapter, write about what you know and what more you'd like to know.**

Grant Wiggins, coauthor of *Understanding by Design*

By hitting the soccer ball with her head, this athlete changes the direction of the soccer ball.

BIGIDEA

A net force causes an object's motion to change.

What do you already know about how the force of one object can affect the movement of another object? ✎ **What more would you like to know?**

_____

_____

_____

_____

_____

Big Questions

? How do you describe the motion of an object? Chapter 1

? How do objects react to forces? Chapter 2

✎ **After reading the chapters, write what you have learned about the Big Idea.**

_____

_____

_____

_____

Energy can take different forms but is always conserved.

What do you already know about what happens to the mass and energy of a candle as it burns?
✎ **What more would you like to know?**

_____

_____

_____

_____

_____

_____

_____

Big Question:

❷ **How do machines make it easier to do work?** Chapter 3

❷ **How is energy conserved in a transformation?** Chapter 4

❷ **How does heat flow from one object to another?** Chapter 5

❷ **How does an electric circuit work?** Chapter 6

❷ **How are electricity and magnetism related?** Chapter 7

✎ **After reading the chapters, write what you have learned about the Big Idea.**

_____

_____

_____

_____

_____

_____

_____

As these skydivers fall, they don't lose any energy—the energy just takes different forms.

HOW CAN YOU DESCRIBE THIS COASTER'S MOTION?

How do you describe the motion of an object?

First there is the long, slow climb up the hill. Then the big plunge down. Your body momentarily leaves the seat. The coaster enters a loop the loop and you are upside down! Up and down faster, slower until you finally stop—PHEW!

Classify **What kinds of motion happen during a roller coaster ride?**

_____

_____

_____

_____

_____

_____

_____

> **UNTAMED SCIENCE** Watch the **Untamed Science** video to learn more about motion.

1 Getting Started

Check Your Understanding

1. **Background** Read the paragraph below and then answer the question.

Jenny is watching television. Suddenly, a warning from the National Weather Service appears on the screen. A thunderstorm is heading in her direction. At that instant, Jenny sees a bolt of lightning in the distant sky. Jenny hopes the storm will be over in time for her soccer game.

> Direction is the line along which something moves.
>
> Instant is a point or very short space in time.
>
> Time is the period of duration between two events.

• What might happen if the storm were to change direction?

_____

_____

> **MY READING WEB** If you had trouble completing the question above, visit **My Reading Web** and type in *Motion.*

Vocabulary Skill

High-Use Academic Words Knowing these academic words will help you become a better reader in all subject areas. Look for these words as you read this chapter.

Word	Definition	Example
system	*n.* an established way of doing something	People have different *systems* for keeping their music collections organized.
equation	*n.* a statement of equality between two quantities, as shown by the equal sign (=).	The *equation* for the area of a circle is $A = \pi \times r^2$.
conclude	*v.* to decide by reasoning	After investigating the evidence, they *concluded* that everyone should wear a bicycle helmet.

2. **Quick Check** Choose the word from the table that best completes the sentence.

• After waiting for 20 minutes, he _____ that his friend was not coming.

motion

speed

velocity

acceleration

Chapter Preview

LESSON 1
- motion
- reference point
- International System of Units
- distance

🔄 Compare and Contrast

△ Measure

LESSON 2
- speed
- average speed
- instantaneous speed
- velocity
- slope

🔄 Identify Supporting Evidence

△ Calculate

LESSON 3
- acceleration

🔄 Identify the Main Idea

△ Graph

> **VOCAB FLASH CARDS** For extra help with vocabulary, visit **Vocab Flash Cards** and type in *Motion.*

3

Describing Motion

🔑 **When Is an Object in Motion?**

MY PLANET DIARY   VOICES FROM HISTORY

Nicolaus Copernicus

Why would anyone think that Earth moves around the sun? After all, on a clear day you can see the sun move across the sky. But Polish astronomer Nicolaus Copernicus realized that an object revolving around you from left to right looks the same as an object standing still while you rotate from right to left. In *On the Revolution of the Heavenly Spheres*, he wrote

Every apparent change in respect of position is due to motion of the object observed, or of the observer, or indeed to an unequal change of both.

This book was published in 1543. It was a summary of more than 30 years of Copernicus's studies on the solar system.

Write your answer to the question below.

For thousands of years, many people thought Earth was the center of the universe. Name one possible reason why they thought this.

_____

_____

_____

_____

_____

_____

▶ PLANET DIARY Go to **Planet Diary** to learn more about motion.

Lab zone® Do the Inquiry Warm-Up *What Is Motion?*

When Is an Object in Motion?

Deciding if an object is in motion isn't as easy as you might think. For example, you are probably sitting in a chair as you read this book. Are you moving? Parts of you are. Your eyes blink and your chest moves up and down. But you would probably say that you are not moving. An object is in **motion** if its position changes relative to another object. Because your position relative to your chair does not change, you could say that you are not in motion.

Vocabulary
- motion • reference point
- International System of Units • distance

Skills
- ⟲ Reading: Compare and Contrast
- △ Inquiry: Measure

Reference Points To decide if you are moving, you use your chair as a reference point. A **reference point** is a place or object used for comparison to determine if something is in motion. 🔑 **An object is in motion if it changes position relative to a reference point.** Objects that are fixed relative to Earth—such as a building, a tree, or a sign—make good reference points.

You may already know what happens if your reference point is moving relative to Earth. Have you ever been in a school bus parked next to another bus? Suddenly, you think that your bus is moving backward. When you look out the window again for a fixed point, you find that your bus isn't moving at all—the other bus is moving forward! Your bus seemed to be moving backward because you had used the other bus as a reference point.

know?

Because of Earth's spin, the stars appear to move in circular arcs across the night sky. Only the North Star remains in a fixed position. Historically, sailors have used the North Star to help them navigate.

FIGURE 1 ···
> ART IN MOTION **Reference Point**
The top photo was taken shortly before the bottom photo.

✏️ **Answer the following questions.**

1. **Interpret Photos** Did the car that the boy is in move, or did the car in the background move? Explain your answer.

_____

_____

_____

_____

2. **Identify** What objects in this photo make good reference points?

_____

_____

_____

5

Relative Motion

If you use your chair as your reference point as you sit and read, you are not moving. If you choose another object as a reference point, you may be moving.

Suppose you use the sun as a reference point instead of your chair. If you compare your position to the sun, you are moving quite rapidly because you and your chair are on Earth, which revolves around the sun. Earth moves about 30 kilometers every second. So you, your chair, this book, and everything else on Earth are moving that quickly as well. Going that fast, you could travel from New York City to Los Angeles in about two minutes! Relative to the sun, both you and your chair are in motion. But because you are moving with Earth, you do not seem to be moving.

Compare and Contrast
A tree is (stationary/in motion) relative to Earth. A tree is (stationary/in motion) relative to the sun.

apply it!

The people in the photo are riding on a spinning carousel.

① Interpret Photos Are the people moving relative to each other? Are they moving relative to objects on the ground? Explain.

_____

_____

_____

_____

_____

_____

_____

_____

② Explain How is your choice of reference point important when describing the motion of the people?

_____

_____

_____

_____

_____

_____

Measuring Distance

To describe motion completely, you need to use units of measurement. Scientists use a system of measurement called the **International System of Units** or, in French, *Système International* (SI). **Distance** is the length of the path between two points. The SI unit for length is the meter (m). The distance from the floor to a doorknob is about 1 meter.

Scientists use other units to measure distances much smaller or much larger than a meter. For example, the width of the spider shown in **Figure 2** can be measured in centimeters (cm). The prefix *centi-* means "one hundredth." A centimeter is one hundredth of a meter, so there are 100 centimeters in a meter. For lengths smaller than a centimeter, the millimeter (mm) is used. The prefix *milli-* means "one thousandth," so there are 1,000 millimeters in a meter. Distances much longer than a meter can be measured in kilometers (km). The prefix *kilo-* means "one thousand," so there are 1,000 meters in a kilometer. A straight line between San Francisco and Boston would measure about 4,300 kilometers.

FIGURE 2 ....

Measuring Distance

The unit of length that you use to measure distance depends on the size of the distance.

✎ **Answer the following questions.**

1. **Review** Fill in the following common conversions for length.

   1 m = _____ mm

   1 m = _____ cm

   1 km = _____ m

2. **Measure** What is the distance in centimeters from points A to B on the spider? _____

3. CHALLENGE How many of these spiders would fit side by side in the length of 1 meter?

   _____

   _____

Ⓐ   Ⓑ

Lab® Do the Quick Lab
zone   *Identifying Motion.*

🔑 Assess Your Understanding

1a. **Review** A _____ is a place or object used for comparison to determine if something is in motion.

b. **Explain** Why is it important to know if your reference point is moving?

_____

_____

_____

_____

got it?

○ **I get it!** Now I know that an object is in motion if _____

_____

_____

_____

○ **I need extra help with** _____

Go to **MY SCIENCE** Ⓢ **COACH** *online for help with this subject.*

2 Speed and Velocity

UNLOCK THE BIG ?

🔑 **How Do You Calculate Speed?**

🔑 **How Do You Describe Velocity?**

🔑 **How Do You Graph Motion?**

my planet diary

BLOG

Posted by: Mallory

Location: Fountain Valley, California

Once my sister talked me into going to the roller-skating rink with her. I hate skating, but against my better judgment, I agreed to go. I can skate, but I don't go very fast. At the rink, there were these speed skaters, or, as I like to call them, "assassin skaters." The assassin skaters went ridiculously fast. They were probably going approximately 20 miles per hour in the same direction as me. They zipped past me, just barely missing me.

The worst part about going skating was getting stuck behind a group of skaters or a couple. They went so slowly that you had to speed up to get around them.

Communicate Answer the questions. Discuss your answers with a partner.

1. Do all the skaters in the rink move at the same speed? Explain.

_____

_____

_____

2. Describe a sport or activity in which speed is important.

_____

_____

_____

_____

▷ PLANET DIARY Go to **Planet Diary** to learn more about speed and velocity.

Lab zone Do the Inquiry Warm-Up *How Fast and How Far?*

Vocabulary
- speed • average speed
- instantaneous speed
- velocity • slope

Skills
- Reading: Identify Supporting Evidence
- Inquiry: Calculate

How Do You Calculate Speed?

You might describe the motion of an airplane as fast or the motion of a snail as slow. By using these words, you are describing the object's speed. The **speed** of an object is the distance the object moves per unit of time. Speed is a type of rate. A rate tells you the amount of something that occurs or changes in one unit of time.

The Speed Equation 🔑 **To calculate the speed of an object, divide the distance the object travels by the amount of time it takes to travel that distance.** This relationship can be written as an equation.

$$\text{Speed} = \frac{\text{Distance}}{\text{Time}}$$

The speed equation contains a unit of distance divided by a unit of time. If you measure distance in meters and time in seconds, the SI unit for speed is meters per second, or m/s. (The slash is read as "per.") For example, at its cruising altitude, an airplane might travel at a constant speed of 260 m/s. This means that the airplane will travel a distance of 260 meters in 1 second. The speed of a snail is about 1 cm/s. This means that the snail will travel a distance of 1 centimeter in 1 second. The speed of the airplane is much greater than the speed of the snail because the airplane travels much farther than the snail in the same amount of time.

Vocabulary High-Use Academic Words Complete the following sentence. The relationship between speed, distance, and time can be written as a(n)

_____

apply it!

The cyclist shown in the diagram is moving at a constant speed of 10 m/s during his ride.

❶ **Identify** Draw arrows on the scale to mark how far the cyclist travels after 1, 2, 3, 3.5, and 4 seconds.

❷ [CHALLENGE] How long will it take the cyclist to travel 400 meters?

10   20   30   40

Distance (m)

FIGURE 1 ·····················

Average Speed

Triathletes A and B are competing in a triathlon. The first two legs of the race are swimming and biking.

✏️ **Calculate** Use the data in the boxes below to calculate each triathlete's average speed during the swimming and biking legs of the race.

Average Speed

When a plane is at its cruising altitude, it can travel at a constant speed for many hours. But the speed of most moving objects is not constant. In a race known as the triathlon, the competitors (or triathletes) first swim, then bike, and finally run. The speeds of the triathletes change throughout the race. They travel slowest when they swim, a little faster when they run, and fastest when they bike.

Although the triathletes do not travel at a constant speed, they do have an average speed throughout the race. To calculate **average speed,** divide the total distance traveled by the total time. For example, suppose a triathlete swims a distance of 3 kilometers in 1 hour. Then the triathlete bikes a distance of 50 kilometers in 3 hours. Finally, the triathlete runs a distance of 12 kilometers in 1 hour. The average speed of the triathlete is the total distance divided by the total time.

Total distance = 3 km + 50 km + 12 km = 65 km

Total time = 1 h + 3 h + 1 h = 5 h

$$\text{Average speed} = \frac{65 \text{ km}}{5 \text{ h}} = 13 \text{ km/h}$$

The triathlete's average speed is 13 kilometers per hour.

Leg 1 *Swimming*

Total distance: 3.0 km
Triathlete A's total time: 0.8 h
Triathlete B's total time: 1.0 h

Triathlete A's average speed =

Triathlete B's average speed =

Leg 2 *Biking*

Total distance: 50.0 km
Triathlete A's total time: 3.0 h
Triathlete B's total time: 2.5 h

Triathlete A's average speed =

Triathlete B's average speed =

Instantaneous Speed Suppose Triathlete B passes Triathlete A during the biking leg. At that moment, Triathlete B has a greater instantaneous speed than Triathlete A. **Instantaneous speed** is the speed at which an object is moving at a given instant in time. It is important not to confuse instantaneous speed with average speed. The triathlete with the greatest average speed, not the greatest instantaneous speed, wins the race.

apply it!

The triathletes run in the third and final leg of the triathlon.

❶ Calculate Use the data from all three legs to solve for each triathlete's average speed.

> **Leg 3** *Running*
> Total distance: 12.0 km
> Triathlete A's total time: 1.2 h
> Triathlete B's total time: 1.0 h

Total distance =	
Triathlete A's total time =	
Triathlete A's average speed =	
Triathlete B's total time =	
Triathlete B's average speed =	

❷ Identify Which triathlete finishes first? _____

Do the Lab Investigation
Stopping on a Dime.

🔑 Assess Your Understanding

1a. Identify The (instantaneous/average) speed is the speed of the object at a given instant in time. The (instantaneous/average) speed is the speed of the object over a longer period of time.

b. Apply Concepts The speedometer in a car gives the car's _____ speed.

got it?

○ **I get it!** Now I know to calculate the speed of an object, I need to _____

_____

○ **I need extra help with** _____

Go to MY SCIENCE COACH *online for help with this subject.*

How Do You Describe Velocity?

Knowing the speed at which something travels does not tell you everything about its motion. To describe an object's motion, you also need to know its direction. For example, suppose you hear that a thunderstorm is traveling at a speed of 25 km/h. Should you prepare for the storm? That depends on the direction of the storm's motion. Because storms usually travel from west to east in the United States, you need not worry if you live west of the storm. You should take cover if you live east of the storm.

When you know both the speed and direction of an object's motion, you know the velocity of the object. Speed in a given direction is called **velocity.** You know the velocity of the storm when you know that it is moving 25 km/h eastward.

At times, describing the velocity of moving objects can be very important. For example, air traffic controllers must keep close track of the velocities of the aircraft under their control. These velocities change as airplanes move overhead and on the runways. An error in determining a velocity, either in speed or in direction, could lead to a collision.

Velocity is also important to airplane pilots. For example, the stunt pilots in **Figure 2** make spectacular use of their control over the velocity of their aircraft. Stunt pilots use this control to stay in close formation while flying graceful maneuvers at high speeds.

Identify Supporting Evidence Underline the reason why velocity is important to air traffic controllers.

FIGURE 2 ·······························

Velocity
These stunt pilots are performing at an air show.

✎ **Explain** Why is velocity and not just speed important to these pilots?

_____

_____

_____

_____

_____

_____

_____

_____

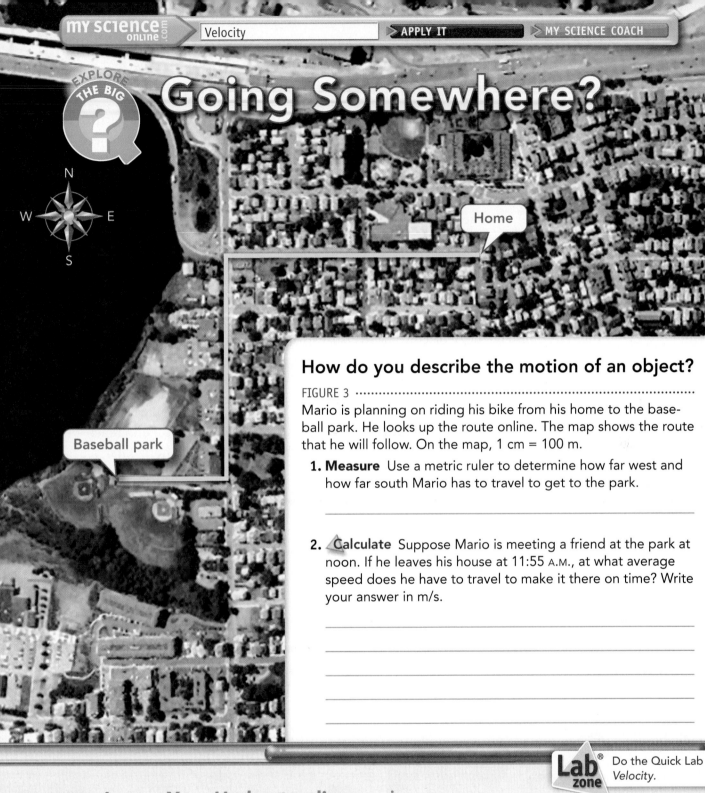

Going Somewhere?

EXPLORE THE BIG ?

How do you describe the motion of an object?

FIGURE 3 ·······································

Mario is planning on riding his bike from his home to the base-ball park. He looks up the route online. The map shows the route that he will follow. On the map, 1 cm = 100 m.

1. **Measure** Use a metric ruler to determine how far west and how far south Mario has to travel to get to the park.

_____

2. **Calculate** Suppose Mario is meeting a friend at the park at noon. If he leaves his house at 11:55 A.M., at what average speed does he have to travel to make it there on time? Write your answer in m/s.

_____

_____

_____

_____

Home

Baseball park

Lab zone | Do the Quick Lab *Velocity.*

🔑 Assess Your Understanding

2. ANSWER THE BIG ? How do you describe the motion of an object?

_____

_____

_____

_____

got it?

○ **I get it!** Now I know that the velocity of an object is the _____

_____

○ **I need extra help with** _____

Go to my science ⓢ COACH online for help with this subject.

How Do You Graph Motion?

The graphs you see in **Figure 4** and **Figure 5** are distance-versus-time motion graphs. 🔑 **You can show the motion of an object on a line graph in which you plot distance versus time.** By tradition, time is shown on the horizontal axis, or *x*-axis. Distance is shown on the vertical axis, or *y*-axis. A point on the line represents the distance an object has traveled during a particular time. The *x* value of the point is time, and the *y* value is distance.

The steepness of a line on a graph is called **slope.** The slope tells you how fast one variable changes in relation to the other variable in the graph. In other words, slope tells you the rate of change. Since speed is the rate that distance changes in relation to time, the slope of a distance-versus-time graph represents speed. The steeper the slope is, the greater the speed. A constant slope represents motion at constant speed.

Calculating Slope

You can calculate the slope of a line by dividing the rise by the run. The rise is the vertical difference between any two points on the line. The run is the horizontal difference between the same two points.

$$\text{Slope} = \frac{\text{Rise}}{\text{Run}}$$

In **Figure 4,** using the points shown, the rise is 400 meters and the run is 2 minutes. To find the slope, you divide 400 meters by 2 minutes. The slope is 200 meters per minute.

FIGURE 4 ·······································

> **INTERACTIVE ART** **Constant Speed**

The graph shows the motion of a jogger.

✎ **Use the graph to answer the questions.**

1. **Read Graphs** What is the jogger's speed?

   _____

2. **Predict** On the same graph, draw a line that represents the motion of a jogger who moves at a constant speed of 100 m/min.

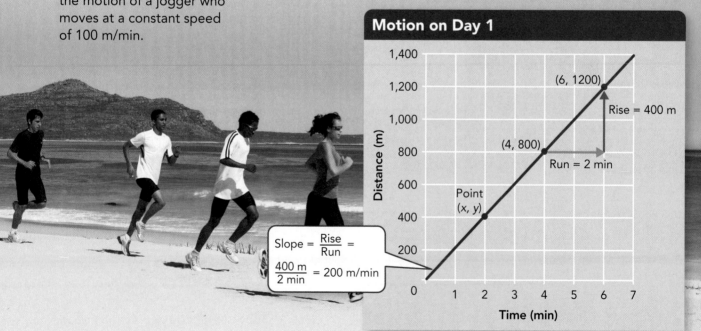

Motion on Day 1

Slope = $\dfrac{\text{Rise}}{\text{Run}}$ =

$\dfrac{400 \text{ m}}{2 \text{ min}}$ = 200 m/min

(6, 1200)

Rise = 400 m

(4, 800)

Run = 2 min

Point (x, y)

Distance (m)

Time (min)

Different Slopes Most moving objects do not travel at a constant speed. For example, the graph in **Figure 5** shows a jogger's motion on the second day of training. The line is divided into three segments. The slope of each segment is different. From the steepness of the slopes you can tell that the jogger ran fastest during the third segment. The horizontal line in the second segment shows that the jogger's distance did not change at all. The jogger was resting during the second segment.

FIGURE 5 ·······························

Changing Speed

The graph shows how the speed of a jogger varies during her second day of training.

✎ **Read Graphs** Find the rise, the run, and the slope for each segment of the graph. Write the answers in the boxes below.

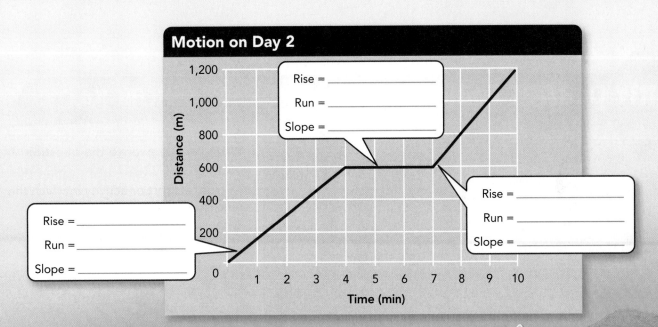

Motion on Day 2

Rise = _____
Run = _____
Slope = _____

Rise = _____
Run = _____
Slope = _____

Rise = _____
Run = _____
Slope = _____

Distance (m)

Time (min)

Lab zone® Do the Quick Lab *Motion Graphs.*

⚷ Assess Your Understanding

3a. Identify The _____ of a distance-versus-time graph shows you the speed of a moving object.

b. Calculate The rise of a line on a distance-versus-time graph is 900 m and the run is 3 min. What is the slope of the line?

_____

_____

c. Apply Concepts Is it possible for a distance-versus-time graph to be a vertical line? Explain.

_____

_____

_____

_____

_____

_____

got it? ···

○ **I get it!** Now I know to show the motion of an object on a line graph, you _____

○ **I need extra help with** _____

Go to my science ⑤ coach *online for help with this subject.*

Acceleration

UNLOCK THE BIG ?

🔑 **What Is Acceleration?**

🔑 **How Do You Graph Acceleration?**

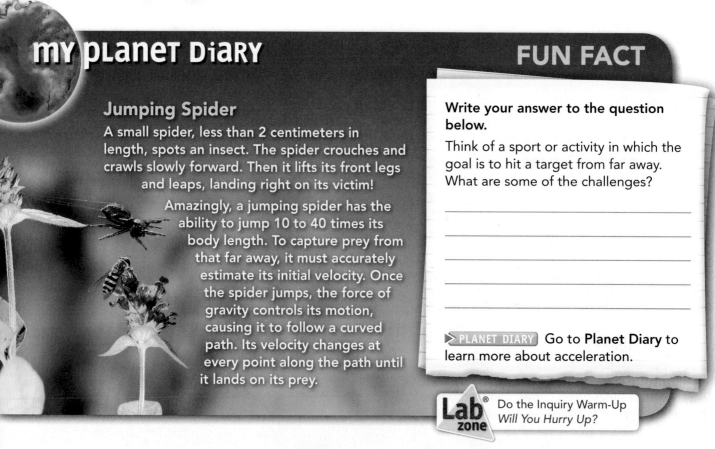

my pLaneT DiaRY

Jumping Spider

A small spider, less than 2 centimeters in length, spots an insect. The spider crouches and crawls slowly forward. Then it lifts its front legs and leaps, landing right on its victim!

Amazingly, a jumping spider has the ability to jump 10 to 40 times its body length. To capture prey from that far away, it must accurately estimate its initial velocity. Once the spider jumps, the force of gravity controls its motion, causing it to follow a curved path. Its velocity changes at every point along the path until it lands on its prey.

FUN FACT

Write your answer to the question below.

Think of a sport or activity in which the goal is to hit a target from far away. What are some of the challenges?

_____

_____

_____

_____

_____

▶ **PLANET DIARY** Go to **Planet Diary** to learn more about acceleration.

Lab zone® Do the Inquiry Warm-Up
Will You Hurry Up?

What Is Acceleration?

Suppose you are a passenger in a car stopped at a red light. When the light changes to green, the driver steps on the accelerator. As a result, the car speeds up, or accelerates. In everyday language, acceleration means "the process of speeding up."

Acceleration has a more precise definition in science. Scientists define **acceleration** as the rate at which velocity changes. Recall that velocity describes both the speed and direction of an object. A change in velocity can involve a change in either speed or direction—or both. 🔑 **In science, acceleration refers to increasing speed, decreasing speed, or changing direction.**

Vocabulary
• acceleration

Skills
🔊 Reading: Identify the Main Idea
△ Inquiry: Graph

Changing Speed Whenever an object's speed changes, the object accelerates. A car that begins to move from a stopped position or speeds up to pass another car is accelerating. People can accelerate too. For example, you accelerate when you coast down a hill on your bike.

Just as objects can speed up, they can also slow down. This change in speed is sometimes called deceleration, or negative acceleration. A car decelerates as it comes to a stop at a red light. A water skier decelerates as the boat slows down.

Changing Direction Even an object that is traveling at a constant speed can be accelerating. Recall that acceleration can be a change in direction as well as a change in speed. Therefore, a car accelerates as it follows a gentle curve in the road or changes lanes. Runners accelerate as they round the curve in a track. A softball accelerates when it changes direction as it is hit.

Many objects continuously change direction without changing speed. The simplest example of this type of motion is circular motion, or motion along a circular path. For example, the seats on a Ferris wheel accelerate because they move in a circle.

🔊 **Identify the Main Idea**
Underline the main idea in the section called Changing Speed.

FIGURE 1 ·················

Acceleration
During the game of soccer, a soccer ball can show three types of acceleration—increasing speed, decreasing speed, and changing direction.

✎ **Interpret Photos** Label the type of acceleration that is occurring in each of the photos.

17

0.0s   1.0s   2.0s   3.0s

0 m/s   8 m/s   16 m/s   24 m/s

FIGURE 2 ·······························

Acceleration

The airplane is accelerating at a rate of 8 m/s².

✏️ **Predict** Determine the speed of the airplane at 4.0 s and 5.0 s. Write your answers in the boxes next to each airplane.

Calculating Acceleration

Acceleration describes the rate at which velocity changes. If an object is not changing direction, you can describe its acceleration as the rate at which its speed changes. To determine the acceleration of an object moving in a straight line, you calculate the change in speed per unit of time. This is summarized by the following equation.

$$\text{Acceleration} = \frac{\text{Final Speed} - \text{Initial Speed}}{\text{Time}}$$

If speed is measured in meters per second (m/s) and time is measured in seconds, the SI unit of acceleration is meters per second per second, or m/s². Suppose speed is measured in kilometers per hour and time is measured in hours. Then the unit for acceleration is kilometers per hour per hour, or km/h².

To understand acceleration, imagine a small airplane moving down a runway. **Figure 2** shows the airplane's speed after each second of the first three seconds of its acceleration. To calculate the acceleration of the airplane, you must first subtract the initial speed of 0 m/s from its final speed of 24 m/s. Then divide the change in speed by the time, 3 seconds.

$$\text{Acceleration} = \frac{24 \text{ m/s} - 0 \text{ m/s}}{3 \text{ s}}$$

$$\text{Acceleration} = 8 \text{ m/s}^2$$

The airplane accelerates at a rate of 8 m/s². This means that the airplane's speed increases by 8 m/s every second. Notice in **Figure 2** that after each second of travel, the airplane's speed is 8 m/s greater than its speed in the previous second.

FIGURE 3 ······························

Deceleration

An airplane touches down on the runway with a speed of 70 m/s. It decelerates at a rate of –5 m/s².

✏️ **Predict** Determine the speed of the airplane after each second of its deceleration. Write your answers in the table to the right.

Time (s)	1	2	3	4
Speed (m/s)				

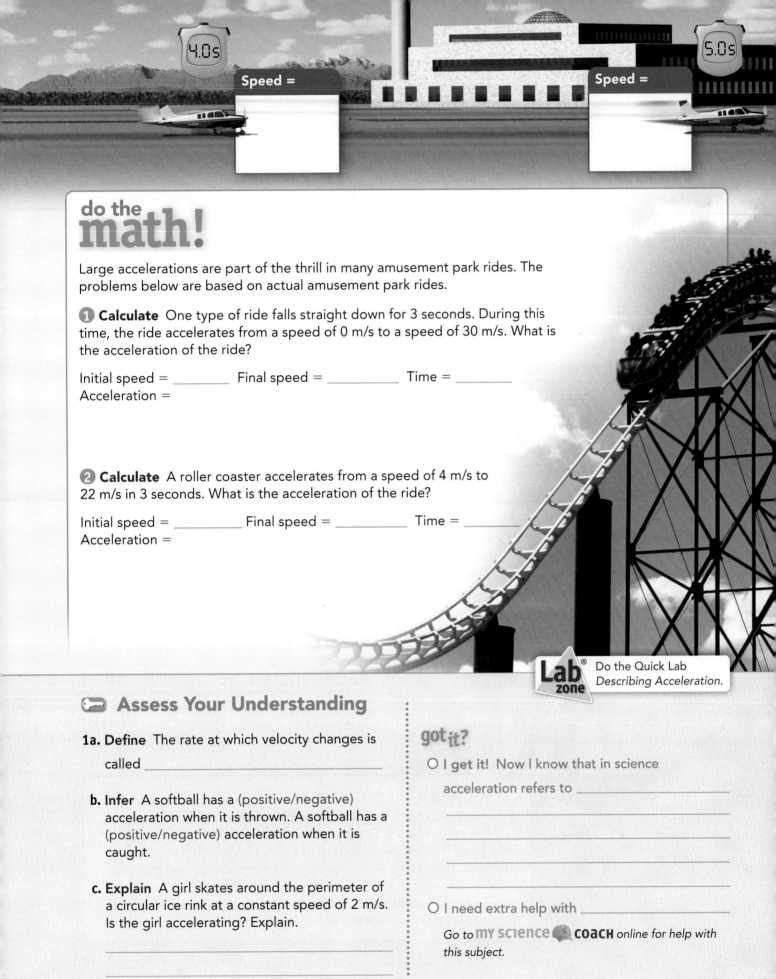

Speed =

4.0 s

Speed =

5.0 s

do the math!

Large accelerations are part of the thrill in many amusement park rides. The problems below are based on actual amusement park rides.

1 Calculate One type of ride falls straight down for 3 seconds. During this time, the ride accelerates from a speed of 0 m/s to a speed of 30 m/s. What is the acceleration of the ride?

Initial speed = _____ Final speed = _____ Time = _____
Acceleration =

2 Calculate A roller coaster accelerates from a speed of 4 m/s to 22 m/s in 3 seconds. What is the acceleration of the ride?

Initial speed = _____ Final speed = _____ Time = _____
Acceleration =

Lab zone Do the Quick Lab
Describing Acceleration.

🔑 Assess Your Understanding

1a. Define The rate at which velocity changes is

called _____

b. Infer A softball has a (positive/negative) acceleration when it is thrown. A softball has a (positive/negative) acceleration when it is caught.

c. Explain A girl skates around the perimeter of a circular ice rink at a constant speed of 2 m/s. Is the girl accelerating? Explain.

_____

_____

got it?

O **I get it!** Now I know that in science

acceleration refers to _____

_____

_____

_____

_____

O **I need extra help with** _____

Go to **MY SCIENCE** Ⓢ **COACH** *online for help with this subject.*

19

How Do You Graph Acceleration?

Suppose you bike down a long, steep hill. At the top of the hill, your speed is 0 m/s. As you start down the hill, your speed increases. Each second, you move at a greater speed and travel a greater distance than the second before. During the five seconds it takes you to reach the bottom of the hill, you are an accelerating object. 🔑 **You can use both a speed-versus-time graph and a distance-versus-time graph to analyze the motion of an accelerating object.**

FIGURE 4 ···

▷ VIRTUAL LAB Speed-Versus-Time Graph

The data in the table show how your speed changes during each second of your bike ride.

✎ **Use the data to answer the questions.**

Time (s)	Speed (m/s)
0	0
1	2
2	4
3	6
4	8
5	10

1. **Graph** Use this data to plot a line graph. Plot time on the horizontal axis. Plot speed on the vertical axis. Give the graph a title.

2. **Calculate** What is the slope of the graph?

Analyzing a Speed-Versus-Time Graph

Look at the speed-versus-time graph that you made in **Figure 4.** What can you learn about your motion by analyzing this graph? First, since the line slants upward, the graph shows that your speed was increasing. Next, since the line is straight, you can tell that your acceleration was constant. A slanted, straight line on a speed-versus-time graph means that the object is accelerating at a constant rate. Your acceleration is the slope of the line.

FIGURE 5 ·······································

▸ INTERACTIVE ART **Distance-Versus-Time Graph**

The data in the table show how your distance changes during each second of your bike ride.

✎ **Use the data to answer the questions.**

Time (s)	Distance (m)
0	0
1	1
2	4
3	9
4	16
5	25

1. **Graph** Use this data to create a line graph. Plot time on the horizontal axis. Plot distance on the vertical axis. Give the graph a title.

2. [CHALLENGE] How does the distance change with time?

_____

_____

_____

_____

Analyzing a Distance-Versus-Time Graph

Look at the distance-versus-time graph that you made in **Figure 5.** The curved line tells you that during each second, you traveled a greater distance than the second before. For example, you traveled a greater distance during the third second than you did during the first second.

The curved line in **Figure 5** also tells you that during each second your speed was greater than the second before. Recall that the slope of a distance-versus-time graph is the speed of an object. From second to second, the slope of the line in **Figure 5** gets steeper. Since the slope is increasing, you can conclude that your speed was also increasing. You were accelerating.

Lab Do the Quick Lab
zone *Graphing Acceleration.*

🔑 Assess Your Understanding

got it? ··

○ **I get it!** Now I know that the two types of graphs that you can use to analyze the motion of an

accelerating object are _____

_____

○ **I need extra help with** _____

Go to MY SCIENCE ⒮ COACH *online for help with this subject.*

1 Study Guide

Which term, speed or velocity, gives you more information about an object's motion? Why?

LESSON 1 Describe Motion

🔑 An object is in motion if it changes position relative to a reference point.

Vocabulary
• motion
• reference point
• International System of Units
• distance

LESSON 2 Speed and Velocity

🔑 To calculate the speed of an object, divide the distance the object travels by the amount of time it takes to travel the distance.

🔑 When you know both the speed and direction of an object's motion, you know the velocity of the object.

🔑 You can show the motion of an object on a line graph in which you plot distance versus time.

Vocabulary
• speed   • average speed
• instantaneous speed   • velocity   • slope

LESSON 3 Acceleration

🔑 In science, acceleration refers to increasing speed, decreasing speed, or changing direction.

🔑 You can use both a speed-versus-time graph and a distance-versus-time graph to analyze the motion of an accelerating object.

Vocabulary
• acceleration

Review and Assessment

LESSON 1 Describing Motion

1. What is the SI unit of distance?

　a. foot 　　　　b. meter

　c. mile 　　　　d. kilometer

2. A change in position with respect to a reference point is _____

3. Classify Suppose you are in a train. List some objects that make good reference points to determine whether or not the train is moving.

_____

Use the illustration to answer Questions 4 and 5.

4. Compare and Contrast Suppose you are standing on the sidewalk. Describe the direction of your motion relative to the car and the plane.

_____

_____

_____

5. Compare and Contrast Suppose you are riding in the plane. Describe the direction of your motion relative to the person standing on the sidewalk and the car.

_____

_____

_____

_____

LESSON 2 Speed and Velocity

6. What quantity can you calculate if you know that a car travels 30 kilometers in 20 minutes?

　a. average speed 　　b. direction

　c. velocity 　　　　d. instantaneous speed

7. On a graph of distance versus time, the slope of the line indicates the _____ of an object.

The graph shows the motion of a remote-control car. Use the graph to answer Questions 8 and 9.

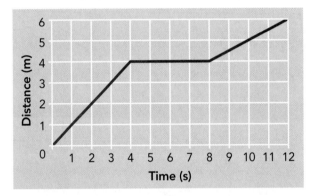

8. Read Graphs During which time period was the car moving the fastest?

_____

9. Calculate What was the speed of the car during the first four seconds?

_____

_____

10. Apply Concepts A family takes a car trip. They travel for an hour at 80 km/h and then 2 hours at 40 km/h. Find their average speed during the trip.

_____

_____

_____

_____

LESSON 3 **Acceleration**

11. The rate at which velocity changes is

    a. acceleration.   **b.** direction.

    c. speed.   **d.** velocity.

12. You can calculate the acceleration of an object moving in a straight line by dividing the

_____ by the time.

The graph below shows the speed of a downhill skier during a period of several seconds. Use the graph to answer Question 13.

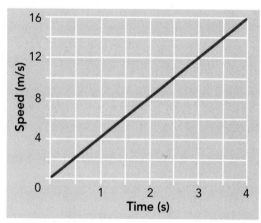

13. Read Graphs What is the skier's acceleration?

_____

_____

_____

14. math! A ball is dropped from a window and takes 2 seconds to reach the ground. It starts from rest and reaches a final speed of 20 m/s. What is the ball's acceleration?

_____

_____

_____

_____

15. 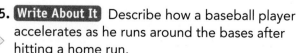 **Write About It** Describe how a baseball player accelerates as he runs around the bases after hitting a home run.

 APPLY THE BIG ? **How do you describe the motion of an object?**
....

16. The distance-versus-time graph is for two runners in a 50-meter race. Describe the motion of the runners in as much detail as you can. Which runner won the race? How do you know? Suppose the graph showed the runners' motion until they came to a stop. Describe how the graph would change.

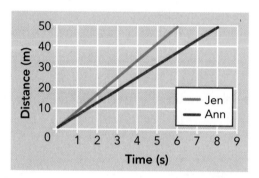

_____

_____

_____

_____

_____

_____

_____

_____

_____

_____

_____

_____

_____

_____

_____

_____

_____

_____

Standardized Test Prep

Multiple Choice

Circle the letter of the best answer.

1. The graph below shows the motion of a runner.

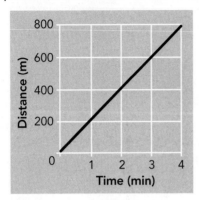

What could the runner do to make the slope of the line rise?

A   stop running

B   decrease speed

C   maintain the same speed

D   increase speed

2. Members of the Fairview Track Running Club are running a 5-kilometer race. What is the distance of the race in meters?

A   0.5 m

B   50 m

C   500 m

D   5000 m

3. What condition is necessary for an object to make a good reference point?

A   The object is moving at a constant speed.

B   The object is accelerating.

C   The object is fixed with respect to Earth.

D   The object is large.

4. Two objects traveling at the same speed have different velocities if they

A   start at different times.

B   travel different distances.

C   have different masses.

D   move in different directions.

5. Your family is driving to the beach. You travel 200 kilometers in the first two hours. During the next hour, you stop for lunch and only travel 25 kilometers. What was your average speed?

A   60 km/h

B   75 km/h

C   100 km/h

D   225 km/h

Constructed Response

Use the graph to answer Question 6. Write your answer on a separate sheet of paper.

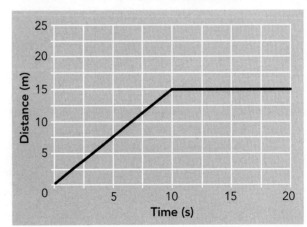

6. The graph above shows the motion of a person. Describe the motion.

THE RACE FOR SPEED

As soon as people started driving automobiles, someone started racing them. We've been trying to go faster ever since.

So how fast can we go? The official top land speed record was set by a man named Andy Green in Blackrock, Nevada, in 1997. Green and his vehicle, named the *Thrust SSC*, reached a speed of 1,288 km/h. That's faster than the speed of sound! In fact, the *Thrust SSC* produced a sonic boom. A sonic boom sounds a lot like an explosion. Thunder is a natural sonic boom.

How did the *Thrust SSC* go so fast? It used two turbo jet engines. So Green's previous experience as a fighter pilot came in handy when he was learning to drive this car.

▲ Andy Green and the jet-propelled *Thrust SSC*.

Graph It There are lots of other speed records. Research the wheel-driven land speed record and the rail speed record, to start. Make a graph or chart that compares all of the speed records you can find. Share your results with your class.

STOP SIGN

If you've ever watched a movie about jet pilots or race car drivers, you've probably heard someone talk about "pulling Gs." But what does that mean? A G-force is an informal unit of measurement used in aeronautics and space engineering. One G-force is the average acceleration due to gravity at Earth's surface. You experience one G-force all the time.

In the 1940s and 1950s, Colonel John Paul Stapp experienced a lot more than one G-force. At what is now Edwards Air Force Base, Colonel Stapp strapped himself into a device that scientists called the Gee Whiz. This was a rocket sled that hurled volunteers forward before bringing them to a sudden stop along the track. In one of his runs, Colonel Stapp was subjected to 46 Gs! His work had an impact on everything from seat belts to the restraints worn by astronauts.

Share It Research what happens when people experience extreme G-forces. Find out what physical symptoms they are likely to experience and how those symptoms can be prevented. Design a safety pamphlet describing your findings.

WHY WON'T THIS ACROBAT LAND ON HER HEAD?

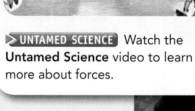

> UNTAMED SCIENCE Watch the **Untamed Science** video to learn more about forces.

How do objects react to forces?

This teen is part of a traveling youth circus that performs in New England. As a circus trouper, she may do stunts such as tumbling and swinging on a trapeze. These stunts often appear to be gravity-defying and dangerous, but the troupers know how to perform in a way that lets them land safely.

△ Develop Hypotheses **How does this athlete land on her feet?**

_____

_____

_____

_____

_____

_____

2 Getting Started

Check Your Understanding

1. **Background** Read the paragraph below and then answer the question.

The dashboard of a car displays your speed so that you know how fast you're going. Since this reading doesn't change when you turn, you don't know the car's velocity. If the car did show you your change in velocity, you could calculate the car's acceleration.

> **Speed** is the distance an object travels per unit of time.
>
> **Velocity** is speed in a given direction.
>
> **Acceleration** is the rate at which velocity changes with time.

• What are three ways to accelerate (change velocity)?

_____

_____

▶ **MY READING WEB** If you had trouble completing the question above, visit **My Reading Web** and type in *Forces*.

Vocabulary Skill

Latin Word Origins Many science words in English come from Latin. For example, the word *solar*, which means "of the sun," comes from the Latin *sol*, which means "sun."

Latin Word	Meaning of Latin Word	Example
fortis	strong	force, *n.* a push or pull exerted on an object
iners	inactivity	inertia, *n.* the tendency of an object to resist any change in its motion
centrum	center	centripetal force, *n.* a force that causes an object to move in a circle

2. **Quick Check** Choose the word that best completes the sentence.

• A _____ always points toward the center of a circle.

force

friction

gravity

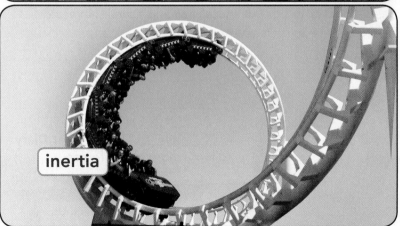

inertia

Chapter Preview

LESSON 1
- force
- newton
- net force

🔄 Relate Text and Visuals
△ Make Models

LESSON 2
- friction
- sliding friction
- static friction
- fluid friction
- rolling friction
- gravity
- mass
- weight

🔄 Identify Supporting Evidence
△ Design Experiments

LESSON 3
- inertia

🔄 Ask Questions
△ Infer

LESSON 4
- momentum
- law of conservation of momentum

🔄 Identify the Main Idea
△ Calculate

LESSON 5
- free fall
- satellite
- centripetal force

🔄 Relate Cause and Effect
△ Create Data Tables

≫ VOCAB FLASH CARDS For extra help with vocabulary, visit **Vocab Flash Cards** and type in *Forces.*

The Nature of Force

🔑 **How Are Forces Described?**

🔑 **How Do Forces Affect Motion?**

my pLaneT DiaRY

MISCONCEPTIONS

Forced to Change

Misconception: Any object that is set in motion will slow down on its own.

Fact: A force is needed to change an object's state of motion.

A soccer ball sits at rest. You come along and kick it, sending it flying across the field. It eventually slows to a stop. You applied a force to start it moving, and then it stopped all on its own, right?

No! Forces cause *all* changes in motion. Just as you applied a force to the ball to speed it up from rest, the ground applied a force to slow it down to a stop. If the ground didn't apply a force to the ball, it would keep rolling forever without slowing down or stopping.

Answer the questions below.

1. Give an example of a force you apply to slow something down.

   _____

   _____

2. Where might it be possible to kick a soccer ball and have it never slow down?

   _____

   _____

   _____

▶ PLANET DIARY Go to **Planet Diary** to learn more about forces.

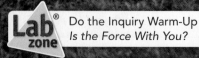

Do the Inquiry Warm-Up
Is the Force With You?

Vocabulary
- force • newton
- net force

Skills
- Reading: Relate Text and Visuals
- Inquiry: Make Models

How Are Forces Described?

In science, the word *force* has a simple and specific meaning. A **force** is a push or a pull. When one object pushes or pulls another object, the first object exerts a force on the second object. You exert a force on a computer key when you push it. You exert a force on a chair when you pull it away from a table.

🗝 **Like velocity and acceleration, a force is described by its strength and by the direction in which it acts.** Pushing to the left is a different force from pushing to the right. The direction and strength of a force can be represented by an arrow. The arrow points in the direction of the force, as shown in **Figure 1.** The length of the arrow tells you the strength of the force—the longer the arrow, the greater the force. The strength of a force is measured in the SI unit called the **newton** (N), after scientist Sir Isaac Newton.

FIGURE 1 ·······

Describing Forces

Forces act on you whenever your motion changes. In the photos at the right, two men are celebrating an Olympic victory. Forces cause them to pull each other in for a hug, lean over, and fall into the pool.

✏️ **Identify** In the box within each photo, draw an arrow that represents the force acting on the person on the right. The first one is done as an example.

Do the Quick Lab
What Is Force?

🗝 **Assess Your Understanding**

got it? ······

○ I get it! Now I know that forces are described by _____

_____

○ I need extra help with _____

Go to my science ⬤ coach *online for help with this subject.*

FIGURE 2 ···

▷ INTERACTIVE ART Net Force

The change in motion of an object is determined by
the net force acting on the object.

✎ ▲Make Models **Calculate and draw an arrow for the
net force for each situation in the boxes below.**

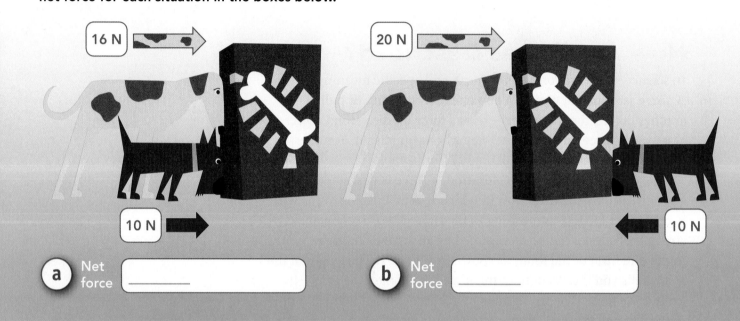

a Net force _____

b Net force _____

How Do Forces Affect Motion?

Often more than one force acts on an object at the same time. The
combination of all the forces on an object is called the **net force.**
The net force determines if and how an object will accelerate.

You can find the net force on an object by adding together the
strengths of all the individual forces acting on the object. Look at
Figure 2a. The big dog pushes on the box with a force of 16 N to
the right. The small dog pushes on the box with a force of 10 N to
the right. The net force on the box is the sum of these forces. The
box will accelerate to the right. In this situation, there is a nonzero
net force. 🔑 **A nonzero net force causes a change in the object's
motion.**

What if the forces on an object aren't acting in the same
direction? In **Figure 2b,** the big dog pushes with a force of 20 N.
The small dog still pushes with a force of 10 N, but now they're
pushing against each other. When forces on an object act in
opposite directions, the strength of the net force is found by
subtracting the strength of the smaller force from the strength
of the larger force. You can still think of this as *adding* the forces
together if you think of all forces that act to the right as positive
forces and all forces that act to the left as negative forces. The box
will accelerate to the right. When forces act in opposite directions,
the net force is in the same direction as the larger force.

·············· ✎ ··············

🔄 **Relate Text and Visuals** Use
the information in the text to
determine the net force of these
two force arrows.

3 N   5 N

Circle the net force below.

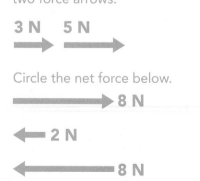

⟶ 8 N

⟵ 2 N

⟵ 8 N

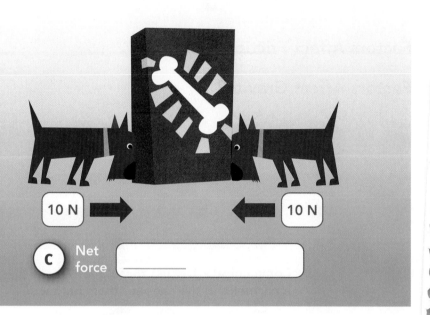

c. Net force [_____]

Use what you know about net force to describe the motion of the box in **Figure 2c.** Assume that the box starts at rest.

_____
_____
_____
_____

apply it!

❶ You pull on your dog's leash to the right with a 12 N force. Your dog pulls to the left with a 6 N force. Sketch this situation, including labeled force arrows, below.

❷ What is the net force on the leash? Calculate it. Draw and label it in the space above.

_____

 Do the Quick Lab
Modeling Unbalanced Forces.

🔑 Assess Your Understanding

1a. Calculate You push on a desk with a force of 120 N to the right. Your friend pushes on the same desk with a force of 90 N to the left. What is the net force on the desk?

_____
_____

b. Predict Your friend increases her force on the desk by 30 N. She doesn't change the direction of her push. What happens to the net force on the desk? Will the desk accelerate?

_____
_____

got it? ....

⚪ I get it! Now I know that changes in motion are caused by _____

⚪ I need extra help with _____

Go to **my science COACH** online for help with this subject.

Friction and Gravity

🔑 **What Factors Affect Friction?**

🔑 **What Factors Affect Gravity?**

my planet Diary

CAREERS

Space Athletes

Have you ever seen pictures of astronauts playing golf on the moon or playing catch in a space station? Golf balls and baseballs can float or fly farther in space, where gravitational forces are weaker than they are on Earth. Imagine what professional sports would be like in reduced gravity!

You may not have to imagine much longer. At least one company specializes in airplane flights that simulate a reduced gravity environment. Similar to NASA training flights that astronauts use when preparing to go into space, these flights allow passengers to fly around the cabin. In environments with reduced gravity, athletes can perform jumps and stunts that would be impossible on Earth. As technology improves, permanent stadiums could be built in space for a whole new generation of athletes.

Communicate Discuss these questions with a partner and then answer them below.

1. Sports can be more fun in reduced gravity. What jobs could be harder or less fun to do in space? Why?

_____

_____

_____

2. What kinds of sports do you think could be more fun in space? Why?

_____

_____

_____

▶ PLANET DIARY Go to **Planet Diary** to learn more about everyday forces.

Lab zone Do the Inquiry Warm-Up *Observing Friction.*

Vocabulary
- friction • sliding friction • static friction
- fluid friction • rolling friction • gravity
- mass • weight

Skills
- Reading: Identify Supporting Evidence
- Inquiry: Design Experiments

What Factors Affect Friction?

If you slide a book across a table, the surface of the book rubs against the surface of the table. The force that two surfaces exert on each other when they rub against each other is called **friction.**

🔑 **Two factors that affect the force of friction are the types of surfaces involved and how hard the surfaces are pushed together.** The football player in **Figure 1** is pushing on a blocking sled. If his coach wanted to make it harder to move the sled, the coach could change the surface of the sled. Covering the bottom of the sled with rubber would increase friction and make the sled harder to move. In general, smooth surfaces produce less friction than rough surfaces.

What would happen if the football player switched to a much heavier sled? He would find the heavier sled harder to push because it pushes down harder against the ground. Similarly, if you rubbed your hands together forcefully, there would be more friction than if you rubbed your hands together lightly. Friction increases when surfaces push harder against each other.

Friction acts in a direction opposite to the direction of the object's motion. Without friction, a moving object will not stop until it strikes another object.

Vocabulary Latin Word Origins
Friction comes from the Latin word *fricare*. Based on the definition of friction, what do you think *fricare* means?
- ○ to burn
- ○ to rub
- ○ to melt

FIGURE 1 ·········
> ART IN MOTION **Friction and Different Surfaces**
The strength of friction depends on the types of surfaces involved. ✎ **Sequence** Rank the surfaces above by how hard it would be to push a sled over them, from easiest (1) to hardest (3). (Each surface is flat.) What does this ranking tell you about the amount of friction over these surfaces?

_____

_____

Sliding Friction

Sliding friction occurs when two solid surfaces slide over each other. Sliding friction is what makes moving objects slow down and stop. Without sliding friction, a penguin that slid down a hill wouldn't stop until he hit a wall!

✏️ **Classify** Label five examples of sliding friction and compare with a classmate.

Friction acts opposite the direction of motion.

Direction of motion →

← Friction

Static Friction

Static friction acts between objects that aren't moving. Think about trying to push a couch across the room. If you don't push hard enough, it won't move. The force that's keeping you from moving it is static friction. Once you push hard enough to overcome static friction, the couch starts moving and there is no more static friction. However, there is sliding friction.

✏️ **Classify** Label five examples of static friction and compare with a classmate.

Draw an arrow representing the frictional force at work.

Fluid Friction

Fluids, such as water and air, are materials that flow easily. **Fluid friction** occurs when a solid object moves through a fluid. Fluid friction is easier to overcome than sliding friction. This is why sidewalks become slippery when they get wet.

✏️ **Classify** Label five examples of fluid friction and compare with a classmate.

Draw an arrow representing the frictional force at work.

Rolling Friction

When an object rolls across a surface, **rolling friction** occurs. Rolling friction is much easier to overcome than sliding friction for similar materials. That's why it's easy to push a bike along the sidewalk when the wheels can turn, but much harder to push the bike if you're applying the brakes and the tires slide, not roll.

✏️ **Classify** Label five examples of rolling friction and compare with a classmate.

Draw an arrow representing the frictional force at work.

apply it!

Your family is moving and isn't sure how to best overcome friction while moving furniture. You have a spring scale, wood blocks to represent your furniture, and sandpaper, aluminum foil, marbles, and olive oil as possible surfaces to slide your furniture over.

⚠ **Design Experiments** **Design an experiment that will help you determine which material will reduce friction the most.**

You know that friction occurs between surfaces when they slide against each other. If you measure the applied force required to push something across a surface, you know that your applied force would (increase/decrease) as friction increased.

STEP ① Measure How would you determine your applied force in this experiment?

_____

_____

_____

STEP ② Control Variables What variables would you have to control to keep your results accurate?

_____

_____

_____

STEP ③ Create Data Tables Draw the data table you would use when performing this experiment.

Lab zone® Do the Lab Investigation *Sticky Sneakers.*

🔑 Assess Your Understanding

1a. List Name four types of friction and give an example of each.

_____

_____

_____

_____

b. Classify What types of friction occur between your bike tires and the ground when you ride over cement, ride through a puddle, and apply your brakes?

_____

got it?

○ **I get it!** Now I know that friction is affected by

_____

_____

_____

○ **I need extra help with** _____

_____

Go to **MY SCIENCE ⓢ COACH** *online for help with this subject.*

What Factors Affect Gravity?

A skydiver would be surprised if she jumped out of a plane and did not fall. We are so used to objects falling that we may not have thought about why they fall. One person who thought about it was Sir Isaac Newton. He concluded that a force acts to pull objects straight down toward the center of Earth. **Gravity** is a force that pulls objects toward each other.

Universal Gravitation Newton realized that gravity acts everywhere in the universe, not just on Earth. It is the force that makes the skydivers in **Figure 2** fall to the ground. It is the force that keeps the moon orbiting around Earth. It is the force that keeps all the planets in our solar system orbiting around the sun.

What Newton realized is now called the law of universal gravitation. The law of universal gravitation states that the force of gravity acts between all objects in the universe that have mass. This means that any two objects in the universe that have mass attract each other. You are attracted not only to Earth but also to the moon, the other planets in the solar system, and all the objects around you. Earth and the objects around you are attracted to you as well. However, you do not notice the attraction among small objects because these forces are extremely small compared to the force of Earth's attraction.

FIGURE 2 ············

Observing Gravity
Newton published his work on gravity in 1687.

✏ **Observe** What observations might you make today that would lead you to the same conclusions about gravity? Write down your ideas below.

_____

_____

_____

_____

_____

_____

Factors Affecting Gravity A gravitational force exists between any two objects in the universe. However, you don't see your pencil fly toward the wall the way you see it fall toward Earth. That's because the gravitational force between some objects is stronger than the force between others. You observe only the effects of the strongest gravitational forces. 🔑 **Two factors affect the gravitational attraction between objects: mass and distance.** Mass is a measure of the amount of matter in an object. The SI unit of mass is the kilogram.

The more mass an object has, the greater its gravitational force. Earth's gravitational force is strong because the mass of Earth is so large. The more massive planets in **Figure 3** experience a greater gravitational force than the less massive planets. Gravitational force also depends on the distance between objects. As distance increases, gravitational force decreases. That's why Earth can exert a visible gravitational force on a pencil in your room and not on a pencil on the moon.

✎ **Identify Supporting Evidence** Underline the factors that determine how strong the gravitational force is between two objects.

FIGURE 3 ·····

Gravitational Attraction
Gravitational attraction depends on two factors: mass and distance. Suppose there was a solar system that looked like this.
✎ **Interpret Diagrams** Use the diagram below to compare the gravitational force between different planets and their sun. Assume all planets are made of the same material, so bigger planets have more mass.

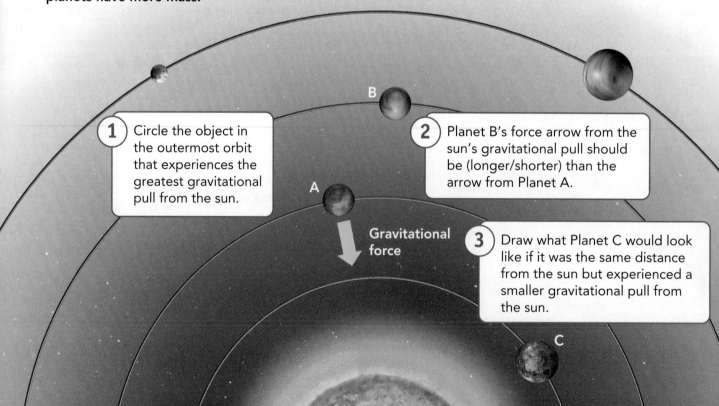

1. Circle the object in the outermost orbit that experiences the greatest gravitational pull from the sun.

2. Planet B's force arrow from the sun's gravitational pull should be (longer/shorter) than the arrow from Planet A.

Gravitational force

3. Draw what Planet C would look like if it was the same distance from the sun but experienced a smaller gravitational pull from the sun.

Earth
60 N

Moon
____N

Mars
____N

Weight and Mass
Mass is sometimes confused with weight. Mass is a measure of the amount of matter in an object. **Weight** is a measure of the force of gravity on an object. When you stand on a bathroom scale, it displays the gravitational force Earth is exerting on you.

At any given time, your mass is the same on Earth as it would be on any other planet. But weight varies with the strength of the gravitational force. The dog in **Figure 4** has a different weight at different places in the solar system. On the moon, he would weigh about one sixth of what he does on Earth. On Mars, he would weigh just over a third of what he does on Earth.

FIGURE 4 ·······························
Weight and Mass
The Mars Phoenix Lander weighs about 3,400 N on Earth. It weighs about 1,300 N on Mars. ✎ Predict **The first scale shows the dog's weight on Earth. Predict its weight on the moon and on Mars. Enter those weights in the boxes on the other two scales.**

Lab ® Do the Quick Lab
zone *Calculating.*

🔑 Assess Your Understanding

2a. Describe What happens to the gravitational force between two objects when their masses are increased? What happens when the distance between the objects increases?

_____

_____

_____

b. Relate Cause and Effect If the mass of Earth increased, what would happen to your weight? What about your mass?

_____

_____

_____

got it? ···
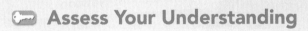

○ **I get it!** Now I know that the factors that affect the gravitational force between objects are _____

_____

○ **I need extra help with** _____

Go to MY SCIENCE ⬤ᶳ COACH *online for help with this subject.*

43

Newton's Laws of Motion

UNLOCK
THE BIG
?

🔑 **What Is Newton's First Law of Motion?**

🔑 **What Is Newton's Second Law of Motion?**

🔑 **What Is Newton's Third Law of Motion?**

my planet Diary

VOICES FROM HISTORY

Horse Force

"If a horse draws a stone tied to a rope, the horse (if I may so say) will be equally drawn back towards the stone...."

—Sir Isaac Newton

Scientists have used everyday examples to explain their ideas for hundreds of years. The quotation is from Newton's *Mathematical Principles of Natural Philosophy*, which was first published in the 1680s. Newton used this book to set down his laws of motion. These three simple laws describe much of the motion around you, and they continue to be studied today.

Answer the question below.
What current scientific discoveries might be taught in schools hundreds of years from now?

_____

_____

_____

_____

_____

▷ PLANET DIARY Go to **Planet Diary** to learn more about Newton.

Lab zone® Do the Inquiry Warm-Up *What Changes Motion?*

What Is Newton's First Law of Motion?

You would be surprised if a rock started rolling on its own or a raindrop paused in midair. If an object is not moving, it will not start moving until a force acts on it. If an object is moving, it will continue at a constant velocity until a force acts to change its speed or its direction. 🔑 **Newton's first law of motion states that an object at rest will remain at rest unless acted upon by a nonzero net force. An object moving at a constant velocity will continue moving at a constant velocity unless acted upon by a nonzero net force.**

Vocabulary
- inertia

Skills
- ⟳ Reading: Ask Questions
- △ Inquiry: Infer

Inertia All objects, moving or not, resist changes in motion. Resistance to change in motion is called **inertia** (in UR shuh). Newton's first law of motion is also called the law of inertia. Inertia explains many common events, including why you move forward in your seat when the car you are in stops suddenly. You keep moving forward because of inertia. A force, such as the pull of a seat belt, is needed to pull you back. Roller coasters like the one in **Figure 1** have safety bars for the same reason.

Inertia Depends on Mass Some objects have more inertia than others. Suppose you need to move an empty backpack and a full backpack. The greater the mass of an object, the greater its inertia, and the greater the force required to change its motion. The full backpack is harder to move than the empty one because it has more mass and therefore more inertia.

FIGURE 1 ···

Inertia
A roller coaster is hard to stop because it has a lot of inertia. ✎ △**Infer Use Newton's first law of motion to explain why you feel tossed around whenever a roller coaster goes over a hill or through a loop.**

_____

_____

_____

_____

_____

Lab zone ® Do the Quick Lab *Around and Around.*

🗝 **Assess Your Understanding**

got it? ···

○ **I get it!** Now I know that Newton's first law of motion states that _____

_____

○ **I need extra help with** _____

Go to my science ⑤ coach *online for help with this subject.*

What Is Newton's Second Law of Motion?

Which is harder to push, a full shopping cart or an empty one? Who can cause a greater acceleration on a shopping cart, a small child or a grown adult?

Changes in Force and Mass Suppose you increase the force on a cart without changing its mass. The acceleration of the cart will also increase. Your cart will also accelerate faster if something falls out. This reduces the mass of the cart, and you keep pushing just as hard. The acceleration of the sled in **Figure 2** will change depending on the mass of the people on it and the force the sled dogs apply. Newton realized these relationships and found a way to represent them mathematically.

Determining Acceleration 🔑 **Newton's second law of motion states that an object's acceleration depends on its mass and on the net force acting on it.** This relationship can be written as follows.

$$\text{Acceleration} = \frac{\text{Net force}}{\text{Mass}}$$

This formula can be rearranged to show how much force must be applied to an object to get it to accelerate at a certain rate.

$$\text{Net force} = \text{Mass} \times \text{Acceleration}$$

FIGURE 2 ·······························

Newton's Second Law
Suppose that four dogs pull a sled carrying two people.
✏️ **Explain** Use words and fill in the pictures to show how you can change the dog/person arrangement to change the sled's acceleration.

How could you increase the sled's acceleration?
_____
_____
_____
_____

How could you decrease the sled's acceleration?
_____
_____
_____
_____

Acceleration is measured in meters per second per second (m/s^2). Mass is measured in kilograms (kg). Newton's second law shows that force is measured in kilograms times meters per second per second ($kg \cdot m/s^2$). This unit is also called the newton (N), which is the SI unit of force. One newton is the force required to give a 1-kg mass an acceleration of $1 \ m/s^2$.

do the math!

Every year in cities around the world, teams create cars, push them across platforms, and hope they will fly. Unfortunately, the cars always end up accelerating down into the water.

1 Calculate If a 100-N net force acts on a 50-kg car, what will the acceleration of the car be?

_____

2 After that same car leaves the platform, gravity causes it to accelerate downward at a rate of $9.8 \ m/s^2$. What is the gravitational force on the car?

_____

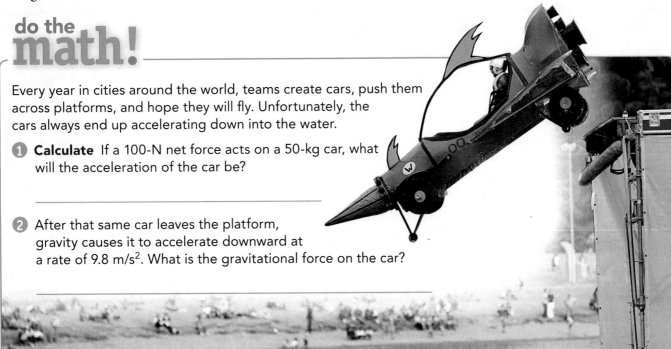

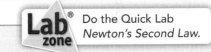

Lab zone® Do the Quick Lab
Newton's Second Law.

🔑 Assess Your Understanding

1a. Review What equation allows you to calculate the force acting on an object?

_____

b. Calculate What is the net force on a 2-kg skateboard accelerating at a rate of $2 \ m/s^2$?

_____

c. Predict If the mass of the skateboard doubled but the net force on it remained constant, what would happen to the acceleration of the skateboard?

_____

_____

_____

got it?

○ **I get it!** Now I know that Newton's second law of motion describes the relationship _____

_____

○ **I need extra help with** _____

Go to **my science** 🅢 **coach** *online for help with this subject.*

FIGURE 3 ·······

Action-Reaction Pairs

A swimmer moves because the water pushes her forward when she pushes back on it.

✎ **Interpret Diagrams** Draw arrows to show the action and reaction forces between the gymnast and the balance beam. Draw your own example in the space provided.

Reaction force   Action force

🕑 **Ask Questions** Action and reaction force pairs are all around you, but they aren't always obvious. Write down a question about a situation in which you can't identify what force pairs are at work.

_____

_____

_____

_____

_____

_____

What Is Newton's Third Law of Motion?

If you leaned against a wall and it didn't push back on you, you'd fall through. The force exerted by the wall is equal in strength and opposite in direction to the force you exert on the wall. 🔑 **Newton's third law of motion states that if one object exerts a force on another object, then the second object exerts a force of equal strength in the opposite direction on the first object.** Another way to state Newton's third law is that for every action there is an equal but opposite reaction.

Action-Reaction Pairs Pairs of action and reaction forces are all around you. When you walk, you push backward on the ground with your feet. Think of this as an action force. (It doesn't matter which force is called the "action" force and which is called the "reaction" force.) The ground pushes forward on your feet with an equal and opposite force. This is the reaction force. You can only walk because the ground pushes you forward! In a similar way, the swimmer in **Figure 3** moves forward by exerting an action force on the water with her hands. The water pushes on her hands with an equal reaction force that propels her body forward.

Detecting Motion If you drop your pen, gravity pulls the pen downward. According to Newton's third law, the pen pulls Earth upward with an equal and opposite reaction force. You see the pen fall. You *don't* see Earth accelerate toward the pen. Remember Newton's second law. If mass increases and force stays the same, acceleration decreases. The same force acts on both Earth and your pen. Since Earth has such a large mass, its acceleration is so small that you don't notice it.

Do Action-Reaction Forces Cancel? You have learned that two equal forces acting in opposite directions on an object cancel each other out and produce no change in motion. So why don't the action and reaction forces in Newton's third law of motion cancel out as well?

Action and reaction forces do not cancel out because they act on different objects. The swimmer in **Figure 3** exerts a backward action force on the water. The water exerts an equal but opposite forward reaction force on her hands. The action and reaction forces act on different objects—the action force acts on the water and the reaction force acts on her hands.

Unlike the swimmer and the water, the volleyball players in **Figure 4** both exert a force on the *same* object—the volleyball. Each player exerts a force on the ball equal in strength but opposite in direction. The forces on the volleyball are balanced. The ball does not move toward one player or the other.

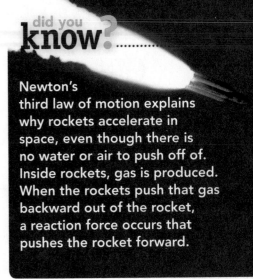

did you
know?..........

Newton's third law of motion explains why rockets accelerate in space, even though there is no water or air to push off of. Inside rockets, gas is produced. When the rockets push that gas backward out of the rocket, a reaction force occurs that pushes the rocket forward.

Force on ball

Forces on hands

Force on ball

FIGURE 4 ·······················

Action-Reaction Forces
All the horizontal forces on the volleyball cancel out.

✎ **Apply Concepts** In the dog illustration above, use Newton's third law of motion to draw and label any missing force arrows for all the objects.

What Makes a Bug Go *Splat*?

How do objects react to forces?

FIGURE 5 ···

▶ **VIRTUAL LAB** Splat! A bug has just flown into the windshield of an oncoming car. The car must have hit the bug much harder than the bug hit the car, right? ✎ **Apply Concepts** Use Newton's laws of motion to make sense of the situation and answer the questions.

A

Buzz!

In order for the bug to fly through the air, a force has to push the bug forward. Identify this force. How does the bug produce it? (*Hint:* Think back to how a swimmer moves through the water.)

_____

_____

_____

_____

_____

The bug was at rest on a tree when it saw the car and decided to fly toward it. If the bug has a mass of 0.05 kg and accelerates at 2 m/s^2, what's the net force on the bug?

_____

10 - LG - SP

B Vroom!

The driver hates killing bugs. When she saw one coming toward the windshield, she braked suddenly and hoped it would get out of the way. (Sadly, it did not.) When she hit the brakes, she felt that she was thrown forward. Use one of Newton's laws to explain why.

_____

_____

_____

_____

_____

C Splat!

The unfortunate bug hits the windshield with a force of 1 N. If you call this the action force, what is the reaction force? Does the car hit the bug any harder than the bug hits the car? Use one of Newton's laws to explain why or why not.

_____

_____

_____

_____

_____

Compare the forces on the bug and the car again. Use another one of Newton's laws to explain why the bug goes *splat* and the car keeps going, without noticeably slowing down.

_____

_____

_____

_____

Lab zone® Do the Quick Lab
Interpreting Illustrations.

🔑 Assess Your Understanding

2a. Identify A dog pulls on his leash with a 10-N force to the left. Identify the reaction force.

_____

_____

_____

_____

b. ANSWER THE BIG ? Using all three of Newton's laws, explain how objects react to forces.

_____

_____

_____

_____

_____

_____

_____

_____

_____

_____

_____

_____

_____

got it? ....

○ **I get it!** Now I know that Newton's third law of motion states that _____

_____

_____

_____

○ **I need extra help with** _____

_____

_____

Go to **MY SCIENCE** ⬤ᔆ **COACH** *online for help with this subject.*

UNLOCK
THE BIG
?

🔑 **What Is an Object's Momentum?**

my planet Diary

Air Hockey Science

Whoosh—you've just scored a goal! The puck is about to go back into play. How can you keep the puck out of your goal and get it back into your opponent's? One of the factors you have to consider is momentum. Momentum is a physical quantity that all moving objects have. If you know about momentum, you can predict how an object will act when it collides with other objects. With some quick scientific thinking, you can get the puck to bounce all over the table and back into your opponent's goal!

Answer the questions below.

1. Why might it be better to try to bounce a puck off the wall rather than shoot it straight into your opponent's goal?

_____

_____

_____

_____

2. Where else could it be helpful to know how objects act after colliding?

_____

_____

_____

▶ PLANET DIARY Go to **Planet Diary** to learn more about momentum.

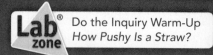

Lab® zone Do the Inquiry Warm-Up
How Pushy Is a Straw?

Vocabulary
- momentum
- law of conservation of momentum

Skills
- Reading: Identify the Main Idea
- Inquiry: Calculate

What Is an Object's Momentum?

Is it harder to stop a rolling bowling ball or a rolling marble? Does your answer depend on the velocities of the objects? All moving objects have what Newton called a "quantity of motion." Today it's called momentum. **Momentum** (moh MEN tum) is a characteristic of a moving object that is related to the mass and the velocity of the object. **The momentum of a moving object can be determined by multiplying the object's mass by its velocity.**

Momentum = Mass × Velocity

Since mass is measured in kilograms and velocity is measured in meters per second, the unit for momentum is kilograms times meters per second (kg·m/s). Like velocity, acceleration, and force, momentum is described by both a direction and a strength. The momentum of an object is in the same direction as its velocity.

The more momentum a moving object has, the harder it is to stop. For example, a 0.1-kg baseball moving at 40 m/s has a momentum of 4 kg·m/s in the direction it's moving.

Momentum = 0.1 kg × 40 m/s

Momentum = 4 kg·m/s

But a 1,200-kg car moving at the same speed as the baseball has a much greater momentum: 48,000 kg·m/s. The velocity of an object also affects the amount of momentum it has. For example, a tennis ball served by a professional tennis player has a large momentum. Although the ball has a small mass, it travels at a high velocity.

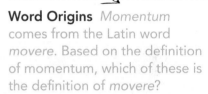

Word Origins *Momentum* comes from the Latin word *movere*. Based on the definition of momentum, which of these is the definition of *movere*?

○ to spin
○ to move
○ to sit

apply it!

△ Calculate In each question below, calculate the desired quantity.

❶ The lioness has a mass of 180 kg and a velocity of 16 m/s to the right. What is her momentum?

_____
_____
_____

❷ The warthog has a mass of 100 kg. What does the warthog's speed have to be for it to have the same momentum as the lioness?

_____

Identify the Main Idea

Circle a sentence that relates the main idea of this section to two colliding cars. Then underline two supporting examples.

FIGURE 1 ·····················

INTERACTIVE ART **Conservation of Momentum**

✎ ◢Calculate **Complete the equations describing the momentum of each collision. Identify the direction in each case.**

Conservation of Momentum

Imagine you're driving a go-cart. If you ran into another go-cart that was at rest and got stuck to it, what do you think would happen to your momentum? Before you hit the other go-cart, your momentum was just your mass times your velocity. How has the additional mass changed that momentum? It actually hasn't changed it at all!

A quantity that is conserved is the same after an event as it was before. The **law of conservation of momentum** states that, in the absence of outside forces like friction, the total momentum of objects that interact does not change. The amount of momentum two cars have is the same before and after they interact.

🔑 **The total momentum of any group of objects remains the same, or is conserved, unless outside forces act on the objects.**

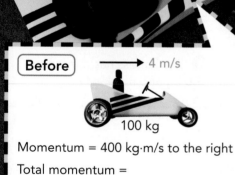

Before → 4 m/s   → 2 m/s

100 kg   100 kg

Momentum = 400 kg·m/s to the right

Momentum = 200 kg·m/s to the right

Total momentum = _____ kg·m/s _____

After → 2 m/s   → 4 m/s

Momentum = _____ kg·m/s to the right

Momentum = _____ kg·m/s to the right

Total momentum = _____ kg·m/s _____

"Non-Sticky" Collisions

Look at this example of a collision. When two objects of the same mass don't stick together and outside forces (such as friction) are negligible, the objects just trade velocities. The car that is going faster before the collision will end up slowing down, and the car that is going slower before the collision will end up speeding up.

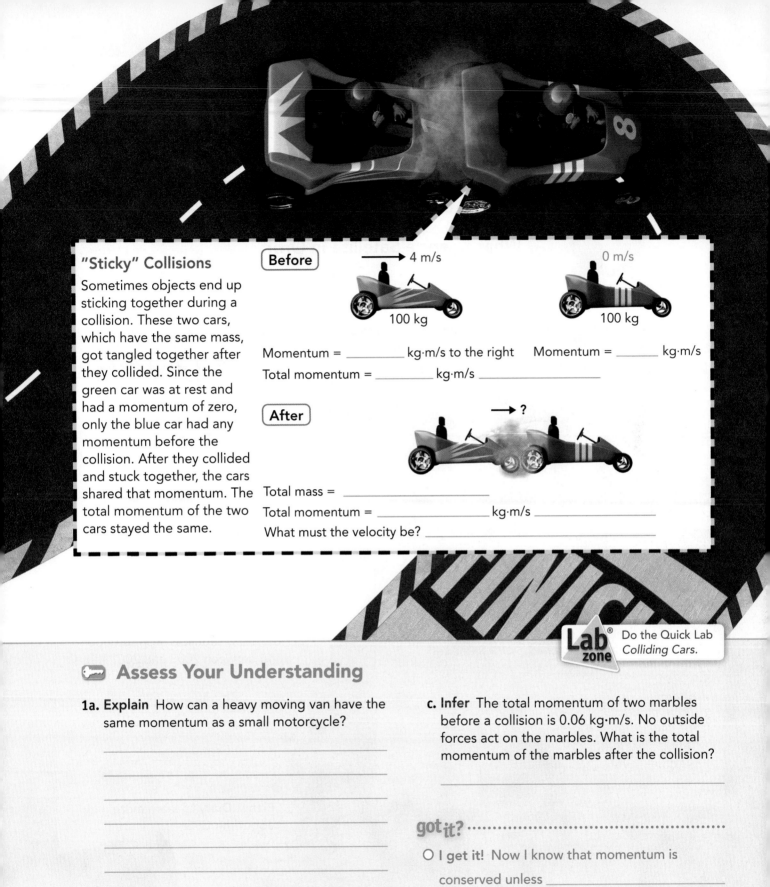

"Sticky" Collisions

Sometimes objects end up sticking together during a collision. These two cars, which have the same mass, got tangled together after they collided. Since the green car was at rest and had a momentum of zero, only the blue car had any momentum before the collision. After they collided and stuck together, the cars shared that momentum. The total momentum of the two cars stayed the same.

Before

4 m/s

0 m/s

100 kg

100 kg

Momentum = _____ kg·m/s to the right   Momentum = _____ kg·m/s

Total momentum = _____ kg·m/s _____

After

→ ?

Total mass = _____

Total momentum = _____ kg·m/s _____

What must the velocity be? _____

Lab zone Do the Quick Lab *Colliding Cars.*

🔑 Assess Your Understanding

1a. Explain How can a heavy moving van have the same momentum as a small motorcycle?

_____

_____

_____

_____

_____

_____

b. Calculate What is the momentum of a 750-kg car traveling at a velocity of 25 m/s?

_____

_____

c. Infer The total momentum of two marbles before a collision is 0.06 kg·m/s. No outside forces act on the marbles. What is the total momentum of the marbles after the collision?

_____

_____

got it? ···

○ **I get it!** Now I know that momentum is

conserved unless _____

_____

○ **I need extra help with** _____

Go to MY SCIENCE ⬤ COACH online for help with this subject.

Free Fall and Circular Motion

🗝 What Is Free Fall?

🗝 What Keeps a Satellite in Orbit?

my planet Diary

Finding Yourself

The GPS (Global Positioning System) is a "constellation" of satellites that orbit 10,600 miles above Earth. The GPS makes it possible for people with ground receivers to pinpoint their geographic location. The first GPS satellites were placed in orbit in 1978. These early satellites were expected to operate for approximately five years. Newer satellites have an expected lifespan of seven to eight years.

GPS Satellites in Orbit		
Years	Number of GPS Satellites Launched	Number of Operating GPS Satellites
1978–1982	6	6
1983–1987	4	8
1988–1992	17	21
1993–1997	12	27
1998–2002	5	28
2003–2007	11	31

SCIENCE STATS

Interpret Data Use the data in the table to answer the questions below.

1. What is the total number of satellites launched from 1978 to 2007? How many were still operating as of 2007?

_____

_____

_____

_____

2. How many satellites stopped operating between 2003 and 2007?

_____

_____

_____

_____

▷ PLANET DIARY Go to **Planet Diary** to learn more about the GPS.

Lab zone Do the Inquiry Warm-Up *What Makes an Object Move in a Circle?*

Vocabulary
- free fall • satellite
- centripetal force

Skills
- Reading: Relate Cause and Effect
- Inquiry: Create Data Tables

What Is Free Fall?

When the only force acting on an object is gravity, the object is said to be in **free fall.** The force of gravity causes the object to accelerate. **Free fall is motion where the acceleration is caused by gravity.** When something falls on Earth, there is fluid friction from the air around it. This friction acts against gravity, reducing the acceleration of falling objects. Air friction increases as an object falls. If an object falls for long enough, increased air friction will reduce its acceleration to zero. The object will continue to fall, but it will fall at a constant velocity.

Near the surface of Earth, the acceleration due to gravity is 9.8 m/s^2. If there were no air friction, a falling object would have a velocity of 9.8 m/s after one second and 19.6 m/s after two seconds. Since air friction reduces acceleration, an object falling on Earth for one second will actually have a velocity that is less than 9.8 m/s.

FIGURE 1 ···

Free Fall

The photo shows a tennis ball and a crumpled piece of paper of different masses as they fall during a fraction of a second. If the only force acting on them were gravity, they would fall at exactly the same rate and line up perfectly. However, air friction is also present. Air friction has a greater effect on the paper's acceleration than on the tennis ball's acceleration. This causes the tennis ball to fall faster.

do the math! ·····················

✎ Create Data Tables
Suppose you had a chamber with no air, eliminating the force of air friction. Complete the table below for an object that is dropped from rest. Remember the formula Velocity = Acceleration × Time. The acceleration due to gravity is 9.8 m/s^2.

Time (s)	Velocity (m/s)
0	_____
1	_____
2	_____
3	_____
4	_____

Lab zone Do the Quick Lab
Which Lands First?

🔑 Assess Your Understanding

got it? ···

○ I get it! Now I know that free fall is _____
_____

○ I need extra help with _____
Go to **my science** 🔵 **COACH** *online for help with this subject.*

What Keeps a Satellite in Orbit?

Objects don't always fall down in straight lines. If you throw a ball horizontally, the ball will move away from you while gravity pulls the ball to the ground. The horizontal and vertical motions act independently, and the ball follows a curved path toward the ground. If you throw the ball faster, it will land even farther in front of you. The faster you throw an object, the farther it travels before it lands.

Satellite Motion This explains how satellites, which are objects that orbit around other objects in space, follow a curved path around Earth. What would happen if you were on a high mountain and could throw a ball as fast as you wanted? The faster you threw it, the farther away it would land. But, at a certain speed, the curved path of the ball would match the curved surface of Earth. Although the ball would keep falling due to gravity, Earth's surface would curve away from the ball at the same rate. The ball would fall around Earth in a circle, as shown in Figure 2.

⟲ **Relate Cause and Effect**
On the next page, underline the effect a centripetal force has on an object's motion. Circle the effect of turning off a centripetal force.

FIGURE 2 ·······················

Satellite Motion
A satellite launched from Earth enters orbit because the curve of its path matches the curved surface of Earth.

✎ **Make Models** On the picture at the right, draw arrows representing the gravitational force on the ball at each point.

[CHALLENGE] Explain why Earth's atmosphere would prevent this baseball from ever actually being thrown into orbit. Why is this not a problem for satellites?

_____

_____

_____

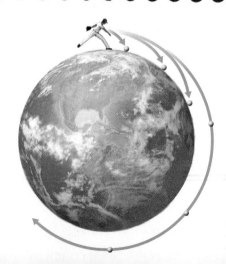

🔑 **Satellites in orbit around Earth continuously fall toward Earth, but because Earth is curved they travel around it.** In other words, a satellite is a falling object that keeps missing the ground! It falls around Earth rather than onto it. Once it has entered a stable orbit, a satellite does not need fuel. It continues to move ahead due to its inertia. At the same time, gravity continuously changes the satellite's direction. Most satellites are launched at a speed of about 7,900 m/s. That's more than 17,000 miles per hour!

Centripetal Force Many manufactured satellites orbit Earth in an almost circular path. Recall that an object traveling in a circle is accelerating because it constantly changes direction. If an object is accelerating, a force must be acting on it. A force that causes an object to move in a circular path is a **centripetal force** (sen TRIP ih tul). The word *centripetal* means "center-seeking." Centripetal forces always point toward the center of the circle an object is moving in. If you could turn off a centripetal force, inertia would cause the object to fly off in a straight line. For example, the string of a yo-yo being swung in a circle provides a centripetal force. Cutting the string would cut off the centripetal force, and the yo-yo would fly off in a straight line.

apply it!

Identify What is creating the centripetal force in each situation below?

1 A tetherball swinging around a pole

_____

2 Mars orbiting around the sun

_____

3 A child standing on a merry-go-round

_____

Lab zone Do the Quick Lab *Orbiting Earth.*

🔑 **Assess Your Understanding**

1a. Identify What is the force that causes objects to move in circles?

_____

b. Predict If Earth's gravity could be turned off, what would happen to satellites that are currently in orbit? Explain your reasoning.

_____

_____

_____

_____

got it?

◯ **I get it!** Now I know that satellites stay in orbit because _____

_____

_____

◯ **I need extra help with** _____

_____

Go to **my science** 🇸 **coach** *online for help with this subject.*

2 Study Guide

Changes in motion are caused by _____. _____ laws describe these changes in motion.

LESSON 1 The Nature of Force

🔑 Like velocity and acceleration, a force is described by its strength and by the direction in which it acts.

🔑 A nonzero net force causes a change in the object's motion.

Vocabulary
- force   • newton
- net force

LESSON 2 Friction and Gravity

🔑 Two factors that affect the force of friction are the types of surfaces involved and how hard the surfaces are pushed together.

🔑 Two factors affect the gravitational attraction between objects: their masses and distance.

Vocabulary
- friction   • sliding friction
- static friction   • fluid friction
- rolling friction   • gravity
- mass   • weight

LESSON 3 Newton's Laws of Motion

🔑 Objects at rest will remain at rest and objects moving at a constant velocity will continue moving at a constant velocity unless they are acted upon by nonzero net forces.

🔑 The acceleration of an object depends on its mass and on the net force acting on it.

🔑 If one object exerts a force on another object, then the second object exerts a force of equal strength in the opposite direction on the first object.

Vocabulary
- inertia

LESSON 4 Momentum

🔑 The momentum of a moving object can be determined by multiplying the object's mass by its velocity.

🔑 The total momentum of any group of objects remains the same, or is conserved, unless outside forces act on the objects.

Vocabulary
- momentum
- law of conservation of momentum

LESSON 5 Free Fall and Circular Motion

🔑 Free fall is motion where the acceleration is caused by gravity.

🔑 Satellites in orbit around Earth continuously fall toward Earth, but because Earth is curved they travel around it.

Vocabulary
- free fall   • satellite   • centripetal force

Review and Assessment

LESSON 1 The Nature of Force

1. When a nonzero net force acts on an object, the force

   a. changes the motion of the object.

   b. must be greater than the reaction force.

   c. does not change the motion of the object.

   d. is equal to the weight of the object.

2. The SI unit of force is the _____

3. Calculate What is the net force on the box? Be sure to specify direction.

15 N ⟶

⟵ 10 N

_____

LESSON 2 Friction and Gravity

4. Friction always acts

   a. in the same direction as motion.

   b. opposite the direction of motion.

   c. perpendicular to the direction of motion.

   d. at a 30° angle to the direction of motion.

5. The factors that affect the gravitational force between two objects are _____

_____

6. List What are two ways you can increase the frictional force between two objects?

_____

_____

7. 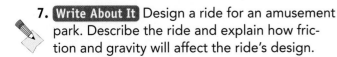 **Write About It** Design a ride for an amusement park. Describe the ride and explain how friction and gravity will affect the ride's design.

LESSON 3 Newton's Laws of Motion

8. Which of Newton's laws of motion is also called the law of inertia?

   a. First   **b.** Second

   c. Third   **d.** Fourth

9. Newton's second law states that force is equal to _____

10. Interpret Diagrams Look at the diagram below of two students pulling a bag of volleyball equipment. The friction force between the bag and the floor is 4 N. What is the net force acting on the bag? What is the acceleration of the bag?

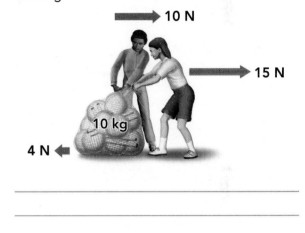

⟶ 10 N

⟶ 15 N

10 kg

4 N ⟵

_____

_____

_____

11. Apply Concepts Suppose you are an astronaut making a space walk outside your space station and your jet pack runs out of fuel. How can you use your empty jet pack to get you back to the station?

_____

_____

_____

_____

_____

_____

_____

LESSON 4 Momentum

12. Momentum is calculated by multiplying

    a. mass times velocity. **b.** weight times mass.

    c. force times speed.   **d.** inertia times force.

13. The SI unit of momentum is _____

14. Explain How can two objects of different masses have the same momentum?

_____

_____

_____

_____

_____

15. Design Experiments Design an experiment in which you could show that momentum is not conserved in a collision between two marbles when friction is present.

_____

_____

_____

_____

_____

_____

_____

_____

_____

16. **Write About It** Pick two sports. Explain how knowing about momentum could help you predict what will happen in the game when you watch these sports on TV.

LESSON 5 Free Fall and Circular Motion

17. Satellites remain in orbit around Earth because

    a. the moon's gravitational pull on them is equal to Earth's pull.

    b. no forces act on them.

    c. their motors keep them moving in circles.

    d. the curve of their paths as they fall matches the curve of Earth.

18. Centripetal forces always point _____

_____

19. Calculate Determine the velocity of an object that started from rest and has been in free fall for 10 seconds. Assume there is no air resistance.

_____

APPLY THE BIG ❓ How do objects react to forces?

20. Forces are all around you. Describe an example of each of Newton's laws of motion that you experience before you get to school in the morning.

_____

_____

_____

_____

_____

_____

_____

_____

_____

_____

Standardized Test Prep

Multiple Choice

Circle the letter of the best answer.

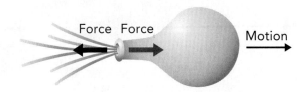

Force Force   Motion →

1. In the balloon diagram above, why don't the two forces cancel each other out?

   A They are not equal.
   B They both act on the air.
   C They both act on the balloon.
   D They act on different objects.

2. What force makes it less likely for a person to slip on a dry sidewalk than on an icy sidewalk?

   A gravity
   B friction
   C inertia
   D momentum

3. A 5-kg cat accelerates at a rate of 2 m/s^2. What is the net force acting on the cat?

   A 10 N
   B 7 N
   C 3 N
   D 2.5 N

4. According to Newton's first law, what will plates at rest on a tablecloth do when the tablecloth is pulled out from under them? (Ignore outside forces such as friction.)

   A fly off the table and hit the ground
   B accelerate with the tablecloth
   C resist the change in motion and stay at rest
   D accelerate in the opposite direction from the tablecloth

5. In a game of tug-of-war, you pull on the rope with a force of 100 N to the right and your friend pulls on the rope with a force of 100 N to the left. What is the net force on the rope?

   A 200 N to the right
   B 200 N to the left
   C 0 N
   D 100 N to the right

Constructed Response

Use your knowledge of science to help you answer Question 6. Write your answer on a separate sheet of paper.

6. Use all three of Newton's laws of motion to describe what happens when a car starts off at rest, is pushed across a platform, and then accelerates downward.

safety restraints

Did you wear your seat belt the last time you rode in a car? Seat belts are safety restraints designed to protect you from injury while you travel in a moving vehicle, whether you stop suddenly to avoid a crash or are stopped suddenly by a crash.

Without a seat belt, inertia would cause the driver and passengers in a car that suddenly stopped to continue traveling forward. Without a restraint, a 75-kilogram driver driving at 50 km/h would experience 12,000 newtons of force in a crash! A safety restraint prevents that forward motion and keeps the driver and passengers safe.

Safety harnesses and seat belts are available in many different designs. Most seat belts are three-point harnesses. Five- and seven-point harnesses are used in vehicles like race cars and fighter jets.

Debate It Most states have laws that require drivers and passengers to wear seat belts. Research the seat belt laws in your state, and participate in a class debate about whether the seat belts are strong enough.

Race car drivers travel at higher speeds than most drivers experience. A five-point harness provides extra security at these high speeds. ▼

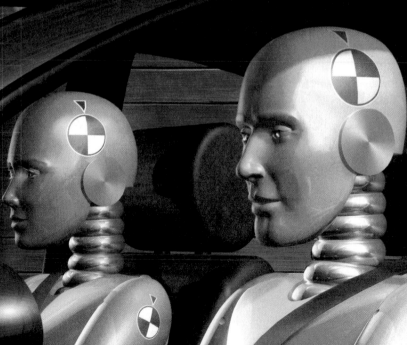

SUPERLUBRICITY

Get a Grip!

There is a substance that doesn't play by the rules of friction. You might be surprised to know it is graphite—the same material found in your pencils, and it has a quality called superlubricity!

When two pieces of graphite slide across each other, if the layers are properly arranged, friction almost disappears. This property makes graphite an excellent dry lubricant. Unlike oils and water- or silicon-based lubricants, graphite won't wet or damage the materials being lubricated.

Scientists are studying graphite because, while they can observe superlubricity, they still can't really describe how it works. Studies are being done to figure out the models of superlubricity, or how it works in different situations.

Colored scanning tunneling micrograph of the surface of graphite. The hexagonal pattern of the graphite surface is related to the way the carbon atoms are arranged. ▼

Test It Find more information about graphite and superlubricity. Design an experiment using lead (which contains graphite) from your pencils to test the friction of graphite sliding across other materials. Keep track of your results and present your findings in a series of graphs and charts.

Graphite is a form of carbon. When it is properly prepared, two layers of graphite can slide across each other with almost no friction. ▶

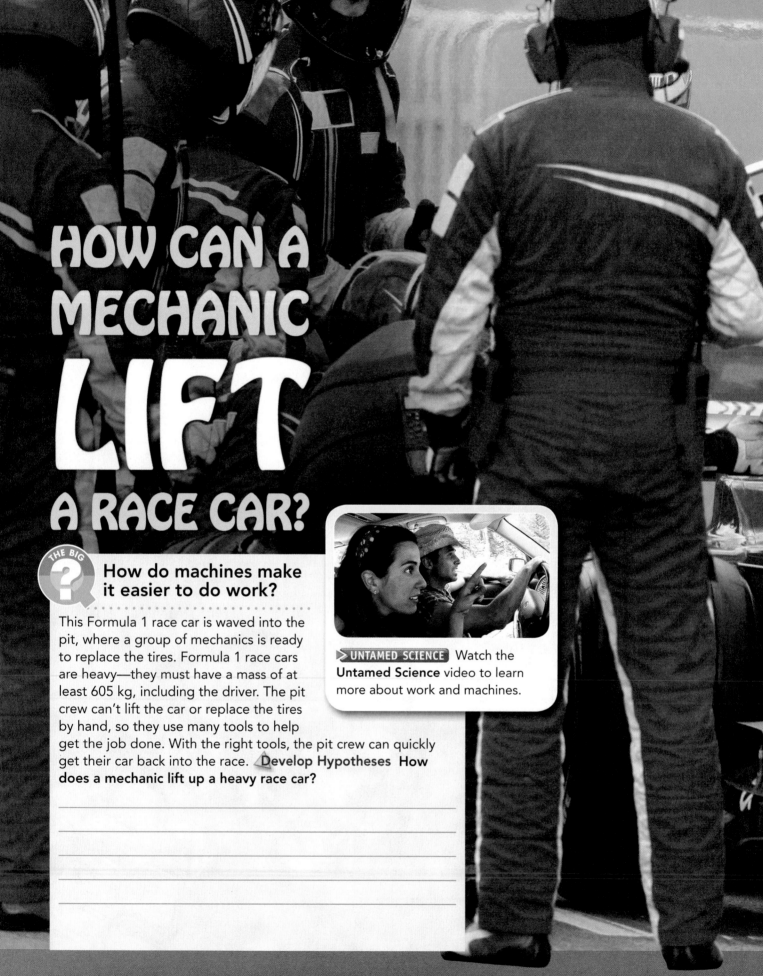

HOW CAN A MECHANIC LIFT A RACE CAR?

How do machines make it easier to do work?

This Formula 1 race car is waved into the pit, where a group of mechanics is ready to replace the tires. Formula 1 race cars are heavy—they must have a mass of at least 605 kg, including the driver. The pit crew can't lift the car or replace the tires by hand, so they use many tools to help get the job done. With the right tools, the pit crew can quickly get their car back into the race. **Develop Hypotheses** How does a mechanic lift up a heavy race car?

UNTAMED SCIENCE Watch the **Untamed Science** video to learn more about work and machines.

Work and Machines

3 Getting Started

Check Your Understanding

1. **Background** Read the paragraph below and then answer the question.

> Charles wants to move his bed across the room, but the weight of the bed is too great for him to lift it. However, he can generate enough force to push the bed.

> A **force** is a push or pull exerted on an object.
>
> **Weight** is a measure of the force of gravity on an object.

- What forces are acting on the bed as Charles pushes it across the floor?

_____

_____

▶ MY READING WEB If you had trouble completing the question above, visit **My Reading Web** and type in *Work and Machines.*

Vocabulary Skill

Identify Multiple Meanings Some familiar words have more than one meaning. Words you use every day may have different meanings in science. Look at the different meanings of the words below.

Word	Everyday Meaning	Scientific Meaning
work	*n.* A job or responsibility Example: She carried her backpack to work every day.	*n.* The product of a force and the distance over which that force is exerted Example: It takes twice as much work to lift a suitcase 2 meters as it does to lift it 1 meter.
machine	*n.* A motorized device Example: A washing machine contains a large rotating basin.	*n.* Any device that makes work easier Example: A wheelbarrow is a machine that lets you lift more weight than you normally could.

2. **Quick Check** Circle the sentence below that uses the scientific meaning of the word *work.*

- Jim did **work** on the bed to move it out of his room.
- Tina had a lot of **work** to do at the end of the semester.

work

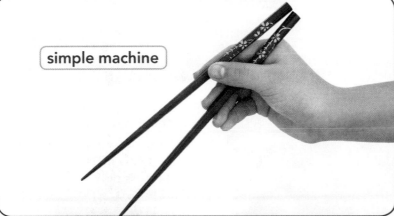

simple machine

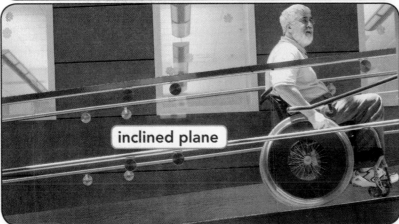

inclined plane

pulley

Chapter Preview

LESSON 1
- work
- joule
- power
- watt

⟳ **Identify Supporting Evidence**
△ **Calculate**

LESSON 2
- machine
- input force
- output force
- mechanical advantage
- efficiency

⟳ **Compare and Contrast**
△ **Predict**

LESSON 3
- simple machine
- inclined plane
- wedge
- screw
- lever
- fulcrum

⟳ **Relate Cause and Effect**
△ **Infer**

LESSON 4
- pulley
- wheel and axle
- compound machine

⟳ **Summarize**
△ **Classify**

> **VOCAB FLASH CARDS** For extra help with vocabulary, visit **Vocab Flash Cards** and type in *Work and Machines.*

1 Work and Power

🗝 **How Is Work Defined?**

🗝 **What Is Power?**

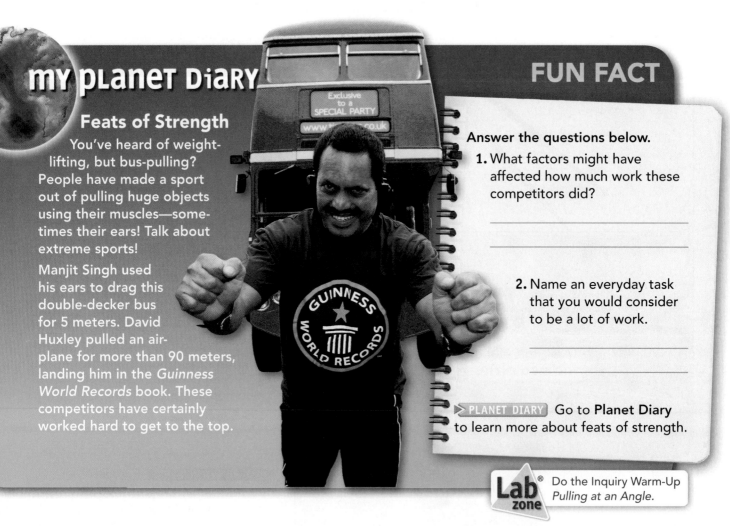

my planet Diary

Feats of Strength

You've heard of weight-lifting, but bus-pulling? People have made a sport out of pulling huge objects using their muscles—sometimes their ears! Talk about extreme sports!

Manjit Singh used his ears to drag this double-decker bus for 5 meters. David Huxley pulled an airplane for more than 90 meters, landing him in the *Guinness World Records* book. These competitors have certainly worked hard to get to the top.

FUN FACT

Answer the questions below.

1. What factors might have affected how much work these competitors did?

_____

_____

2. Name an everyday task that you would consider to be a lot of work.

_____

_____

> **PLANET DIARY** Go to **Planet Diary** to learn more about feats of strength.

Lab zone Do the Inquiry Warm-Up *Pulling at an Angle.*

How Is Work Defined?

If you push a child on a swing, you are doing work on the child. If you pull your books out of your backpack, you do work on your books. In scientific terms, you do **work** any time you exert a force on an object that causes the object to move some distance.

🗝 **Work is done on an object when the object moves in the same direction in which the force is exerted.**

Vocabulary
- work   • joule
- power   • watt

Skills
- Reading: Identify Supporting Evidence
- Inquiry: Calculate

No Work Without Motion Suppose you push on a car that is stuck in the mud. You certainly exert a force on the car, so it might seem as if you do work. But if the force you exert does not make the car move, you are not doing any work on it. To do work on an object, the object must move some distance as a result of your force. If the object does not move, no work is done, no matter how much force is exerted.

Force in the Same Direction Think about carrying your backpack to school in the morning. You know that you exert a force on your backpack when you carry it, but you do not do any work on it. To do work on an object, the force you exert must be in the same direction as the object's motion. When you carry an object while walking at constant velocity, you exert an upward force on the object. The motion of the object is in the horizontal direction. Since the force is vertical and the motion is horizontal, you don't do any work.

Figure 1 shows three different ways to move a cello. You can lift it off the ground and carry it, you can push it parallel to the ground, or you can pull it at an angle to the ground. The weight of the cello is the same in each situation, but the amount of work varies.

FIGURE 1 ···

Force, Motion, and Work
The amount of work that you do on something depends on the direction of your force and the object's motion. ✎ **Describe** Suppose you are moving a rolling suitcase. Describe three ways of moving it that require different amounts of work.

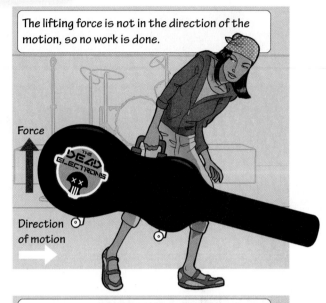
The lifting force is not in the direction of the motion, so no work is done.

Force

Direction of motion

The force acts in the same direction as the motion, so the maximum work is done.

Direction of motion

Force

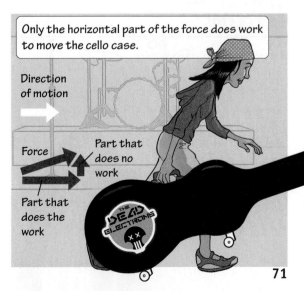
Only the horizontal part of the force does work to move the cello case.

Direction of motion

Force

Part that does no work

Part that does the work

Two factors affect the amount of work April does to hand her friend an instrument: the force she must apply and the distance she must apply the force through.

FIGURE 2 ⋯⋯⋯⋯⋯⋯⋯⋯

> **INTERACTIVE ART** Amount of Work

When April lifts an instrument up the stairs, she does work.

✎ **Draw Conclusions** In the second panel, where could April's friend stand to reduce the work she does to hand him the trumpet? Circle the step(s). If the stage were higher, what would happen to the amount of work that April does on the trumpet when she lifts it?

_____

did you
know? ⋯⋯⋯⋯⋯⋯⋯⋯

Participants in the Empire State Building Run-Up race up the skyscraper's stairs. For a 500 N person to climb 1,576 steps (320 m) it takes 160,000 J of work. That's enough work to lift an elephant over 3 m!

Calculating Work   Look at **Figure 2**. Which do you think involves more work: lifting a 40-newton tuba up three steps (about 0.5 meters), or lifting a 5-newton trumpet up the same three steps? Your common sense may suggest that lifting a heavier object requires more work than lifting a lighter object. This is true. But is it more work to lift an instrument up three steps or up to the top story of a building? As you might guess, moving an object a greater distance requires more work than moving the same object a shorter distance.

The amount of work you do depends on both the amount of force you exert and the distance the object moves. 🔑 **The amount of work done on an object can be determined by multiplying force times distance.**

$$\text{Work} = \text{Force} \times \text{Distance}$$

When you lift an object, the upward force you exert must be at least equal to the object's weight. So, to lift the trumpet, you would have to exert a force of 5 newtons. The distance you lift the trumpet is 0.5 meters. The amount of work you do on the trumpet can be calculated using the work formula.

$$\text{Work} = \text{Force} \times \text{Distance}$$

$$\text{Work} = 5 \text{ N} \times 0.5 \text{ m}$$

$$\text{Work} = 2.5 \text{ N·m}$$

To lift the tuba, you would have to exert a force of 40 newtons. So the amount of work you do would be 40 newtons × 0.5 meters, or 20 N•m. You do more work

When force is measured in newtons and distance in meters, the SI unit of work is the newton-meter (N m). This unit is also called a **joule** (JOOL) in honor of James Prescott Joule, a physicist who studied work in the mid-1800s. One joule (J) is the amount of work you do when you exert a force of 1 newton to move an object a distance of 1 meter. It takes 2.5 joules of work to lift the trumpet up three steps. Lifting the tuba the same distance requires 20 joules of work.

apply it!

The climber on the right does work on his equipment as he carries it up the mountain.

1 On a warm day, the climber does 3,000 J of work to get his pack up the mountain. On a snowy day, he adds equipment to his pack. If he climbs to the same height, he would do (more/less/the same amount of) work.

2 If the climber's pack stayed the same weight and the climber only climbed halfway up, he would do (more/less/the same amount of) work.

3 **Calculate** How much work does the climber do on his pack if his pack weighs 90 N and he climbs to a height of 30 m?

_____

4 [CHALLENGE] On a different trip, the climber's pack weighs twice as much and he climbs twice as high. How many times more work does he do on this pack than the one in question 3?

_____

Lab zone® Do the Quick Lab
What is Work?

🔑 Assess Your Understanding

1a. Describe A waiter carries a 5-newton tray of food while he walks a distance of 10 meters. Is work done on the tray? Why or why not?

_____

_____

_____

b. Explain You're holding your dog's leash and trying to stand still as he pulls on the leash at an angle. You move forward. (All of/Some of/None of) his force does work on you.

c. Calculate How much work do you do when you push a shopping cart with a force of 50 N for a distance of 5 m?

_____

got it?

○ **I get it!** Now I know that work is _____

○ **I need extra help with** _____

Go to MY SCIENCE ⑤ COACH online for help with this subject.

What Is Power?

If you carry a backpack up a flight of stairs, the work you do is the same whether you walk or run. The amount of work you do on an object is not affected by the time it takes to do the work. But scientists keep track of how fast work is done with a rate called power.

Power is the rate at which work is done.  **Power equals the amount of work done on an object in a unit of time.** You need more power to run up the stairs with your backpack than to walk because it takes you less time to do the same work.

You can think of power in another way. An object that has more power than another object does more work in the same time. It can also mean doing the same amount of work in less time.

✎ **Identify Supporting Evidence** Underline details and examples that support the main idea of this section.

Calculating Power

Whenever you know how fast work is done, you can calculate power. Power is calculated by dividing the amount of work done by the amount of time it takes to do the work. This can be written as the following formula.

$$\text{Power} = \frac{\text{Work}}{\text{Time}}$$

Since work is equal to force times distance, you can rewrite the equation for power as follows.

$$\text{Power} = \frac{\text{Force} \times \text{Distance}}{\text{Time}}$$

FIGURE 3

Work and Power

April carried her moving boxes up a flight of stairs. Notice how much time it took her.

✎ **Estimate** Suppose April ran instead. Fill in the second panel to show how much time it would take her.

Power Units

You may have heard car advertisements mention horsepower. The term isn't misleading. It's the same kind of power you just learned how to calculate. When work is measured in joules and time in seconds, the SI unit of power is the joule per second (J/s). This unit is also known as the watt (W). One joule of work done in one second is one **watt** of power. In other words, 1 J/s = 1 W. A watt is very small, so power is often measured in larger units such as kilowatts or horsepower. One kilowatt (kW) equals 1,000 watts. One horsepower equals 746 watts.

Vocabulary Identify Multiple Meanings What is the scientific meaning of *power*?

_____

_____

_____

do the math!

When a tow truck pulls a car, it applies a force over a distance. Work is done in a horizontal direction. **Calculate** Complete the table by calculating the power of the tow truck in each case.

Recall the formula for power is

$$Power = \frac{Work}{Time}$$

If a tow truck does 10,000 J of work in 5 seconds, then the power of the truck is calculated as follows.

$$Power = \frac{10,000 \text{ J}}{5 \text{ s}} = 2,000 \text{ W}$$

Tow Truck Power

Work (J)	Time (s)	Power (W)
120,000	60	_____
69,000	30	_____
67,500	45	_____

Lab® zone Do the Quick Lab *Investigating Power.*

🔑 Assess Your Understanding

got it? ....

○ I get it! Now I know that power _____

_____

○ I need extra help with _____

Go to my science ⓢ coach *online for help with this subject.*

Understanding Machines

UNLOCK THE BIG ?

🔑 **What Does a Machine Do?**

🔑 **What Is Mechanical Advantage?**

🔑 **What Is Efficiency?**

my planet Diary

FUN FACT

Sticks and Stones

When you need to peel an apple or open a can of soup, you reach for the right tool to do the job.

Some animals use items such as sticks and rocks to make finding or eating their food easier. For example, woodpecker finches and capuchin monkeys use sticks to get food out of places they can't reach. Sea otters and Egyptian vultures both use rocks as tools. Otters use rocks to pry shellfish away from other rocks. Egyptian vultures use their beaks to pick up rocks and break open eggs to eat.

Communicate Discuss these questions with a partner. Write your answers below.

1. How does the rock make it easier for the chimpanzee in the photo to crack open nuts?

_____

_____

_____

_____

_____

_____

2. What human tools would you use to do the same job?

_____

_____

_____

_____

▷ PLANET DIARY Go to **Planet Diary** to learn more about tools.

 Lab® zone Do the Inquiry Warm-Up *Is It a Machine?*

Vocabulary

- machine • input force • output force
- mechanical advantage • efficiency

Skills

- Reading: Compare and Contrast
- Inquiry: Predict

What Does a Machine Do?

What do you picture when you hear the word *machine*? You may think of machines as complex gadgets with motors, but a machine can be as simple as a ramp. **Machines** are devices that allow you to do work in an easier way. Machines do not reduce the amount of work you do. Instead, they just change the way you do work. In **Figure 1,** April does the same amount of work to move her speaker onto the stage whether or not she uses a ramp. The ramp makes that work easier. 🗝 **A machine makes work easier by changing at least one of three factors: the amount of force you exert, the distance over which you exert your force, or the direction in which you exert your force.**

Input Versus Output When you do work, the force you exert is called the **input force.** You exert your input force over the input distance. In **Figure 1B,** April's input force is the force she uses to pull the speaker up the ramp. The input distance is the length of the ramp. The machine exerts the **output force** over the output distance. The weight of the speaker is the output force. The height of the ramp is the output distance. Input force times input distance equals input work. Output force times output distance equals output work. Since machines do not reduce the work you do, your output work can never be greater than your input work.

FIGURE 1 ·······································
Using Machines
Using a ramp makes it easier for April to move the speaker onto the stage.

✎ **Interpret Diagrams** In Figure 1B, draw a line that represents April's output distance and an arrow that represents her output force.

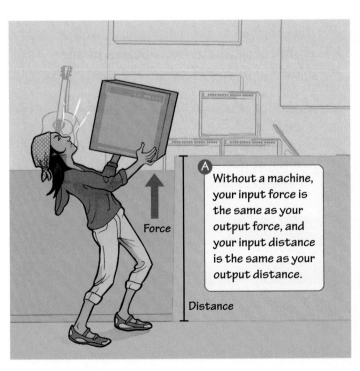

A Without a machine, your input force is the same as your output force, and your input distance is the same as your output distance.

Force

Distance

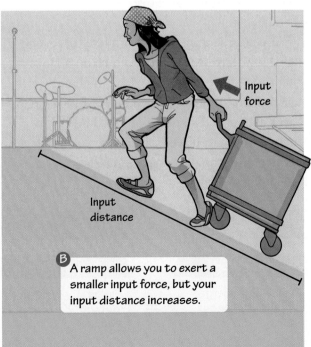

Input force

Input distance

B A ramp allows you to exert a smaller input force, but your input distance increases.

77

FIGURE 2 ···

Making Work Easier

The devices shown all make work easier in different ways. The arrows on the photos show how the machines change input work.

Input force

Output force

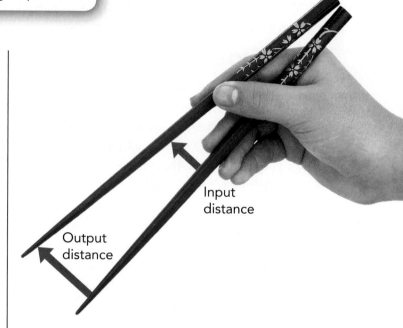

Input distance

Output distance

Changing Force

In some machines, the output force is *greater* than the input force. How can this happen? Recall the formula for work: **Work = Force × Distance.** If the amount of work stays the same, a decrease in force means an increase in distance. So if a machine allows you to use less input force to do the same amount of work, you must apply that smaller input force over a greater distance.

You see machines that work like this every day. How hard would it be to turn on a faucet that didn't have a handle? Since the handle is wider than the shaft of the faucet, your hand turns a greater distance than it would if you turned the shaft directly. Turning the handle a greater distance allows you to use less force.

Changing Distance

In some machines, the output force is less than the input force. This kind of machine allows you to exert your input force over a shorter distance. In order to apply a force over a shorter distance, you need to apply a greater input force. When do you use this kind of machine? Think of a pair of chopsticks. When you use chopsticks to eat, you move the hand holding the chopsticks a short distance. The other end of the chopsticks moves a greater distance, allowing you to pick up and eat a large piece of food with a small movement.

> Complete the equation below. Be sure to describe each quantity as *large* or *small*.

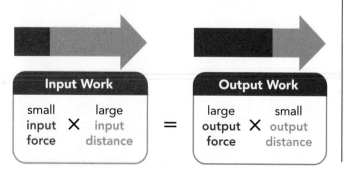

Input Work				Output Work		
small **input force**	×	large input distance	=	large **output force**	×	small output distance

Input Work				Output Work		
_____	×	small input distance	=	small **output force**	×	_____

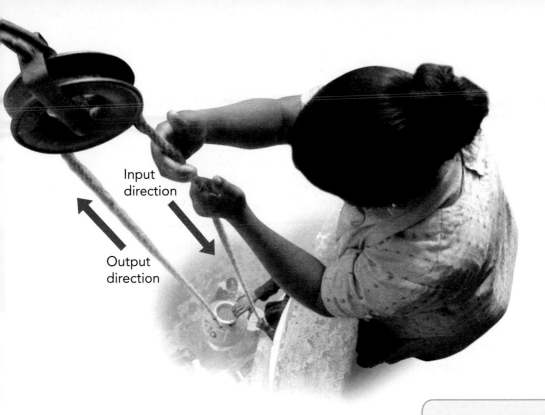

Input
direction

direction

Changing Direction Some machines don't change either force or distance. The photo above shows a machine called a *pulley* attached to a bucket. (You'll learn more about pulleys soon.) The pulley doesn't increase input force or distance. However, by changing the direction of the input force, the pulley makes it much easier to move the bucket to the top of a building—you can just pull down on the rope. Without a pulley, you would have to carry the bucket up a ladder or staircase. A flagpole rigging is also a pulley.

Complete the equation below. Be sure to describe each quantity as *large* or *small*.

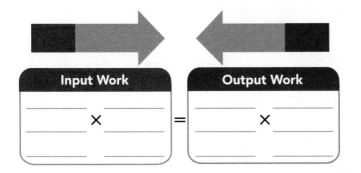

Input Work		Output Work
____ × ____	=	____ × ____

Lab® Do the Quick Lab *Going Up.*
zone

🔑 **Assess Your Understanding**

1a. List Name two examples of machines for which the output force is greater than the input force.

_____

_____

b. Apply Concepts Suppose that you use a pair of chopsticks and apply a force of 1 N over a distance of 0.01 m. How much work do you do? If the output force of the chopsticks is only 0.5 N, how far do the tips of the chopsticks move?

_____

_____

got it? ....

○ **I get it!** Now I know that machines make work easier by _____

_____

_____

○ **I need extra help with** _____

Go to my science ⬡ coach *online for help with this subject.*

What Is Mechanical Advantage?

You've just learned how to describe machines using words, but you can also describe machines with numbers. A machine's **mechanical advantage** is the number of times a machine increases a force exerted on it.  **The ratio of output force to input force is the mechanical advantage of a machine.**

$$\text{Mechanical advantage} = \frac{\text{Output force}}{\text{Input force}}$$

Increasing Force When the output force is greater than the input force, the mechanical advantage of a machine is greater than 1. You exert an input force of 10 newtons on a can opener, and the opener exerts an output force of 30 newtons. The mechanical advantage of the can opener is calculated below.

$$\frac{\text{Output force}}{\text{Input force}} = \frac{30\ N}{10\ N} = 3$$

The can opener triples your input force!

Increasing Distance When a machine increases distance, the output force is less than the input force. The mechanical advantage is less than 1. If input force is 20 newtons and the output force is 10 newtons, the mechanical advantage is shown below.

$$\frac{\text{Output force}}{\text{Input force}} = \frac{10\ N}{20\ N} = 0.5$$

Your input force is cut in half, but your input distance is doubled.

.... 🖉 ....

⊙ **Compare and Contrast** On these two pages, underline the sentences that explain how to distinguish among machines based on their mechanical advantages.

FIGURE 3 ⋯⋯⋯⋯⋯⋯⋯⋯

Mechanical Advantage
Drums are tuned by tightening and loosening bolts. Drum keys make the bolts easier to turn.
🖉 **Identify** Draw an arrow for the key's output force.

When April provides an input force of 10 N, the drum key provides an output force of 15 N.

Input force

Is the output force acting in the same direction as the input force? _____

Calculate the mechanical advantage of the drum key.

Since the drum key increases April's input force, is her input distance greater or smaller than the key's output distance?

THE DEAD ELECTRONS

Changing Direction What can you predict about the mechanical advantage of a machine that changes the direction of the force? If only the direction changes, input force will be the same as the output force. The mechanical advantage will always be 1.

do the math!

The graph shows input and output force data for three different ramps. Use the graph to answer the questions below. (The actual ramps are not pictured. Do not confuse the lines in the graph with the ramps themselves!)

1 Read Graphs If an 80 N input force is exerted on Ramp 2, what is the output force?

_____

2 Interpret Data Find the slope of the line for each ramp.

_____

_____

_____

3 Draw Conclusions Why does the slope represent each ramp's mechanical advantage?

_____

_____

_____

_____

_____

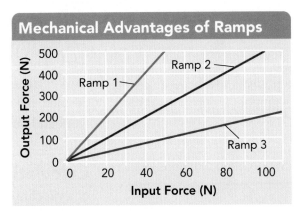

Mechanical Advantages of Ramps

Output Force (N) — 0, 100, 200, 300, 400, 500
Input Force (N) — 0, 20, 40, 60, 80, 100
Ramp 1, Ramp 2, Ramp 3

4 Graph On the graph above, plot a line for a ramp that has a mechanical advantage of 3.

5 CHALLENGE Predict Which ramp is the steepest? How do you know?

_____

_____

_____

_____

_____

_____

Lab zone ® Do the Quick Lab *Mechanical Advantage.*

🔑 Assess Your Understanding

got it? ●

○ I get it! Now I know that mechanical advantage _____

_____

○ I need extra help with _____

Go to my science s coach *online for help with this subject.*

What Is Efficiency?

So far you have assumed that the work you put into a machine is exactly equal to the work done by the machine. In an ideal situation, this would be true. In real situations, however, the output work is always less than the input work.

Overcoming Friction If you have ever tried to cut something with rusty scissors, you know that a large part of your work is wasted overcoming the friction between the parts of the scissors.

All machines waste some work overcoming the force of friction. The less friction there is, the closer the output work is to the input work. The **efficiency** of a machine compares output work to input work. Efficiency is expressed as a percentage. The higher the percentage, the more efficient the machine is. If you know the input work and output work for a machine, you can calculate a machine's efficiency.

Calculating Efficiency 🗝 **To calculate the efficiency of a machine, divide the output work by the input work and multiply the result by 100 percent.** This is summarized by the following formula.

$$\text{Efficiency} = \frac{\text{Output work}}{\text{Input work}} \times 100\%$$

Vocabulary Identify Multiple Meanings Underline the scientific definition of *efficiency* in the text. Then write a sentence that uses the everyday meaning of *efficient*.

_____

_____

_____

_____

_____

apply it!

❶ Calculate the efficiency of this bicycle if the input work to turn the pedals is 45 J and the output work is 30 J. Show your calculations.

_____

_____

_____

❷ Predict What will happen to the efficiency of the bike after the gears have been cleaned and the chain has been oiled?

_____

_____

_____

Real and Ideal Machines

A machine with an efficiency of 100 percent would be an ideal machine. Since all machines lose work to friction, ideal machines do not exist. All machines have an efficiency of less than 100 percent.

How does this affect mechanical advantage? *Ideal* mechanical advantage is your input distance divided by the machine's output distance. It is often related to the measurements of a machine. What you have calculated so far (output force divided by input force) is *actual* mechanical advantage. If machines were ideal and input work was equal to output work, ideal and actual mechanical advantages would be equal. Because of friction, actual mechanical advantage is always less than ideal mechanical advantage.

FIGURE 4 ···
> REAL-WORLD INQUIRY

An Ideal Machine?

The balls of this Newton's cradle may swing for a long time, but they will eventually come to rest.

✎ **Communicate** With a partner, discuss where in this machine work is lost due to friction. Circle these locations on the photo and explain your reasoning.

Lab® zone   Do the Quick Lab *Friction and Efficiency.*

🔑 Assess Your Understanding

2a. Relate Cause and Effect Real machines have an efficiency of less than 100% because some work is wasted to overcome _____

b. Predict What happens to the output work of a bicycle as it gets rusty? How does this affect efficiency?

_____

got it? ···

O **I get it!** Now I know that efficiency _____

_____

O **I need extra help with** _____

Go to my science s coach *online for help with this subject.*

Inclined Planes and Levers

🔑 How Do Inclined Planes Work?

🔑 How Are Levers Classified?

my planeT DiaRY

Is It a Machine?

Which objects in the photo below are machines? If you guessed the truck and the motorbike, you're correct—but not completely! Remember, a device doesn't have to be complicated or motorized in order to be a machine. Look between the truck and the motorbike. The ramp is a machine. Look at the person rolling the bike up the ramp. His hands hold the handlebars. His knees bend to help him walk. These are examples of simple machines. The motorbike and the truck contain many simple machines. There are dozens of machines in this photo, not just the two with motors.

MISCONCEPTIONS

Communicate Discuss these questions with a partner. Then write your answers below.

1. What kind of work is made easier by the ramp in the picture?

   _____

   _____

   _____

2. What are other examples of ramps that you have seen or used?

   _____

   _____

▷ PLANET DIARY Go to **Planet Diary** to learn more about everyday machines.

Lab zone® Do the Inquiry Warm-Up Inclined Planes and Levers.

Vocabulary
- simple machine • inclined plane • wedge
- screw • lever • fulcrum

Skills
↻ Reading: Relate Cause and Effect

△ Inquiry: Infer

How Do Inclined Planes Work?

Machines can be as simple as chopsticks or as complex as motor-bikes. Any complex machine can be broken down into smaller building blocks called simple machines. A **simple machine** is the most basic device for making work easier. Three closely related simple machines—the inclined plane, the wedge, and the screw—form the inclined plane family.

Inclined Plane Lifting a heavy object such as a motorbike is much easier with a ramp. A ramp is an example of a simple machine called an inclined plane. An **inclined plane** is a flat, sloped surface.

How It Works 🔑 **An inclined plane allows you to exert your input force over a longer distance.** As a result, the input force needed is less than the output force. The input force you use on an inclined plane is the force with which you push or pull an object along the slope. The inclined plane's output force is equal to the object's weight.

Mechanical Advantage You can determine the ideal mechanical advantage of an inclined plane by dividing the length of the incline by its height.

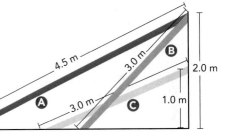

4.5 m · 3.0 m · B · 2.0 m · A · 3.0 m · C · 1.0 m

apply it!

❶ Imagine you were pushing a wheelchair up the ramps in the drawing above. Which would be the hardest to use? Why?

_____

❷ Calculate the ideal mechanical advantage of each ramp using the following formula.

$$\text{Ideal mechanical advantage} = \frac{\text{Length of ramp}}{\text{Height of ramp}}$$

_____

_____

_____

❸ The ramp with the (smallest/greatest) mechanical advantage is the steepest.

FIGURE 1
Wedges

During a forest fire, select trees are cut down to prevent the fire from spreading.

✏️ **Review** In the white circle below, draw and label the input force acting on the wedge and the output forces it exerts.

Input force

Output force

Output force

Wedge

If you've ever sliced an apple with a knife or pulled up a zipper, you are familiar with another simple machine known as a wedge. A **wedge** is a device that is thick at one end and tapers to a thin edge at the other end.

How It Works

Think of a wedge as an inclined plane (or two back-to-back inclined planes) that moves. 🔑 **When you use a wedge, instead of moving an object along the inclined plane, you move the inclined plane itself.** For example, when an ax is used to split wood, the ax handle exerts a force on the blade of the ax, which is the wedge. That force pushes the wedge down into the wood. The wedge in turn exerts an output force at a 90° angle to its slope, splitting the wood in two.

Mechanical Advantage

The ideal mechanical advantage of a wedge is determined by dividing the length of the wedge by its width. The longer and thinner a wedge is, the greater its mechanical advantage. When you sharpen a knife, you make the wedge thinner. This increases its mechanical advantage. That is why sharp knives cut better than dull knives.

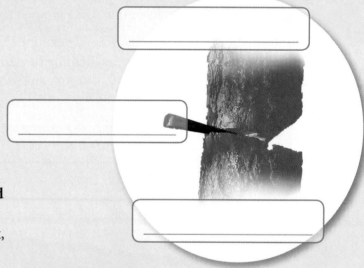

$$\text{Ideal mechanical advantage} = \frac{\text{Length of wedge}}{\text{Width of wedge}}$$

Calculate the ideal mechanical advantage of the firefighter's wedge if it is 4 cm wide and 22 cm long.

_____

_____

Screw Like a wedge, a **screw** is a simple machine that is related to the inclined plane. A screw can be thought of as an inclined plane wrapped around a cylinder.

How It Works When you twist a screw into a piece of wood, you exert an input force on the screw. 🔑 **The threads of a screw act like an inclined plane to increase the distance over which you exert the input force.** As the threads of the screw turn, they exert an output force on the wood. Friction holds the screw in place. Other examples of screws include bolts, drills, and jar lids.

Mechanical Advantage Think of the length around the threads of a screw as the length of an inclined plane and the length of the screw as the height of an inclined plane. The ideal mechanical advantage of the screw is the length around the threads divided by the length of the screw—just as the ideal mechanical advantage of an inclined plane is its length divided by its height. The closer together the threads of a screw are, the greater the mechanical advantage.

FIGURE 2 ··

Screws

The diagram below shows a screw with ten threads.
✏️ **Calculate** What is the mechanical advantage of the screw on the left? CHALLENGE On the smooth screw next to it, draw in the threads to make a screw that is the same length but would be easier to screw into a piece of wood. There is a hint in the text. Find it and circle it.

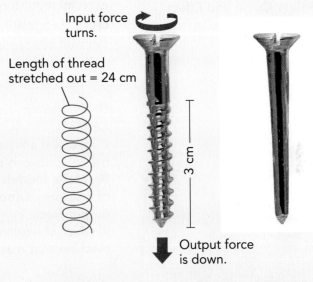

Input force turns.

Length of thread stretched out = 24 cm

3 cm

Output force is down.

$$\text{Ideal mechanical advantage} = \frac{\text{Length around threads}}{\text{Length of screw}}$$

_____

_____

Lab ® Do the Lab Investigation
zone *Angling for Access.*

🔑 **Assess Your Understanding**

1a. List List three closely related simple machines in the inclined plane family. _____

_____

b. Explain A simple inclined plane makes work easier by decreasing the input (force/distance) required to move the object.

c. Compare and Contrast Name one way inclined planes and screws are similar and one way they are different.

_____

_____

_____

_____

_____

got it? ··

○ I get it! Now I know that inclined planes _____

_____

○ I need extra help with _____

Go to MY SCIENCE ⓢ COACH online for help with this subject.

How Are Levers Classified?

Have you ever ridden on a seesaw or used a spoon to eat your food? If so, then you are already familiar with another simple machine called a lever. A **lever** is a rigid bar that is free to pivot, or rotate, on a fixed point. The fixed point that a lever pivots around is called the **fulcrum.**

How It Works To understand how levers work, think about using a spoon. Your wrist acts as the fulcrum. The bowl of the spoon is placed near your food. When you turn your wrist, you exert an input force on the handle, and the spoon pivots on the fulcrum. As a result, the bowl of the spoon digs in, exerting an output force on your food.

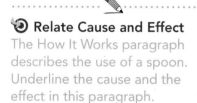

Relate Cause and Effect
The How It Works paragraph describes the use of a spoon. Underline the cause and the effect in this paragraph.

FIGURE 3 ···

Levers

A seesaw is a type of lever in which the fulcrum is located halfway between the input and output forces.

✎ **Make Models** In the space to the left, draw a diagram of a seesaw. Label the fulcrum, the input force, and the output force. [CHALLENGE] The diagrams below show levers in which the fulcrum is not centered. Write the name of a machine that matches each diagram.

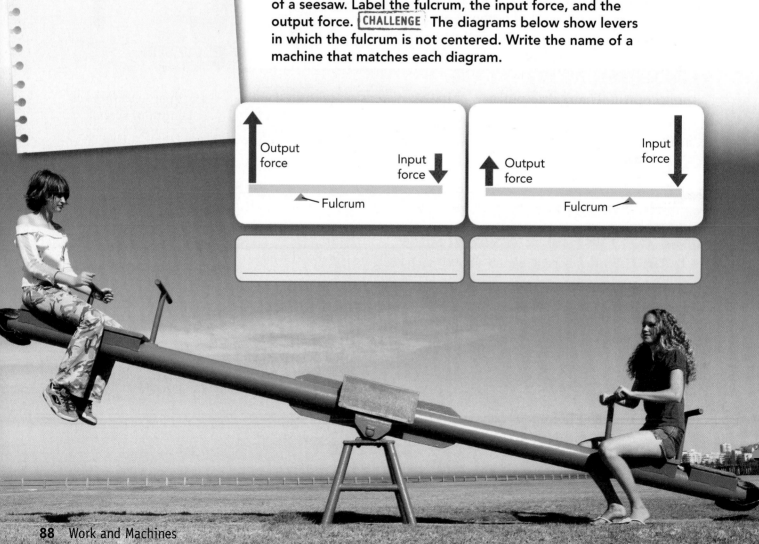

Mechanical Advantage

Using a lever like a spoon doesn't increase your input force or change the direction of your input force. Instead, it increases your input distance. When you use a spoon, you only have to move the handle a short distance in order to scoop up food over a longer distance. However, you need to apply a greater force than you would have without the spoon.

The ideal mechanical advantage of a lever is determined using the following formula.

$$\text{Ideal mechanical advantage} = \frac{\text{Distance from fulcrum to input force}}{\text{Distance from fulcrum to output force}}$$

In the case of the spoon, the distance from the fulcrum to the input force is less than the distance from the fulcrum to the output force. This means that the mechanical advantage is less than 1.

Types of Levers

When a spoon is used as a lever, the input force is located between the fulcrum and the output force. But this is not always the case. **Levers are classified according to the location of the fulcrum relative to the input and output forces.** The three different classes of levers are explained on the next page.

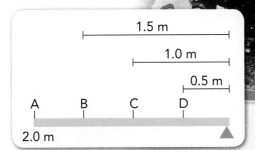

apply it!

A hockey stick is an example of a lever. Your shoulder acts as the fulcrum of the lever. The output force is exerted where the stick hits the puck. You exert the input force where your bottom hand grips the stick. What is the mechanical advantage of a hockey stick

1 that is gripped at point D and hits the puck at point A? _____

2 that is gripped at point D and hits the puck at point B? _____

3 **Infer** Would the mechanical advantage of a hockey stick ever be greater than 1? Explain.

_____
_____
_____
_____
_____
_____
_____

FIGURE 4

▶ ART IN MOTION Three Classes of Levers

The three classes of levers differ in the positions of the fulcrum, input force, and output force. ✎ **Interpret Diagrams** Draw and label the fulcrum, input force, and output force on the second-class and third-class lever photographs.

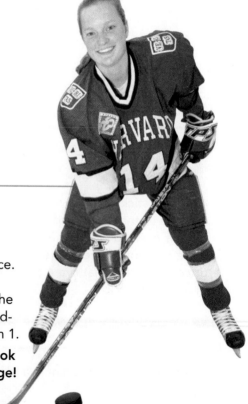

First-Class Levers

First-class levers change the direction of the input force. They also increase force or distance. Force increases if the fulcrum is closer to the output force. Distance increases if the fulcrum is closer to the input force. Examples of first-class levers include seesaws and scissors.

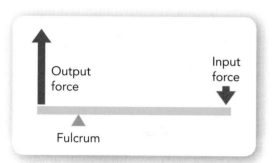

Second-Class Levers

Second-class levers increase force. They do not change the direction of the input force. Examples include doors, nutcrackers, and bottle openers. The mechanical advantage of second-class levers is always greater than 1.

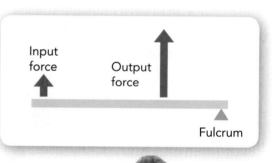

Third-Class Levers

Third-class levers increase distance, but do not change the direction of the input force. Examples include spoons, shovels, and baseball bats. The mechanical advantage of third-class levers is always less than 1.

If you find this one tricky, look for help on the previous page!

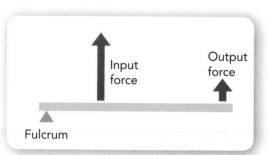

Levers in the Body

Levers can be found throughout your body. ✎ **Classify** In the last two panels of the diagram, draw an arrow representing the output force. Then identify the class of lever for each part of the body.

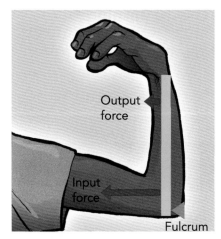

Your biceps muscle provides the input force. The output force is used to lift your arm.

The muscles in the back of your neck provide an input force, and the resulting output force tilts your chin back.

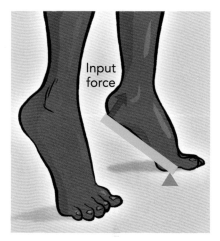

Your calf muscle provides an input force, and the resulting output force raises your body and moves it slightly forward.

 **Lab zone** Do the Quick Lab *Modeling Levers.*

🗝 Assess Your Understanding

2a. Describe Describe how each class of lever makes work easier.

_____

_____

_____

_____

b. Calculate What is the mechanical advantage of a lever with 2 m between the input force and the fulcrum and 1 m between the output force and the fulcrum? _____

c. Infer What class(es) of lever could the lever from the previous question be? Explain.

_____

_____

_____

_____

_____

_____

_____

_____

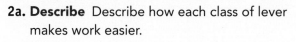 **got it?** ....

○ **I get it!** Now I know that levers are classified by _____

_____

○ **I need extra help with** _____

Go to **MY SCIENCE** 💬 **COACH** *online for help with this subject.*

Putting Machines Together

UNLOCK THE BIG ?

🔑 **What Simple Machines Make Use of Turning?**

🔑 **How Does a Compound Machine Do Work?**

my planet Diary

DISCOVERY

Lidar Alert

One of the oldest forms of transportation in the world—the sailboat—may benefit from new technology: a mobile lidar station. Lidar (short for light detection and ranging) stations sense wind speed and direction using laser beams. The new station, developed by Chinese scientists, fits on a bus that can be parked near bodies of water. Sailors need to know about wind speed and direction to position their sails. With the information they gather from these new lidar stations and the simple machines they use to control their sails, sailors can greatly improve their chances of navigating safely and winning races.

Answer the questions below.

1. Why might sailboat makers incorporate simple machines into their designs?

_____

_____

2. What is another example of pairing advanced technology with simple machines?

_____

_____

_____

> **PLANET DIARY** Go to **Planet Diary** to learn more about boating.

 Lab zone® Do the Inquiry Warm-Up *Machines That Turn.*

Vocabulary
- pulley
- wheel and axle
- compound machine

Skills
↻ Reading: Summarize
△ Inquiry: Classify

What Simple Machines Make Use of Turning?

If you have ever pulled a suitcase with wheels that were stuck, you know that it is easier to move the suitcase when the wheels can turn. 🗝 **Two simple machines take advantage of turning: the pulley and the wheel and axle.**

How a Pulley Works
When you raise a sail on a sailboat, you are using a pulley. A **pulley** is a simple machine made of a grooved wheel with a rope or cable wrapped around it. You use a pulley by pulling on one end of the rope. This is the input force. At the other end of the rope, the output force pulls up on the object you want to move. The grooved wheel turns. This makes it easier to move the rope than if it had just been looped over a stick. To move an object some distance, a pulley can make work easier in two ways. It can decrease the amount of input force needed to lift the object. It can also change the direction of your input force. For example, when you pull down on a flagpole rope, the flag moves up.

↻ **Summarize** In one or two sentences, summarize what you have learned on this page.

_____

_____

_____

_____

FIGURE 1 ....

Simple Machines in Sailboats
You can find many simple machines on a sailboat. Below are some diagrams of different parts of a sailboat. △ **Classify Circle the machines on the diagram that you think are pulleys.**

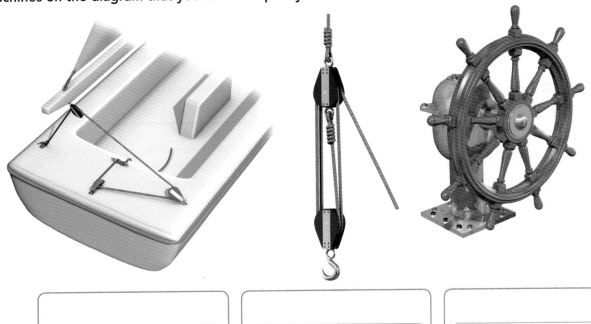

_____   _____   _____

FIGURE 2 ....

> **INTERACTIVE ART** **Types of Pulleys**

Pulley systems are classified by the number and position of the wheels they contain. ✎ **Classify** **Go back to Figure 1 and check your answers. Next to each pulley, label its type.**

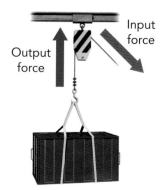

Mechanical advantage = 1

Fixed Pulley

A fixed pulley changes the direction of force but not the amount applied.

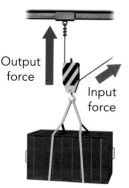

Mechanical advantage = 2

Movable Pulley

A movable pulley decreases the amount of input force needed. It does not change the direction of the force.

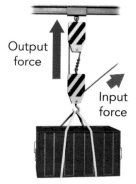

Mechanical advantage = 3

Block and Tackle

A block and tackle is a pulley system made up of fixed and movable pulleys.

Types of Pulleys

A pulley that you attach to a structure is a fixed pulley. Fixed pulleys are used at the tops of flagpoles. A movable pulley is attached directly to the object you are attempting to move. Construction cranes often use movable pulleys. Combining fixed and movable pulleys makes a pulley system called a block and tackle. The direction of the input force of a block and tackle could be either up or down depending on the arrangement of the rope and pulleys. The ideal mechanical advantage of a pulley or pulley system is equal to the number of sections of rope that support the object. Don't include the rope on which you pull downward though, because it does not support the object.

The pulley system shown here allows the painter to raise or lower himself.

❶ Label Suppose the painter pulls down on the rope with just enough force to lift himself. Draw and label arrows to indicate the direction of the input and output forces. Draw one of the arrows longer to indicate which force is greater.

❷ Interpret Diagrams The mechanical advantage of this pulley system is _____ .

❸ CHALLENGE What is the benefit of combining fixed and movable pulleys in a system like this one?

_____

_____

_____

_____

How a Wheel and Axle Works

You use a screwdriver to tighten screws because it is much easier to turn the handle instead of turning the screw itself. A simple machine made of two connected objects that rotate about a common axis is called a **wheel and axle**. The object with the larger radius is the wheel. In a screwdriver, the handle is the wheel and the shaft is the axle. When you turn the wheel, the axle rotates. The axle exerts a larger output force over a shorter distance.

If you apply force to the axle, your output force will be less than your input force. However, it will be exerted over a greater distance. This is how a paddle wheel on a boat works. The boat's motor turns an axle that turns the boat's wheel, pushing the boat forward a greater distance.

Mechanical Advantage

The ideal mechanical advantage of a wheel and axle is the radius of the wheel divided by the radius of the axle. (A radius is the distance from the outer edge of a circle to the circle's center.) The greater the ratio of the wheel radius to the axle radius, the greater the advantage.

FIGURE 3

Wheel and Axle

The screwdrivers have the same shaft radius. The blue screwdriver has a larger handle radius.

✎ **Infer** Circle the screwdriver with the greater mechanical advantage.

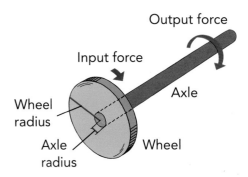

Output force

Input force

Axle

Wheel radius

Axle radius

Wheel

Ideal mechanical advantage = $\dfrac{\text{Radius of wheel}}{\text{Radius of axle}}$

The blue screwdriver has a handle radius of 1.5 cm and a shaft radius of 0.25 cm. What is its mechanical advantage?_____

△ **Classify** Go back to Figure 1 and recheck your answers. If you spot a wheel and axle, draw a box around it.

🔺 Lab zone ® Do the Quick Lab *Building Pulleys.*

🔑 Assess Your Understanding

1a. List List two examples of a wheel and axle. Which of your examples has the greater mechanical advantage?

_____

_____

b. Apply Concepts You exert a 100-N force on a pulley system to lift 300 N. What's the mechanical advantage of this system? How many sections of rope support the weight?

_____

_____

got it? ....

○ **I get it!** Now I know that pulleys and wheels and axles _____

_____

○ **I need extra help with** _____

Go to **MY SCIENCE 🔵ⁱ COACH** *online for help with this subject.*

How Does a Compound Machine Do Work?

Suppose you and your neighbors volunteer to clean up a local park. Will the job be easier if just a few people help or if everyone in the neighborhood works together? Getting a job done is usually easier if many people work on it. Similarly, doing work can be easier if more than one simple machine is used. A machine that combines two or more simple machines is called a **compound machine.**

🔑 **Within a compound machine, the output force of one simple machine becomes the input force of another simple machine.** Think about a stapler. The handle is a lever. Each tip of a staple acts as a wedge. Suppose the lever has a mechanical advantage of 0.8 and the wedge has mechanical advantage of 2. If you input a force of 10 N on the lever, the output force of the lever will be 8 N. That 8 N becomes the input force of the wedge, and the final output force is 8 N times 2, or 16 N.

Recall that mechanical advantage is output force divided by input force. The mechanical advantage of the stapler is 16 N divided by 10 N, or 1.6. There is another way to calculate this value. You can multiply the mechanical advantages of the stapler's component machines, the lever (0.8) and the wedge (2). The ideal mechanical advantage of a compound machine is the product of the ideal mechanical advantages of the simple machines that it consists of.

FIGURE 4 ·······································
Compound Machines
A compound machine consists of two or more simple machines. ✏️ **Identify In the photo at the left, circle and identify three simple machines that make up the apple peeler.**

If the mechanical advantages of the component machines in the peeler are 2, 3, and 12, what is the overall mechanical advantage of the apple peeler?

_____

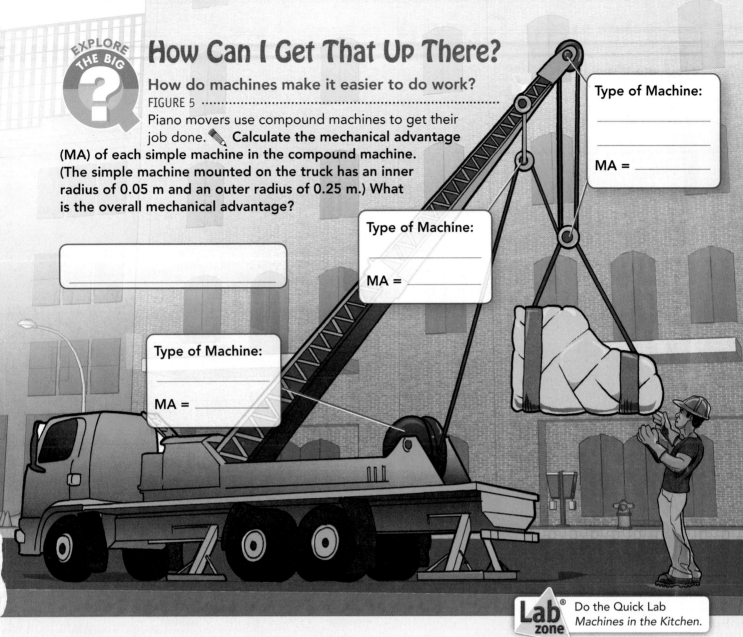

EXPLORE THE BIG ?

How Can I Get That Up There?

How do machines make it easier to do work?

FIGURE 5 ··

Piano movers use compound machines to get their job done. ✎ **Calculate the mechanical advantage (MA) of each simple machine in the compound machine. (The simple machine mounted on the truck has an inner radius of 0.05 m and an outer radius of 0.25 m.) What is the overall mechanical advantage?**

Type of Machine:
_____
_____
MA = _____

Type of Machine:
_____
MA = _____

Type of Machine:
_____
MA = _____

Lab zone® Do the Quick Lab *Machines in the Kitchen.*

🔑 Assess Your Understanding

2a. Calculate What is the mechanical advantage of a pencil sharpener made from a wheel and axle with a mechanical advantage of 3 and a wedge with a mechanical advantage of 4?

_____

b. ANSWER THE BIG ? Explain how simple and compound machines make it easier to do work.

_____
_____
_____

_____
_____
_____

got it?

○ **I get it!** Now I know that compound machines _____
_____

○ **I need extra help with** _____

Go to **my science** ⑤ **coach** online for help with this subject.

3 Study Guide

REVIEW THE BIG

Work is done when a _____ is applied in the direction of motion.

_____ make it easier to do work.

LESSON 1 Work and Power

🗝 Work is done on an object when the object moves in the same direction in which the force is exerted.

🗝 The amount of work done on an object can be determined by multiplying force times distance.

🗝 Power equals the amount of work done on an object in a unit of time.

Vocabulary
• work • joule • power • watt

LESSON 2 Understanding Machines

🗝 A machine makes work easier by changing force, distance, or direction.

🗝 The ratio of output force to input force is the mechanical advantage of a machine.

🗝 To calculate the efficiency of a machine, divide the output work by the input work and multiply the result by 100 percent.

Vocabulary
• machine • input force • output force
• mechanical advantage • efficiency

LESSON 3 Inclined Planes and Levers

🗝 Three closely related simple machines—the inclined plane, the wedge, and the screw—form the inclined plane family.

🗝 Levers are classified according to the location of the fulcrum relative to the input and output forces.

Vocabulary
• simple machine • inclined plane
• wedge • screw • lever • fulcrum

LESSON 4 Putting Machines Together

🗝 Two simple machines make use of turning: the pulley and the wheel and axle.

🗝 Within a compound machine, the output force of one simple machine becomes the input force of another simple machine.

Vocabulary
• pulley
• wheel and axle
• compound machine

Review and Assessment

LESSON 1 Work and Power

1. The amount of work done on an object is found by multiplying

    a. force times distance.   **b.** force times time.

    c. power times efficiency.   **d.** speed times time.

2. The rate at which work is done is called

    _____

3. Calculate You go rock climbing with a pack that weighs 70 N and you reach a height of 30 m. How much work did you do to lift your pack? If you finished the climb in 10 minutes (600 s), what was your power?

    _____

    _____

    _____

4. Apply Concepts What do automobile makers mean when they say their cars are more powerful than their competitors' cars?

    _____

    _____

    _____

5. Write About It Your friend's parents tell him that he needs to do more work around the house. How can your friend use science to explain to them that he does plenty of work just by going through his daily activities?

LESSON 2 Understanding Machines

6. One way a machine can make work easier is by

    a. increasing force   **b.** decreasing time

    c. increasing work   **d.** reducing work

7. The actual mechanical advantage of any machine is its _____ divided by its _____

8. Solve Problems You and your friends are building a treehouse, and you need a machine to get a heavy load of wood from the ground to the top of the tree. You set up a pulley system that allows you to pull down on a rope to lift the wood up. You end up able to lift a load you normally couldn't. In what way(s) does your machine make work easier?

    _____

    _____

    _____

    _____

9. Control Variables You are designing an experiment to test the efficiency of different bikes. What variables do you have to control?

    _____

    _____

    _____

10. Relate Cause and Effect You push on an old skateboard with a force of 20 N. The output force is only 10 N. What is the skateboard's efficiency? How would the efficiency change if the old, rusty ball bearings were replaced with new ones?

    _____

    _____

LESSON 3 Inclined Planes and Levers

11. Which of these is an example of a simple machine from the inclined plane family?

    a. baseball bat   **b.** jar lid

    c. bottle opener   **d.** wheelbarrow

12. The fixed point that a lever pivots around is called the _____

13. **Interpret Diagrams** Which ramp has the greater ideal mechanical advantage?

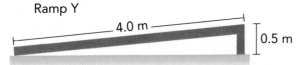

Ramp Y

4.0 m   0.5 m

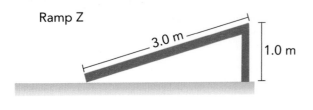

Ramp Z

3.0 m   1.0 m

_____

_____

_____

14. **Make Judgments** Your friend wants to design a wheelbarrow with an ideal mechanical advantage of 5,000. Do you think your friend should consider a different design? Explain.

_____

_____

_____

15. math! On a separate sheet of paper, draw one example of each of the three different classes of levers. For each lever, measure the distance between the fulcrum and the input force, the distance between the fulcrum and the output force, and calculate the ideal mechanical advantage.

LESSON 4 Putting Machines Together

16. Which of these is an example of a wheel and axle?

    a. axe   **b.** seesaw

    c. doorknob   **d.** flagpole rigging

17. A _____ is a system that consists of at least one fixed pulley and one movable pulley.

18. **Apply Concepts** A circular faucet handle is an example of a wheel and axle. How could you increase the mechanical advantage of a circular faucet handle?

_____

_____

_____

APPLY
THE BIG
?Q

How do machines make it easier to do work?

19. This paper cutter is a compound machine. How does it make cutting paper easier? What simple machines make up the paper cutter? Describe how they interact.

_____

_____

_____

_____

_____

_____

Standardized Test Prep

Multiple Choice

Circle the letter of the best answer.

1. The table below shows the input work and output work for four different pulleys. Which pulley has the highest efficiency?

Work of Different Pulleys		
Pulley	**Input Work**	**Output Work**
Fixed pulley A	20,000 J	8,000 J
Fixed pulley B	20,000 J	10,000 J
Movable pulley	20,000 J	12,000 J
Block and tackle	20,000 J	16,000 J

  A Fixed pulley A
  B Fixed pulley B
  C Movable pulley
  D Block and tackle

2. Why does it take more work to carry a 22-N bag of birdseed to the third floor of a house than it takes to move a 16-N bag of cat food to the second floor of a house?

  A Work equals distance divided by force and the birdseed requires less force to lift it.
  B The force exerted on the birdseed is not the direction of motion.
  C The cat food has less mass than the birdseed.
  D The birdseed has greater mass and has to be moved farther.

3. Which is the best scientific definition of a machine?

  A A machine is a timesaving device that uses motors and gears.
  B A machine changes the amount of input force.
  C A machine makes work easier by changing force, distance, or direction.
  D A machine can either be simple or compound.

4. Which of the following will increase the ideal mechanical advantage of a wheel and axle?

  A increasing the wheel's radius
  B decreasing the wheel's radius
  C increasing the axle's radius
  D increasing the wheel's radius and the axle's radius equally

5. Which activity describes work being done on an object?

  A walking a dog on a leash
  B lifting a bag of groceries
  C holding up an umbrella
  D pressing a stamp onto an envelope

Constructed Response

Use your knowledge of science to help you answer Question 6. Write your answer on a separate sheet of paper.

6. Explain why an engineer would design a road to wind around a mountain rather than go straight up the side. Explain how this design would be better.

GOOD THINGS COME IN SMALL PACKAGES

This image shows an artist's idea of how a nanite might look as it helps fight cancer in the body. ▼

Imagine a tiny machine that works right inside your cells, delivering medication to specific sites. Scientists are working to build just such machines. Nanomachines, or nanites, are machines whose size is measured in nanometers. One nanometer is equivalent to one billionth (10^{-9}) of a meter. That's pretty tiny—smaller than most people can imagine. In comparison with these tiny machines, red blood cells, which have a diameter of about 7 micrometers (7×10^{-6} of a meter), look huge!

So how do these tiny machines work? Most nanomachines are made of gold or platinum. They use cylindrical carbon molecules or hydrogen peroxide for fuel. Scientists hope that nanomachines will one day use the fuel of a patient's cell to do work.

Some tube-shaped nanomachines convert energy from light into chemical energy and then into mechanical energy to do work. These machines are injected into human cancer cells in the dark. Before they are injected, the tiny machines are loaded with medicine. When scientists expose the machines to light, a chemical reaction causes a wagging motion inside the tube, which releases the medication in exactly the right spot.

Research It Scientists are working to develop a "submarine" nanomachine. How is this new machine different from other medical nanomachines? Draw the submarine and describe its functions.

A new SET OF WHEELS

Students at the Massachusetts Institute of Technology (MIT) have the chance to help 20 million people by taking a class called Wheelchair Design in Developing Countries.

Over the semester, students will learn how to build a wheelchair. They will also study the needs of people who use wheelchairs in developing countries. What's the real test? Designing devices that will actually improve people's lives!

Analyze It Look at the wheelchairs in the photo. Create a graphic organizer in which you identify things someone would need a wheelchair to do, and how a wheelchair feature could meet that need. For example, the user might need to go up or down a steep hill, so the chair should have good brakes and should not be too heavy. Identify and evaluate the scientific knowledge and concepts students may need to apply when creating their wheelchairs.

SCIENCE ATHLETES
Let the Games Begin

Every year, students from all over the country compete to be the best at everything from chemistry to robot building. What is this scientific pageant of skill and achievement? It's the Science Olympiad!

In the Mission Possible event, teams of students work all year to invent, design, and build a Rube Goldberg machine. A Rube Goldberg machine is a compound machine designed to accomplishe a very simple task— and makes you laugh in the process.

This Rube Goldberg machine takes over 20 steps to perform three tasks. It selects, crushes, and pitches a can into a recycling bin.

Make It Work Divide your class into teams and compete in your own Mission Possible event in which you invent a complex machine to perform a simple task. Score each team's creation!

WHAT
MAKES THESE
SNOWBOARDERS
"FLY"
DOWNHILL?

 THE BIG ?

How is energy conserved in a transformation?

These women are competing in the sport of snowboard cross. They "fly" down a narrow course, filled with jumps, steep sections, and ramps. Disaster looms at every turn. If they don't crash into each other or fall, then the first one across the finish line wins.

△ **Develop Hypotheses** What do you think makes these snowboarders go so fast?

_____

_____

_____

_____

_____

▷ **UNTAMED SCIENCE** Watch the **Untamed Science** video to learn more about energy.

4 Getting Started

Check Your Understanding

1. **Background** Read the paragraph below and then answer the question.

Michael pulls his brother in a wagon. Suddenly, Michael's dog jumps on his brother's lap. Michael continues to pull the wagon, but it is more difficult now. The added mass of the dog means that Michael has to generate more force to accelerate the wagon to the same speed.

> **Mass** is a measure of the amount of matter in an object.
>
> A **force** is a push or pull.
>
> The **speed** of an object is the distance the object travels per unit of time.

• Why is it harder to pull the wagon with the dog in it?

_____

_____

▶ **MY READING WEB** If you had trouble completing the question above, visit **My Reading Web** and type in *Energy.*

Vocabulary Skill

Identify Multiple Meanings Some familiar words may have different meanings in science. Look at the different meanings of the words below.

Word	Everyday Meaning	Scientific Meaning
energy	*n.* the ability to be active or take part in a vigorous activity **Example:** She had enough *energy* to run for miles.	*n.* the ability to do work or cause change **Example:** The wind can move objects because it has *energy.*
power	*n.* the ability to influence others **Example:** The coach has a lot of *power* over his young athletes.	*n.* the rate at which work is done **Example:** A truck's engine has more *power* than a car's engine.

2. **Quick Check Review the sentences below. Then circle the sentence that uses the scientific meaning of the word *energy.***

• A puppy has too much *energy* to be inside the house all day.

• A wrecking ball has enough *energy* to knock down a building.

kinetic energy

gravitational potential energy

600 N

400 N

mechanical energy

energy transformation

Chapter Preview

LESSON 1

- energy
- kinetic energy
- potential energy
- gravitational potential energy
- elastic potential energy

⟳ Relate Cause and Effect
△ Calculate

LESSON 2

- mechanical energy
- nuclear energy
- thermal energy
- electrical energy
- electromagnetic energy
- chemical energy

⟳ Identify the Main Idea
△ Classify

LESSON 3

- energy transformation
- law of conservation of energy

⟳ Identify Supporting Evidence
△ Infer

> VOCAB FLASH CARDS For extra help with vocabulary, visit **Vocab Flash Cards** and type in *Energy.*

What Is Energy?

🔑 **How Are Energy, Work, and Power Related?**

🔑 **What Are Two Types of Energy?**

my planeT DiaRY

Wind Farms

Did you know that wind can be used to produce electricity? A wind farm is a group of very large wind-mills, or turbines, placed in a location that gets a lot of wind. The energy of the wind causes the propellers of the turbines to spin. The turbines are connected to generators. When the turbines are spinning, the generators produce electricity. The amount of electricity produced depends on the size of the propellers, the number of turbines, and the strength of the wind.

FUN FACT

Write your answer to the question below.

Analyze Costs and Benefits What are some advantages and disadvantages of using wind energy to create electricity?

_____

_____

_____

_____

_____

▶ PLANET DIARY Go to **Planet Diary** to learn more about energy.

Lab zone Do the Inquiry Warm-Up *How High Does a Ball Bounce?*

How Are Energy, Work, and Power Related?

Did you put a book in your backpack this morning? If so, then you did work on the book. Recall that work is done when a force moves an object. The ability to do work or cause change is called **energy.**

Work and Energy When you do work on an object, some of your energy is transferred to that object. You can think of work as the transfer of energy. When energy is transferred, the object upon which the work is done gains energy. Energy is measured in joules—the same units as work.

Vocabulary
- energy • kinetic energy • potential energy
- gravitational potential energy • elastic potential energy

Skills
- Reading: Relate Cause and Effect
- Inquiry: Calculate

Power and Energy You may recall that power is the rate at which work is done. **Since the transfer of energy is work, then power is the rate at which energy is transferred, or the amount of energy transferred in a unit of time.**

$$Power = \frac{Energy\ Transferred}{Time}$$

Different machines have different amounts of power. For example, you could use either a hand shovel or a snowblower, like the one in **Figure 1,** to remove snow from your driveway. Each transfers the same amount of energy when it moves the snow the same distance. However, you could move the snow faster using a snowblower than a hand shovel. The snowblower has more power because it transfers the same amount of energy to the snow in less time.

FIGURE 1 ·······
Power
The snowblower has more power than the person with the hand shovel.

✎ **Apply Concepts** You could use an elevator or the stairs to lift a box to the tenth floor. Which has greater power? Why?

_____

_____

_____

_____

_____

Do the Lab Investigation
Can You Feel the Power?

⚷ Assess Your Understanding

got it? ···

○ **I get it!** Now I know that since the transfer of energy is work, then power is _____

_____

○ **I need extra help with** _____

Go to my science ⑤ coach *online for help with this subject.*

What Are Two Types of Energy?

Moving objects, such as the vehicles shown in **Figure 2,** have one type of energy. A rock perched on the edge of a cliff or a stretched rubber band has another type of energy. 🔑 **The two basic types of energy are kinetic energy and potential energy.** Whether energy is kinetic or potential depends on the motion, position, and shape of the object.

Kinetic Energy A moving object can do work when it strikes another object and moves it. For example, a swinging hammer does work on a nail as it drives the nail into a piece of wood. The hammer has energy because it can do work. The energy an object has due to its motion is called **kinetic energy.**

Factors Affecting Kinetic Energy The kinetic energy of an object depends on both its speed and its mass. Suppose you are hit with a tennis ball that has been lightly tossed at you. It probably would not hurt much. What if you were hit with the same tennis ball traveling at a much greater speed? It would hurt! The faster an object moves, the more kinetic energy it has.

Kinetic energy also increases as mass increases. Suppose a tennis ball rolls across the ground and hits you in the foot. Compare this with getting hit in the foot with a bowling ball moving at the same speed as the tennis ball. The bowling ball is much more noticeable because it has more kinetic energy than a tennis ball. The bowling ball has more kinetic energy because it has a greater mass.

FIGURE 2 ··

> **ART IN MOTION** **Kinetic Energy**
The kinetic energy of an object depends on its speed and mass.

✎ **Use the diagram to answer the questions.**

1. **Interpret Diagrams** List the vehicles in order of increasing kinetic energy.

   _____

   _____

   _____

2. **Explain** Describe another example of two objects that have different kinetic energies. Explain why their kinetic energies are different.

   _____

   _____

   _____

   _____

   _____

   _____

   _____

Calculating Kinetic Energy You can use the following equation to solve for the kinetic energy of an object.

$$\text{Kinetic energy} = \frac{1}{2} \times \text{Mass} \times \text{Speed}^2$$

For example, suppose a boy is pulling a 10-kg wagon at a speed of 1 m/s.

$$\text{Kinetic energy of wagon} = \frac{1}{2} \times 10 \text{ kg} \times (1 \text{ m/s})^2$$

$$= 5 \text{ kg·m}^2/\text{s}^2 = 5 \text{ joules}$$

Note that $1 \text{ kg·m}^2/\text{s}^2 = 1$ joule

Do changes in speed and mass have the same effect on the kinetic energy of the wagon? No—changing the speed of the wagon will have a greater effect on its kinetic energy than changing its mass by the same factor. This is because speed is squared in the kinetic energy equation. For example, doubling the mass of the wagon will double its kinetic energy. Doubling the speed of the wagon will quadruple its kinetic energy.

Relate Cause and Effect
What has a greater effect on an object's kinetic energy— doubling its mass or doubling its speed? Explain.

_____

_____

_____

_____

_____

_____

do the math!

A girl and her dog are running. The dog has a mass of 20 kg. The girl has a mass of 60 kg.

1 Calculate Suppose both the dog and the girl run at a speed of 2 m/s. Calculate both of their kinetic energies.

Kinetic energy of dog =

Kinetic energy of girl =

2 Calculate Suppose the dog speeds up and is now running at a speed of 4 m/s. Calculate the dog's kinetic energy.

Kinetic energy of dog =

3 Draw Conclusions Are your answers to Questions 1 and 2 reasonable? Explain.

_____

_____

_____

_____

Quantity	SI Unit
Force	_____
Height	_____
Work	_____
Mass	_____
Energy	_____

Potential Energy

Potential Energy An object does not have to be moving to have energy. Some objects have energy as a result of their shapes or positions. When you lift a book up to your desk from the floor or compress a spring by winding a toy, you transfer energy to it. The energy you transfer is stored, or held in readiness. It might be used later if the book falls or the spring unwinds. Energy that results from the position or shape of an object is called **potential energy.** This type of energy has the potential to do work.

Gravitational Potential Energy Potential energy related to an object's height is called **gravitational potential energy.** The gravitational potential energy of an object is equal to the work done to lift it to that height. Remember that work is equal to force multiplied by distance. The force you use to lift the object is equal to its weight. The distance you move the object is its height above the ground. You can calculate an object's gravitational potential energy using this equation.

$$\text{Gravitational potential energy} = \text{Weight} \times \text{Height}$$

For example, suppose a book has a weight of 10 newtons (N). If the book is lifted 2 meters off the ground, the book has 10 newtons times 2 meters, or 20 joules, of gravitational potential energy.

FIGURE 3

Gravitational Potential Energy

The rock climbers have gravitational potential energy.

✏ **Use the diagram to answer the questions.**

1. **Identify** Circle the rock climber with the greatest potential energy. Calculate this potential energy. The height to be used is at the rock climber's lowest foot.

_____

_____

_____

_____

2. **CHALLENGE** Where would the rock climbers at the top have to be to have half as much potential energy?

_____

_____

Elastic Potential Energy An object has a different type of potential energy due to its shape. **Elastic potential energy** is the energy associated with objects that can be compressed or stretched. For example, when the girl in **Figure 4** presses down on the trampoline, the trampoline changes shape. The trampoline now has potential energy. When the girl pushes off of the trampoline, the stored energy sends the girl upward.

FIGURE 4 ···

Elastic Potential Energy
The energy stored in a stretched object, such as the trampoline, is elastic potential energy.

✎ **Interpret Diagrams** Rank the amount of elastic potential energy of the trampoline from greatest to least. A ranking of one is the greatest. Write your answers in the circles. Then explain your answers in the space to the right.

 Do the Quick Lab *Mass, Velocity, and Kinetic Energy.*

🔑 Assess Your Understanding

1a. Identify The energy an object has due to its motion is called (kinetic/potential) energy. Stored energy that results from the position or shape of an object is called (kinetic/potential) energy.

b. Summarize What are the two factors that affect an object's kinetic energy?

c. Apply Concepts What type of energy does a cup sitting on a table have? Why?

got it? ··

○ I get it! Now I know that the two basic types of energy are _____

○ I need extra help with _____

　　Go to my science ⓢ coach online for help with this subject.

Forms of Energy

UNLOCK
THE BIG
?

🔑 **How Can You Find an Object's Mechanical Energy?**

🔑 **What Are Other Forms of Energy?**

MY PLANET DIARY

BLOG

Posted by: Lauren

Location: Carlisle, Massachusetts

The first hurricane that I ever saw was a big one! The storm had weakened by the time it arrived in Massachusetts, but the wind was still so powerful it easily flung around our lawn chairs. The trees bent and swayed in the wind. When it was over, branches were scattered across our lawn. The wind even ripped up a tree, blocking our road. The storm did a lot of damage, but we were lucky to be safe inside while watching this awesome force of nature.

Write your answer to the question.

What is some evidence that the storm Lauren described had energy?

_____

_____

_____

_____

_____

> PLANET DIARY Go to **Planet Diary** to learn more about forms of energy.

Lab zone® Do the Inquiry Warm-Up
What Makes a Flashlight Shine?

How Can You Find an Object's Mechanical Energy?

What do a falling basketball, a moving car, and a trophy on a shelf all have in common? They all have mechanical energy. The form of energy associated with the motion, position, or shape of an object is called **mechanical energy.**

Vocabulary

- mechanical energy
- nuclear energy
- thermal energy
- electrical energy
- electromagnetic energy
- chemical energy

Skills

- Reading: Identify the Main Idea
- Inquiry: Classify

Calculating Mechanical Energy An object's mechanical energy is a combination of its potential energy and its kinetic energy. For example, the basketball in **Figure 1** has both potential energy and kinetic energy. The higher the basketball moves, the greater its potential energy. The faster the basketball moves, the greater its kinetic energy. 🔑 **You can find an object's mechanical energy by adding together the object's kinetic energy and potential energy.**

Mechanical energy = Potential energy + Kinetic energy

Sometimes an object's mechanical energy is its kinetic energy or potential energy only. A car moving along a flat road has kinetic energy only. A trophy resting on a shelf has gravitational potential energy only. But both have mechanical energy.

Potential energy = 20 J
Kinetic energy = 2 J
Mechanical energy =

B

FIGURE 1 ···
Mechanical Energy
The basketball has mechanical energy because of its speed and position above the ground.
✏️ **Calculate** Solve for the mechanical energy of the basketball at point A and point B.

A

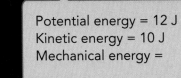

Potential energy = 12 J
Kinetic energy = 10 J
Mechanical energy =

✏️ **Draw Conclusions** Why does the ball's gravitational potential energy increase from points A to B?

_____

_____

_____

_____

_____

115

mechanical energy can do work on another object. In fact, you can think of mechanical energy, like all forms of energy, as the ability to do work. For example, a basketball does work on the net as it falls through the hoop. The net moves as a result. The more mechanical energy an object has, the more work it can do.

apply it!

The bowling ball does work on the pins when it hits them.

❶ Why is the bowling ball able to do work?

_____

_____

_____

_____

❷ How should you throw the ball to maximize the amount of work it does on the pins?

_____

_____

_____

_____

_____

_____

❸ CHALLENGE In the type of bowling shown in the photo, the ball has a mass of 7.0 kg. In candlepin bowling, the ball has a mass of about 1.0 kg. Does the ball with the greater mass always have the greater mechanical energy? Explain.

_____

_____

_____

_____

_____

Lab zone® Do the Quick Lab *Determining Mechanical Energy.*

🔑 Assess Your Understanding

1a. Define Mechanical energy is the form of energy associated with the _____ ,

_____ , or _____ of an object.

b. Calculate At a certain point the kinetic energy of a falling apple is 5.2 J and its potential energy is 3.5 J. What is its mechanical energy?

_____

c. Infer If an object's mechanical energy is equal to its potential energy, how much kinetic energy does the object have? Explain.

_____

_____

_____

_____

_____

got it? ··

○ **I get it!** Now I know you can find an object's mechanical energy by _____

_____

○ **I need extra help with** _____

Go to MY SCIENCE ⓢ COACH online for help with this subject.

What Are Other Forms of Energy?

So far, you have read about energy that involves the motion, position, or shape of an object. But an object can have other forms of kinetic and potential energy. These other forms are associated with the particles that make up objects. These particles are far too small to see with the naked eye. 🗝 **Forms of energy associated with the particles of objects include nuclear energy, thermal energy, electrical energy, electromagnetic energy, and chemical energy.**

Nuclear Energy All objects are made up of particles called atoms. The region in the center of an atom is called the nucleus. A type of potential energy called **nuclear energy** is stored in the nucleus of an atom. Nuclear energy is released during a nuclear reaction. One kind of nuclear reaction, known as nuclear fission, occurs when a nucleus splits. A nuclear power plant, like the one shown in **Figure 2,** uses fission reactions to produce electricity. Another kind of reaction, known as nuclear fusion, occurs when the nuclei of atoms fuse, or join together. Nuclear fusion reactions occur constantly in the sun, releasing huge amounts of energy. Only a tiny portion of this energy reaches Earth as heat and light.

🖉

⊙ Identify the Main Idea
Underline the main idea under the red heading Nuclear Energy.

FIGURE 2 ⋯⋯⋯⋯⋯⋯⋯⋯⋯⋯⋯⋯⋯⋯⋯⋯⋯⋯⋯⋯

Nuclear Energy
Controlled nuclear fission reactions occur at some power plants. Nuclear fusion reactions occur in the sun.

🖉 **Compare and Contrast Use the Venn diagram to compare and contrast nuclear fission and nuclear fusion.**

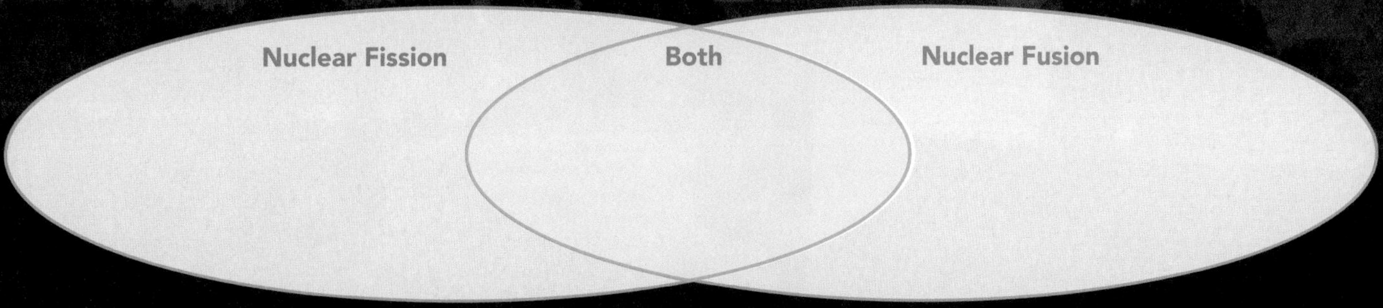

Nuclear Fission   Both   Nuclear Fusion

Thermal Energy

The particles that make up objects are constantly in motion. This means that they have kinetic energy. These particles are arranged in specific ways in different objects, so they also have potential energy. The total kinetic and potential energy of the particles in an object is called **thermal energy.**

The higher the temperature of an object, the more thermal energy the object has. For example, suppose you heat a pot of water. As heat is applied to the water, the particles in the water move faster on average. The faster the particles move, the greater their kinetic energy and the higher the temperature. Therefore, a pot of water at 75°C, for example, has more thermal energy than the same amount of water at 30°C.

Electrical Energy

When you receive a shock from a metal doorknob, you experience electrical energy. The energy of electric charges is **electrical energy.** Depending on whether the charges are moving or stored, electrical energy can be a form of kinetic or potential energy. Lightning is a form of electrical energy. You rely on electrical energy from batteries or electrical lines to run devices such as computers, handheld games, and digital audio players.

FIGURE 3 ·······················
> INTERACTIVE ART **Forms of Energy**
Many objects in this restaurant have more than one form of energy.

✎ **Classify** Circle three objects. Describe two forms of energy each object has.

Electromagnetic Energy The light you see is one type of electromagnetic energy. **Electromagnetic energy** is a form of energy that travels through space in waves. The source of these waves is vibrating electric charges. These waves do not require a medium, so they can travel through a vacuum, or empty space. This is why you can see the sun and stars.

The microwaves you use to cook your food and the X-rays doctors use to examine patients are also types of electromagnetic energy. Other forms of electromagnetic energy include ultraviolet rays, infrared (or heat) waves, and radio waves. Cell phones send and receive messages using microwaves.

Chemical Energy Chemical energy is in the foods you eat, in the matches you use to light a candle, and even in the cells of your body. **Chemical energy** is potential energy stored in chemical bonds. Chemical bonds are what hold atoms together. Often when these bonds are broken, this stored energy is released. For example, when you digest food, bonds are broken to release energy for your body to use.

Vocabulary Identify Multiple Meanings Review the multiple meaning words in the Getting Started section and complete the sentence. During a lightning storm, electric charges move between the clouds and the ground, releasing stored

_____

Lab zone® Do the Quick Lab Sources of Energy.

🔑 **Assess Your Understanding**

2a. Explain Why do the particles of objects have both kinetic and potential energy?

_____
_____
_____
_____
_____
_____
_____

b. Classify The energy you get from eating a peanut butter and jelly sandwich is in the form of _____ energy.

got it?

○ **I get it!** Now I know the forms of energy associated with the particles of objects include _____
_____
_____

○ **I need extra help with** _____

Go to **my science** ⬤ᔆ **COACH** online for help with this subject.

119

Energy Transformations and Conservation

UNLOCK THE BIG ?

🔑 How Are Different Forms of Energy Related?

🔑 What Is the Law of Conservation of Energy?

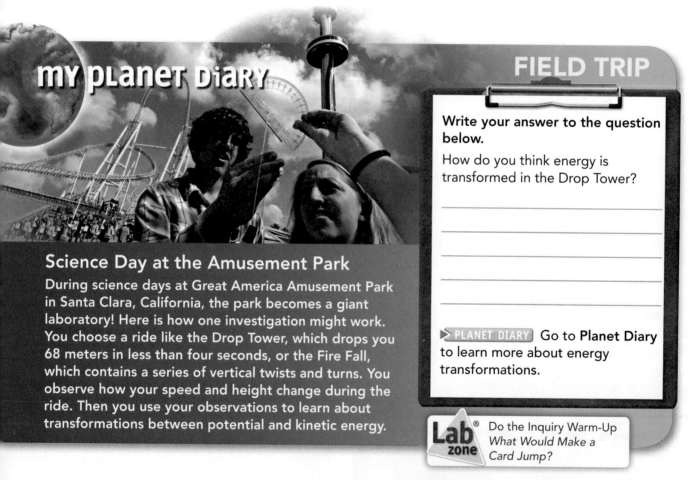

my planet diary

Science Day at the Amusement Park

During science days at Great America Amusement Park in Santa Clara, California, the park becomes a giant laboratory! Here is how one investigation might work. You choose a ride like the Drop Tower, which drops you 68 meters in less than four seconds, or the Fire Fall, which contains a series of vertical twists and turns. You observe how your speed and height change during the ride. Then you use your observations to learn about transformations between potential and kinetic energy.

FIELD TRIP

Write your answer to the question below.

How do you think energy is transformed in the Drop Tower?

_____

_____

_____

_____

_____

▶ PLANET DIARY Go to **Planet Diary** to learn more about energy transformations.

Lab zone Do the Inquiry Warm-Up *What Would Make a Card Jump?*

How Are Different Forms of Energy Related?

What does flowing water have to do with electricity? In a hydro-electric power plant, the mechanical energy of moving water is transformed into electrical energy. 🔑 **All forms of energy can be transformed into other forms of energy.** A change from one form of energy to another is called an **energy transformation.** Some energy changes involve single transformations, while others involve many transformations.

Vocabulary
- energy transformation
- law of conservation of energy

Skills
- Reading: Identify Supporting Evidence
- Inquiry: Infer

Single Transformations Sometimes, one form of energy needs to be transformed into another to get work done. For example, a toaster transforms electrical energy to thermal energy to toast your bread. A cell phone transforms electrical energy to electromagnetic energy that travels to other phones.

Your body transforms the chemical energy in food to the mechanical energy you need to move your muscles. Chemical energy in food is also transformed to the thermal energy your body uses to maintain its temperature.

Multiple Transformations Often, a series of energy transformations is needed to do work. For example, the mechanical energy used to strike a match is transformed first to thermal energy. The thermal energy causes the particles in the match to release stored chemical energy, which is transformed to more thermal energy and to the electromagnetic energy you see as light.

In a car engine, another series of energy conversions occurs. Electrical energy produces a spark. The thermal energy of the spark releases chemical energy in the fuel. The fuel's chemical energy in turn becomes thermal energy. Thermal energy is converted to mechanical energy used to move the car, and to electrical energy to produce more sparks.

Identify Supporting Evidence
Underline the energy transformation that must occur for you to talk on your cell phone.

apply it!

A series of energy transformations must occur for you to ride your bike. Write the forms of energy involved in each transformation.

Reactions occur within the sun to transform _____ energy into _____ energy.

Plants transform _____ energy into _____ energy.

Your body also transforms _____ energy into _____ energy when you ride your bike.

Your body transforms _____ energy into _____ energy to maintain your body temperature.

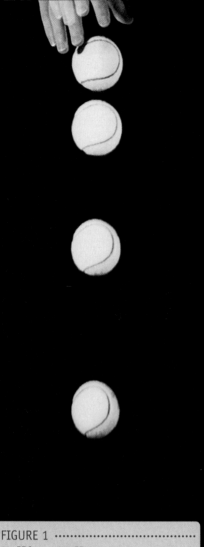

Kinetic and Potential Energy

The transformation between potential and kinetic energy is one of the most common energy transformations. For example, when you stretch a rubber band, you give it elastic potential energy. If you let it go, the rubber band flies across the room. When the rubber band is moving, it has kinetic energy. The potential energy of the stretched rubber has transformed to the kinetic energy of the moving rubber band. Transformations between kinetic and potential energy can also occur in any object that rises or falls. A falling object, a pendulum, and a pole vault are all examples of these transformations.

Falling Object A transformation between potential and kinetic energy occurs in the ball in **Figure 1.** As the height of the ball decreases, it loses potential energy. At the same time, its kinetic energy increases because its speed increases. Its potential energy is transformed into kinetic energy.

Pendulum A pendulum like the one in **Figure 2** swings back and forth. At the highest point in its swing, the pendulum has no movement. As it swings downward, it speeds up. The pendulum is at its greatest speed at the bottom of its swing. As the pendulum swings to the other side, its height increases and its speed decreases. At the top of its swing, it comes to a stop again.

FIGURE 1 ·······
Falling Ball
The ball was photographed at equal time intervals as it fell.

✎ **Interpret Photos** How can you tell that the ball's kinetic energy is increasing?

_____

_____

_____

_____

_____

_____

_____

FIGURE 2 ··
▶ INTERACTIVE ART Pendulum
A continuous transformation between potential and kinetic energy occurs in a pendulum. ✎ **Interpret Diagrams** Label the type of energy the pendulum has at positions A, B, and C.

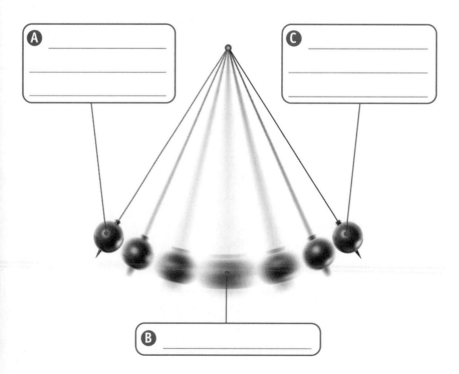

Ⓐ _____

Ⓒ _____

Ⓑ _____

Pole Vault The pole-vaulter in Figure 3 starts out by running forward. When the pole-vaulter plants the pole to jump, his speed decreases and the pole bends. As the pole straightens out, the pole-vaulter is lifted high into the air. Once he is over the bar, the pole-vaulter's speed increases as he falls toward the safety cushion.

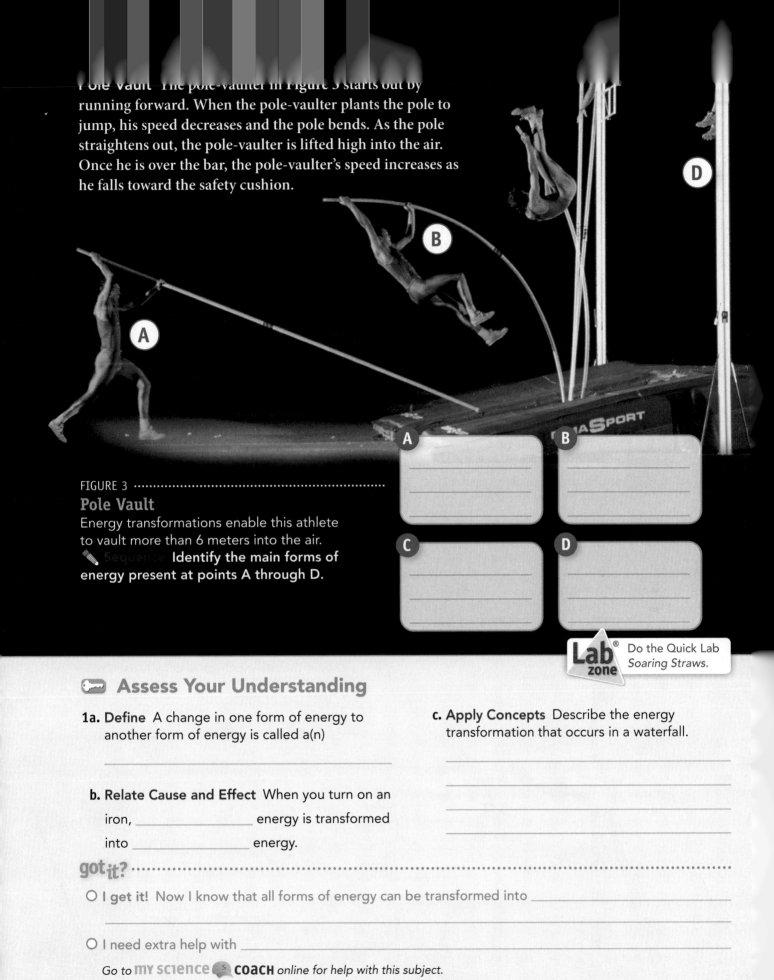

FIGURE 3 ···

Pole Vault
Energy transformations enable this athlete to vault more than 6 meters into the air.

✎ Sequence **Identify the main forms of energy present at points A through D.**

Lab Do the Quick Lab
zone *Soaring Straws.*

🔑 Assess Your Understanding

1a. Define A change in one form of energy to another form of energy is called a(n)

_____

b. Relate Cause and Effect When you turn on an

iron, _____ energy is transformed

into _____ energy.

c. Apply Concepts Describe the energy transformation that occurs in a waterfall.

_____

_____

_____

_____

got it? ··

○ **I get it!** Now I know that all forms of energy can be transformed into _____

_____

○ **I need extra help with** _____

Go to **my science** 💬 **coach** *online for help with this subject.*

What Is the Law of Conservation of Energy?

Once you set a pendulum in motion, does it swing forever? No, it does not. Then what happens to its energy? Is the energy destroyed? Again, the answer is no. The **law of conservation of energy** states that when one form of energy is transformed to another, no energy is lost in the process. 🔑 **According to the law of conservation of energy, energy cannot be created or destroyed.** The total amount of energy is the same before and after any transformation. If you add up all of the new forms of energy after a transformation, all of the original energy will be accounted for. So what happens to the energy of the pendulum once it stops moving?

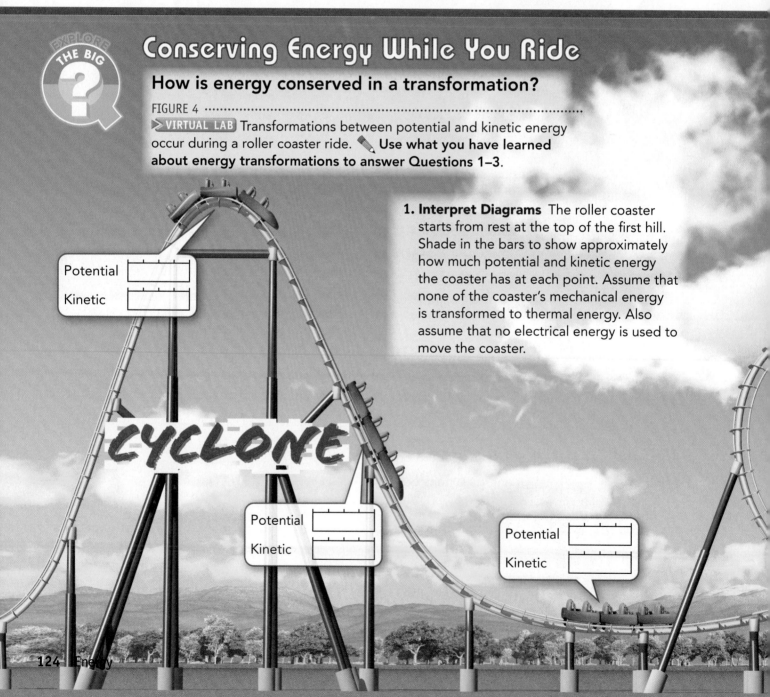

EXPLORE THE BIG ❓

Conserving Energy While You Ride

How is energy conserved in a transformation?

FIGURE 4 ···

▷ VIRTUAL LAB Transformations between potential and kinetic energy occur during a roller coaster ride. ✏ **Use what you have learned about energy transformations to answer Questions 1–3.**

1. **Interpret Diagrams** The roller coaster starts from rest at the top of the first hill. Shade in the bars to show approximately how much potential and kinetic energy the coaster has at each point. Assume that none of the coaster's mechanical energy is transformed to thermal energy. Also assume that no electrical energy is used to move the coaster.

Potential

Kinetic

CYCLONE

Potential

Kinetic

Potential

Kinetic

As the pendulum swings, it encounters friction at the pivot of the string and from the air through which it moves. Whenever a moving object experiences friction, some of its kinetic energy is transformed into thermal energy. So the mechanical energy of the pendulum is not destroyed. It is transformed to thermal energy.

The fact that friction transforms mechanical energy to thermal energy should not surprise you. After all, you take advantage of such thermal energy when you rub your cold hands together to warm them up. Friction is also the reason why no machine is 100 percent efficient. You may recall that the output work of any real machine is always less than the input work. This reduced efficiency occurs because some mechanical energy is always transformed into thermal energy due to friction.

did you know? ....

When ancient animals and plants died, the chemical energy they had stored was trapped within their remains. This trapped energy is the chemical energy found in coal.

2. **Infer** Suppose you had taken thermal energy into account in Step 1. Would the total length of the shaded portion of the bars increase, decrease, or stay the same as as result?

○ Increase ○ Decrease ○ Stay the same

3. **CHALLENGE** Why is the first hill of a roller coaster always the tallest?

_____

_____

_____

_____

Potential [ ]
Kinetic [ ]

Potential [ ]
Kinetic [ ]

Lab zone — Do the Quick Lab *Law of Conservation of Energy.*

🔑 **Assess Your Understanding**

2. **ANSWER THE BIG Q** How is energy conserved in a transformation?

_____

_____

_____

_____

got it? ....

○ I get it! Now I know that according to the law of conservation of energy, energy _____

_____

_____

○ I need extra help with _____

Go to my science ⁵ coach *online for help with this subject.*

4 Study Guide

The total amount of _____ is the same before and after any transformation.

LESSON 1 What Is Energy?

🔑 Since the transfer of energy is work, then power is the rate at which energy is transferred, or the amount of energy transferred in a unit of time.

🔑 The two basic types of energy are kinetic energy and potential energy.

Vocabulary
- energy
- kinetic energy
- potential energy
- gravitational potential energy
- elastic potential energy

LESSON 2 Forms of Energy

🔑 You can find an object's mechanical energy by adding together the object's kinetic energy and potential energy.

🔑 Forms of energy associated with the particles of objects include nuclear energy, thermal energy, electrical energy, electromagnetic energy, and chemical energy.

Vocabulary
- mechanical energy   • nuclear energy   • thermal energy
- electrical energy   • electromagnetic energy
- chemical energy

LESSON 3 Energy Transformations and Conservation

🔑 All forms of energy can be transformed into other forms of energy.

🔑 According to the law of conservation of energy, energy cannot be created or destroyed.

Vocabulary
- energy transformation
- law of conservation of energy

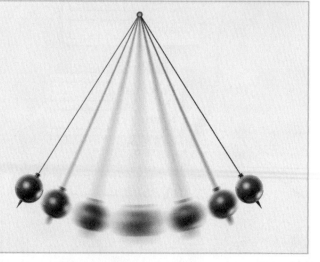

Review and Assessment

LESSON 1 What Is Energy?

1. When you stretch a rubber band, you give it

  a. kinetic energy.   **b.** electrical energy.

  c. potential energy.   **d.** chemical energy.

2. To calculate power, divide the amount of energy transferred by _____

3. **Compare and Contrast** In the illustration below, which vehicle has the greatest kinetic energy? Explain your answer.

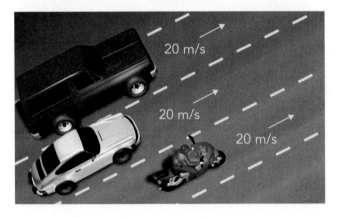

  20 m/s

  20 m/s

  20 m/s

_____

_____

_____

4. **Apply Concepts** If a handsaw does the same amount of work on a log as a chainsaw does, which has more power? Why?

_____

_____

_____

_____

5. **math!** A 1,350-kg car travels at 12 m/s. What is its kinetic energy?

_____

_____

LESSON 2 Forms of Energy

6. What is the energy stored in the nucleus of an atom called?

  a. electrical energy   **b.** chemical energy

  c. thermal energy   **d.** nuclear energy

7. An object's mechanical energy is the sum of its

_____

8. **Classify** When you heat a pot of water over a flame, what form of energy is added to the water?

_____

The graph shows the kinetic energy of a 500-N diver during a dive from a 10-m platform. Use the graph to answer Questions 9 and 10.

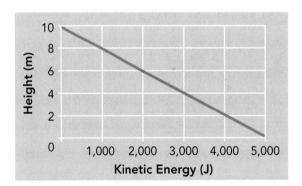

9. **Read Graphs** How does the diver's kinetic energy change as the diver falls? Why?

_____

_____

_____

_____

10. **Calculate** What is the diver's gravitational potential energy just before the dive?

_____

_____

4 Review and Assessment

Energy Transformations and Conservation

11. As a car skids to a stop, friction transforms kinetic energy to

    a. thermal energy.   **b.** potential energy.

    c. chemical energy.   **d.** electrical energy.

12. The law of conservation of energy states that

_____

_____

_____

_____

13. Classify Describe the energy transformation that occurs in a digital clock.

_____

_____

_____

14. Apply Concepts Explain why a spinning top will not remain in motion forever.

_____

_____

_____

15. Infer Why does a bouncing ball rise to a lower height with each bounce?

_____

_____

_____

_____

_____

_____

16. **Write About It** An eagle flies from its perch in a tree to the ground to capture and eat its prey. Describe its energy transformations.

APPLY
THE BIG
?

How is energy conserved in a transformation?

17. The golfer in the photo is taking a swing. The golf club starts at point A and ends at point E. (1) Describe the energy transformations of the club from points A to E. (2) The kinetic energy of the club at point C is more than the potential energy of the club at point B. Does this mean that the law of conservation of energy is violated? Why or why not?

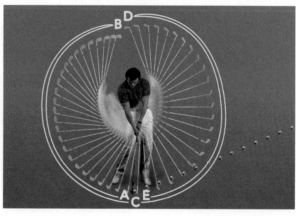

_____

_____

_____

_____

_____

_____

_____

_____

_____

_____

_____

_____

_____

_____

Standardized Test Prep

Multiple Choice

Circle the letter of the best answer.

1. The table gives the kinetic and potential energy of a 6-kg cat doing various activities.

Activity	Kinetic Energy (J)	Potential Energy (J)
Running	200	0
Leaping	150	100
Climbing a tree	3	300
Sleeping on a chair	0	30

During which activity does the cat have the greatest mechanical energy?

A climbing a tree   B leaping
C running   D sleeping on a chair

2. Why does wind have energy?

A It can change direction.
B It can do work.
C It moves through space as waves.
D It is electrically charged.

3. What is the SI unit used to express gravitational potential energy?

A newton
B kilowatt
C horsepower
D joule

4. What causes a pendulum to eventually slow down and stop swinging?

A friction
B kinetic energy
C weight
D potential energy

5. Which energy transformation takes place when wood is burned?

A Nuclear energy is transformed to thermal energy.
B Thermal energy is transformed to electrical energy.
C Chemical energy is transformed to thermal energy.
D Mechanical energy is transformed to thermal energy.

Constructed Response

Use the table below to answer Question 6.
Write your answer on a separate sheet of paper.

Time	Speed at Bottom of Swing (m/s)
8:00 a.m.	2.2
10:00 a.m.	1.9
12:00 p.m.	1.7
2:00 p.m.	1.6

6. A large pendulum at a science museum is set in motion at the beginning of the day. The table shows how its speed at the bottom of the swing changes during the day. Use this data to determine how the height of the pendulum's swing changes. Explain your answer.

CHARGE IT!

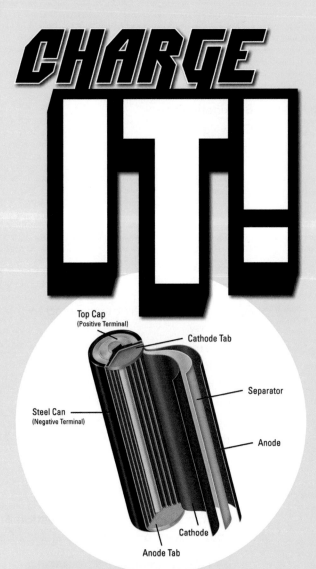

Top Cap
(Positive Terminal)

Cathode Tab

Separator

Steel Can
(Negative Terminal)

Anode

Cathode

Anode Tab

Have you ever noticed how many batteries you use every day? There are batteries in cars, flashlights, cell phones, laptop computers, and even bug zappers! Discarded batteries add up to a lot of waste. Fortunately, rechargeable batteries can help keep the energy flowing and reduce the number of batteries that get thrown out. Can you imagine how many nonrechargeable batteries a cell phone would go through in a month?

Batteries transform chemical energy into electrical energy. To refuel a rechargeable battery, you plug it into a power source—such as an outlet in the wall. The electrical energy reverses the chemical changes, storing the electrical energy as chemical energy. The battery is once again "charged up" and ready to go!

Research It Gasoline-powered cars and hybrid cars have rechargeable batteries. Research how the batteries in gasoline-powered cars and hybrid cars are recharged.

▲ The inside of this rechargeable battery has three long thin layers. A separator separates a positive electrode from a negative electrode. Using the battery causes lithium ions to move from the positive material to the negative one. Applying an electrical charge moves the ions back to the positive electrode.

Museum of Science®

CATCH AND NO RELEASE

A spider's web is more than just a sticky net hanging across an open space. The strong, elastic nature of spider silk ensures that an insect cannot leave once it strikes the web. To make their webs, spiders produce two kinds of silk—dragline silk and capture-spiral silk.

Dragline silk makes up the web's large frame. When an insect crashes into a spider's web, the dragline silk absorbs the force of impact and spreads it out over the entire area of the frame. No matter the mass or speed of the insect, the dragline silk is strong enough to absorb the force.

Capture-spiral silk is the sticky silk at the center of the web. It is more elastic than dragline silk so it stretches and then returns to its shape when an insect strikes it. As it stretches, it transforms the insect's kinetic energy into elastic potential energy. As a result, the insect slows down gradually and doesn't immediately bounce off the web. Once the insect comes to a stop, the stickiness of the capture-spiral thread keeps the prey from leaving.

Spider silk is only one-tenth the diameter of human hair, but it is very strong. In fact, a thread of spider silk can resist more force than a piece of steel of the same size. Think of that next time you get tangled up in a spider's web.

Research It Identify an object that could be made from spider silk instead of steel or Kevlar. Then write a proposal that includes a list of spider silk's advantages and a request for funding to build a prototype of the object.

WHAT MIGHT THESE COLORS MEAN?

THE BIG ❓

How does heat flow from one object to another?

The image at the right is called a thermogram. A special camera measures the electromagnetic radiation of an object and creates a temperature "map." A thermographic camera can be used to find people in a fire, detect when a racehorse might be injured, and spot tumors in humans. By noticing excessive heat in motors, transformers, and pumps, the camera can detect equipment problems before they fail, saving millions of dollars.

Infer Since a thermogram shows temperature, what might the colors you see indicate?

_____

_____

_____

_____

▷ **UNTAMED SCIENCE** Watch the **Untamed Science** video to learn more about heat.

Thermal Energy and Heat

5 Getting Started

Check Your Understanding

1. **Background** Read the paragraph below and then answer the question.

Kiera is swimming in the ocean. Since she is moving, she has **kinetic energy.** Energy is measured in **joules.** Her brother, who swims at the same speed but has more mass, has more kinetic energy. If he slows down, he will have the same amount of kinetic energy as Kiera. While swimming, she notices that it is easier to float in salt water because it has a higher **density** than fresh water.

Kinetic energy is energy an object has due to its motion.

A **joule** is a unit of work equal to one newton-meter.

Density is the ratio of the mass of a substance to its volume.

• What are the two ways you can increase kinetic energy?

> **MY READING WEB** If you had trouble completing the question above, visit **My Reading Web** and type in *Thermal Energy and Heat.*

Vocabulary Skill

Identify Multiple Meanings Some words have several meanings. Words you use every day may have different meanings in science.

Word	Everyday Meaning	Scientific Meaning
conductor	*n.* the director of an orchestra **Example:** The *conductor* signaled to the musicians to begin playing.	*n.* a material that conducts heat well **Example:** Metal is a good *conductor.*
heat	*v.* to make warm or hot **Example:** The fireplace began to *heat* the room.	*n.* thermal energy moving from a warmer object to a cooler object **Example:** When the door was left open, *heat* transferred from the warm room to the cool air outside.

2. **Quick Check** Circle the sentence below that uses the scientific meaning of the word *conductor.*

• The *conductor* got a standing ovation after the concert.

• It is easier to cook eggs in a pan that is a good *conductor.*

MON	TUES	WED
25°	26°	24°
18°	19°	17°

temperature

convection

radiation

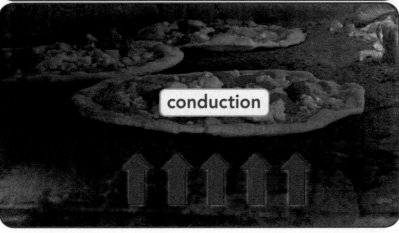

conduction

Chapter Preview

LESSON 1
- temperature
- Fahrenheit scale
- Celsius scale
- Kelvin scale
- absolute zero
- heat

  ⊙ Identify Supporting Evidence
  △ Communicate

LESSON 2
- convection
- convection current
- radiation
- conduction

  ⊙ Compare and Contrast
  △ Infer

LESSON 3
- conductor
- insulator
- specific heat
- thermal expansion

  ⊙ Identify the Main Idea
  △ Calculate

> VOCAB FLASH CARDS For extra help with vocabulary, visit **Vocab Flash Cards** and type in *Thermal Energy and Heat.*

Temperature, Thermal Energy, and Heat

🔑 **What Determines the Temperature of an Object?**

🔑 **What Is Thermal Energy?**

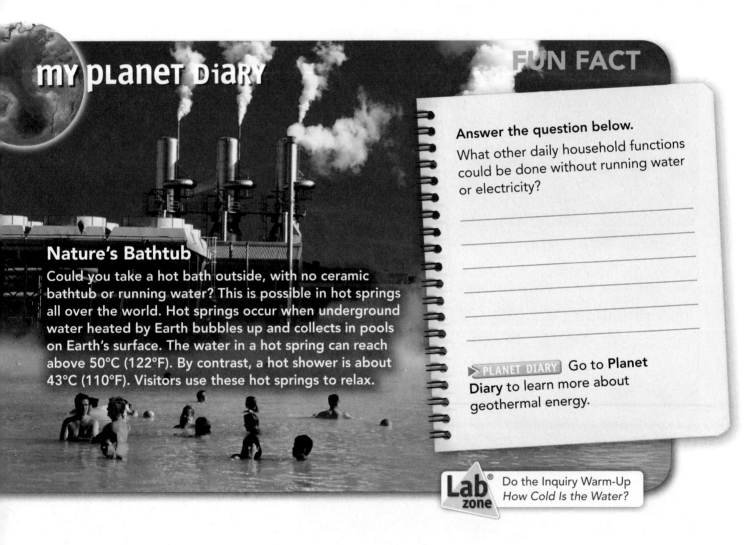

my planet diary

Nature's Bathtub

Could you take a hot bath outside, with no ceramic bathtub or running water? This is possible in hot springs all over the world. Hot springs occur when underground water heated by Earth bubbles up and collects in pools on Earth's surface. The water in a hot spring can reach above 50°C (122°F). By contrast, a hot shower is about 43°C (110°F). Visitors use these hot springs to relax.

FUN FACT

Answer the question below.
What other daily household functions could be done without running water or electricity?

_____

_____

_____

_____

_____

> PLANET DIARY Go to **Planet Diary** to learn more about geothermal energy.

Lab ® Do the Inquiry Warm-Up
zone *How Cold Is the Water?*

What Determines the Temperature of an Object?

You may have used a thermometer to take your temperature when you were sick. **Temperature** is a measure of how hot or cold something is compared to a reference point. (One reference point is the freezing point of water.) What makes an object hot or cold?

Vocabulary
- temperature
- Celsius scale
- absolute zero
- Fahrenheit scale
- Kelvin scale
- heat

Skills
- ↪ Reading: Identify Supporting Evidence
- △ Inquiry: Communicate

Recall that all moving objects have kinetic energy. Matter is made up of tiny particles that are always moving, so these particles have kinetic energy. ⬤ **Temperature is a measure of the average kinetic energy of the particles in an object.** As an object heats up, its particles move faster. As a result, both the average kinetic energy of the particles and the temperature increase.

The United States uses the **Fahrenheit scale** to measure temperature. Most countries use the **Celsius scale.** You can use an equation to convert between scales, but it's simpler to estimate using thermometers like the one in **Figure 1.** Temperatures that line up, like 32°F and 0°C, are equivalent. Many scientists use the **Kelvin scale.** Celsius and Fahrenheit scales are divided into degrees. The Kelvin scale is divided into kelvins (K). A temperature change of 1 K is the same temperature change as 1°C. Zero kelvins, or **absolute zero,** is the lowest temperature possible. At absolute zero, particles have no kinetic energy. Zero K is equal to −273°C.

did you know?

When Anders Celsius invented the Celsius scale, he had 100°C as the *freezing* point of water and 0°C as its *boiling* point.

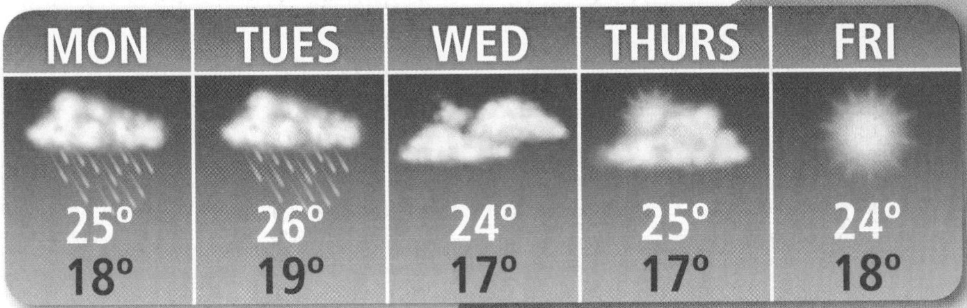

MON	TUES	WED	THURS	FRI
25°	26°	24°	25°	24°
18°	19°	17°	17°	18°

FIGURE 1 ....

▶ ART IN MOTION **Temperature Scales**
The chart above shows a weather report, but it does not identify the temperature scale.

✎ **Interpret Diagrams** Explain why this report would mean something different in Japan than it would in the United States. Fill in the thermometer to show one of the temperatures in Celsius. What is this equivalent to in Fahrenheit?

_____

_____

_____

_____

Lab zone ® Do the Lab Investigation
Build Your Own Thermometer.

⬤ **Assess Your Understanding**

got it? ....

○ **I get it!** Now I know that temperature is
related to _____

_____

○ **I need extra help with** _____

Go to my science ⑤ coach *online for help with this subject.*

What Is Thermal Energy?

Different objects at the same temperature can have different amounts of energy. To understand this, you need to know about thermal energy and about heat. Temperature, thermal energy, and heat are closely related, but they are not the same thing.

Thermal Energy Temperature is a measure of the average kinetic energy of the individual particles in an object. However, it is not a measure of the total amount of energy in an object. 🔑 **Thermal energy is the total energy of all the particles in an object.** It depends on the temperature of an object, the number of particles in it, and how those particles are arranged. This lesson will focus on the first two factors.

The more particles an object has at a given temperature, the more thermal energy it has. For example, a 1-liter pot of tea at 75°C has more thermal energy than a 0.2-liter mug of tea at 75°C because the pot contains more tea particles. On the other hand, the higher the temperature of an object, the more thermal energy the object has. Therefore, if two 1-liter pots of tea have different temperatures, the pot with the higher temperature has more thermal energy.

Identify Supporting Evidence Since thermal energy is the total energy of all the particles in an object, it depends on multiple factors. Underline sentences that support this idea.

apply it!

The total amount of thermal energy an object has depends on its temperature and how many particles it contains.

❶ Identify In the top two panels, circle the chicken pot pie that contains more thermal energy.

❷ Apply Concepts In the last panel, draw in and record the temperature of three pies that have more thermal energy than the one on the left.

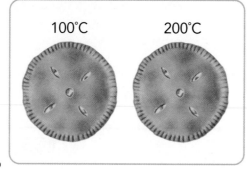

100°C   200°C

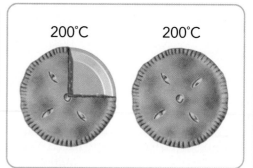

200°C   200°C

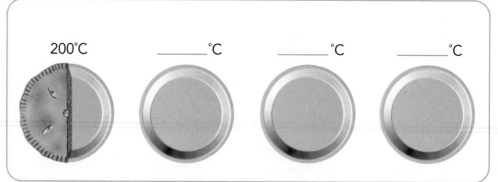

200°C   _____°C   _____°C   _____°C

Heat You might say that an object contains heat, but, strictly speaking, it does not. Objects contain thermal energy. **Heat** is the *transfer* of thermal energy from a warmer object to a cooler object. The warmer object will cool down, and the cooler object will warm up until they are the same temperature. When this happens, heat stops transferring. Heat is measured in the units of energy—joules.

Vocabulary Write a sentence that uses the scientific meaning of *heat*.

_____

_____

_____

FIGURE 2 ·····················

▶ VIRTUAL LAB **Heat**
When you hold your hand over a plate of food, you will feel warmth if heat transfers into you and cold if heat transfers out of you.

✎ **Communicate** In the photo, draw arrows to show the direction of heat transfer for at least two foods. Would your hand feel warmer over some foods than over others? What characteristics of the food might affect how warm or cold your hand feels? Discuss your ideas with a partner.

_____

_____

_____

Lab zone ® Do the Quick Lab *Temperature and Thermal Energy.*

🔑 **Assess Your Understanding**

1a. List What are two factors that determine an object's thermal energy?

_____

_____

b. CHALLENGE Object A has less thermal energy than Object B, but heat flows from Object A to Object B. What conditions would make this possible?

_____

_____

_____

got it?

○ **I get it!** Now I know that the thermal energy in an object is defined as _____

_____

_____

_____

○ **I need extra help with** _____

Go to my science ⓢ coach *online for help with this subject.*

The Transfer of Heat

UNLOCK
THE BIG
?

🔑 **How Is Heat Transferred?**

my planeT DiaRY

Wild Weather

Hurricanes are intense storms that can cause billions of dollars in damage. These storms form when very warm, moist air rises quickly, creating an area of lower air pressure below. As the air rises, the water vapor in the air condenses, releasing a huge amount of thermal energy. This energy causes swirling winds, which draw in more warm water, feeding the storm. If a hurricane's path takes it over land, the storm can cause massive destruction. However, as the storm moves over land, its energy source—the warm ocean water—is depleted, and the storm eventually fizzles out.

DISASTER

Answer the question below.
Why do hurricanes tend to form in warmer climates?

_____

_____

_____

_____

_____

_____

_____

_____

▶ PLANET DIARY Go to **Planet Diary** to learn more about hurricanes.

Labzone® Do the Inquiry Warm-Up *What Does It Mean to Heat Up?*

How Is Heat Transferred?

Heat is transferring around you all the time. If it wasn't, nothing would ever change temperature. Heat doesn't transfer randomly. It travels only in one direction and by three different methods. 🔑 **Heat is transferred from warmer areas to cooler areas by conduction, convection, and radiation.**

Vocabulary
- convection • convection current
- radiation • conduction

Skills
⟳ Reading: Compare and Contrast

△ Inquiry: Infer

Convection

Convection is a type of heat transfer that occurs only in fluids, such as water and air. When air is heated, its particles speed up and move farther apart. This makes the heated air less dense. The heated air rises to float on top of the denser, cooler air. Cooler air flows into its place, heats up, and rises. Previously heated air cools down, sinks, and the cycle repeats. This flow creates a circular motion known as a **convection current.** Convection currents in air cause wind and weather changes.

Radiation

Radiation is the transfer of energy by electromagnetic waves. Radiation is the only form of heat transfer that does not require matter. You can feel the radiation from a fire without touching the flames. The sun's energy travels to Earth through 150 million kilometers of empty space.

Conduction

Conduction transfers heat from one particle of matter to another within an object or between two objects. The fast-moving particles in the floor of the oven collide with the slow-moving particles in the uncooked pizza. This causes the pizza's particles to move faster, making the pizza hotter.

FIGURE 1 ·····························

Heat Transfer

A wood-fire pizza oven demonstrates three types of heat transfer.

✎ **Apply Concepts** Describe a heat transfer that occurs after the pizza comes out of the oven. What kind of transfer is it?

_____

_____

⟳ **Compare and Contrast** Circle statements on the previous page that describe what the different types of heat transfer have in common. Underline their differences on this page.

Where Does Heat Transfer on This Beach?

How does heat flow from one object to another?

FIGURE 2 ···

> **INTERACTIVE ART** Heat transfer goes on all around you all the time, even on the beach. ✎ **Apply Concepts** Fill in the chart below to review the different types of heat transfer. Then, in the illustration, label at least one example of each type of heat transfer. Draw arrows to show how heat is being transferred in each example.

Type of Heat Transfer	Explanation
Conduction	
Convection	
Radiation	

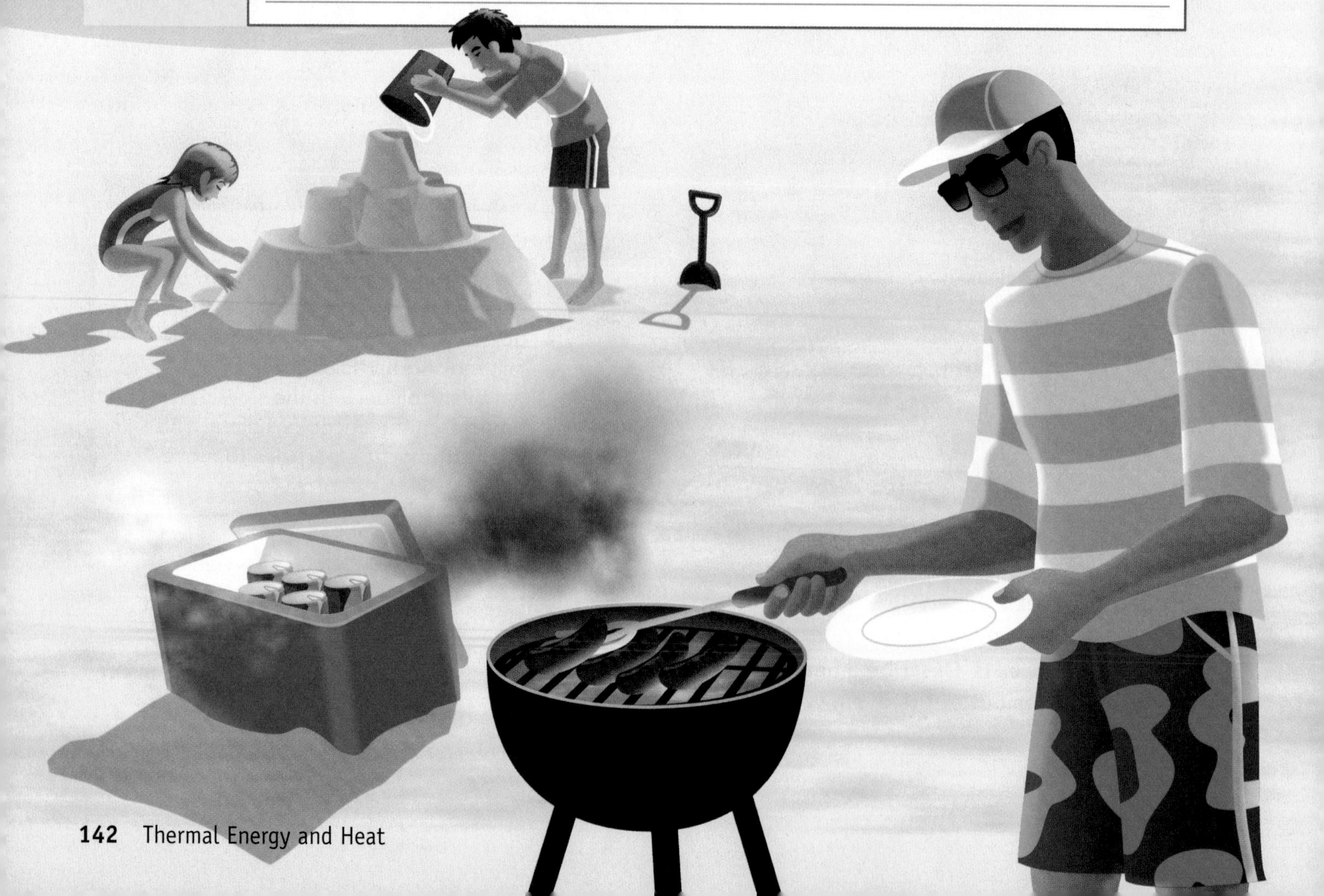

apply it!

Cooking pots come in a variety of shapes and sizes, but you're much more likely to see a wide, squat pot like this

than a tall, narrow pot like this.

⚠ **Infer** Use conduction to explain why this is the case.

_____

_____

_____

_____

_____

_____

_____

Lab zone Do the Quick Lab *Visualizing Convection Currents.*

🔑 Assess Your Understanding

1a. Classify What type of heat transfer occurs when eggs cook in a hot pan? Before toasters, people toasted bread by holding it over a fire. What type of heat transfer occurred then? Name the third type of heat transfer and an example of a food cooked by it.

_____

_____

b. ANSWER THE BIG ❓ How does heat flow from one object to another?

_____

_____

_____

_____

_____

got it?

○ **I get it!** Now I know that the three methods of heat transfer are _____

_____

○ **I need extra help with** _____

Go to MY SCIENCE Ⓢ COACH *online for help with this subject.*

Thermal Properties

UNLOCK THE BIG ? **How Do Different Materials Respond to Heat?**

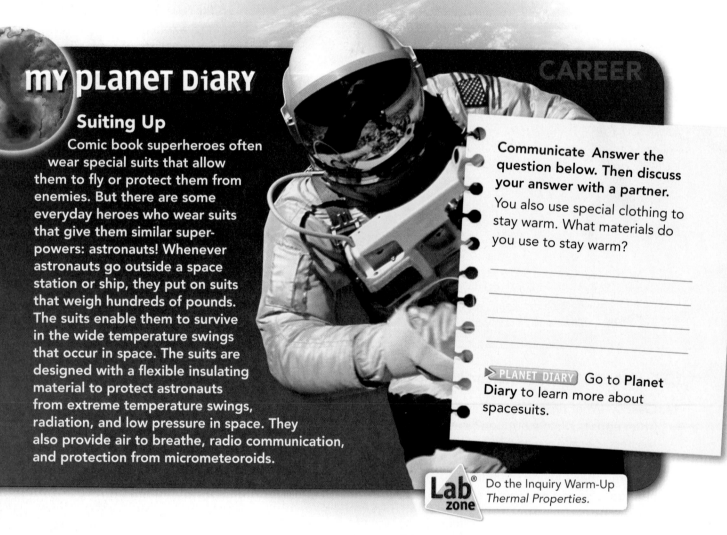

my planet diary

CAREER

Suiting Up

Comic book superheroes often wear special suits that allow them to fly or protect them from enemies. But there are some everyday heroes who wear suits that give them similar super-powers: astronauts! Whenever astronauts go outside a space station or ship, they put on suits that weigh hundreds of pounds. The suits enable them to survive in the wide temperature swings that occur in space. The suits are designed with a flexible insulating material to protect astronauts from extreme temperature swings, radiation, and low pressure in space. They also provide air to breathe, radio communication, and protection from micrometeoroids.

Communicate Answer the question below. Then discuss your answer with a partner.

You also use special clothing to stay warm. What materials do you use to stay warm?

_____

_____

_____

_____

▶ PLANET DIARY Go to **Planet Diary** to learn more about spacesuits.

Lab zone ® Do the Inquiry Warm-Up *Thermal Properties.*

How Do Different Materials Respond to Heat?

When you bake something in the oven, you use dishes made of glass, ceramics, or metal instead of plastic. Some materials can stand up to the heat of an oven better than others. Materials respond to heat in different ways. The thermal properties of an object determine how it will respond to heat.

Vocabulary

- conductor
- insulator
- specific heat
- thermal expansion

Skills

- Reading: Identify the Main Idea
- Inquiry: Calculate

Conductors and Insulators If you walk barefoot from your living room rug to the tile floor of your kitchen, you will notice that the tile feels colder than the rug. But the temperature of the rug and the tile are the same—room temperature! The difference has to do with how materials conduct heat. 🔑 **Some materials conduct heat well, while other materials do not.**

Conductors A material that conducts heat well is called a **conductor**. Metals such as silver are good conductors. Some materials are good conductors because of the particles they contain and how those particles are arranged. A good conductor, such as the tile floor, feels cold to the touch because heat easily transfers out of your skin and into the tile. However, heat also transfers out of conductors easily. A metal flagpole feels much hotter on a summer day than a wooden pole would in the same place because heat easily transfers out of the metal pole and into your hand.

Insulators A wooden pole and your living room rug are good insulators. **Insulators** are materials that do not conduct heat well. Other good insulators include air and wool. For example, wool blankets slow the transfer of heat out of your body.

FIGURE 1 ....

ART IN MOTION Conductors and Insulators
Both conductors and insulators are useful in a kitchen. Conductors easily transfer heat to cook your food. Insulators stay cool enough to be handled.
✏️ **Classify** Circle the conductors in the photo. Below, list objects in a kitchen that can act as insulators.

_____

_____

_____

_____

Specific Heat Imagine running across hot sand toward the ocean. You run to the water's edge, but you don't go any farther—the water is too cold. How can the sand be so hot and the water so cold? After all, the sun heats both of them. The answer is that water requires more heat to raise its temperature than sand does.

When an object is heated, its temperature rises. But the temperature does not rise at the same rate for all objects. The amount of heat required to raise the temperature of an object depends on the object's chemical makeup. 🔑 **To change the temperature of different objects by the same amount, different amounts of thermal energy are required.**

The amount of energy required to raise the temperature of 1 kilogram of a material by 1 kelvin is called its **specific heat.** It is measured in joules per kilogram-kelvin, or J/(kg·K). A material with a high specific heat can absorb a great deal of thermal energy without a great change in temperature.

You can calculate thermal energy changes with a formula.

Energy Change = Mass × Specific Heat × Temperature Change

✎ **Identify the Main Idea**
Circle the main idea on this page. Underline the sentences that support the main idea.

do the math!

You can calculate the amount of thermal energy gained by 2 kg of water as its temperature increases by 3 K.

Energy Change = Mass × Specific Heat × Temp. Change

Energy Change = 2 kg × 4,180 J/(kg·K) × 3 K

Energy Change = 25,080 J

Material	Specific Heat (J/(kg·K))
Copper	385
Water	4,180
Glass	837
Silver	235
Iron	450

① Calculate Use the formula and the table at the right to calculate how much energy is lost by 0.5 kg of silver that cools off by 2 K.

_____

② Interpret Tables How many times more energy must you transfer into a kilogram of glass than a kilogram of silver to raise their temperatures by the same amount?

_____

③ Draw Conclusions The seawater at a beach heats up more slowly than the sand on the beach does. The specific heat of water must be (greater than/less than) the specific heat of sand.

Thermal Expansion To loosen a jar lid, you can hold it under a stream of hot water. This works because the metal lid expands more than the glass does as it gets hotter. As the thermal energy of matter increases, its particles usually spread out, causing the substance to expand. This is true for almost all matter. The expanding of matter when it is heated is known as **thermal expansion.** When matter is cooled, the opposite happens. Thermal energy is released. This causes the particles to slow down and move closer together. As matter cools, it usually decreases in volume, or contracts. Different materials expand and contract at different rates.

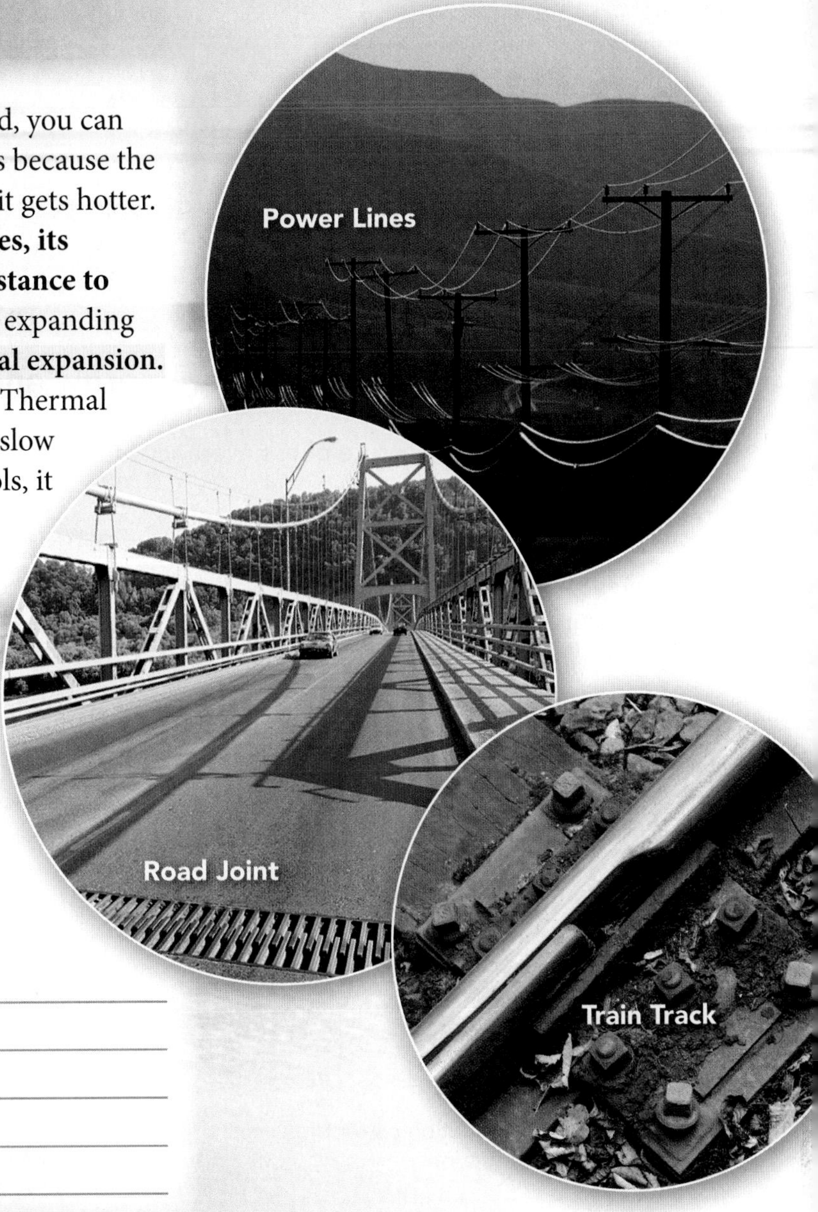

Power Lines

Road Joint

Train Track

FIGURE 2 ·····························

Thermal Expansion
Many objects are specifically designed to allow extra space for thermal expansion, such as road joints and train tracks.

✎ **Predict** Pick one of the examples. What might happen if thermal expansion was not considered when this object was designed?

_____

_____

_____

_____

_____

Lab ® Do the Quick Lab
zone Frosty Balloons.

🔑 Assess Your Understanding

1a. Classify Foam picnic coolers keep food cold on a hot day. Is foam a conductor or an insulator? Explain.

_____

_____

_____

b. Calculate The specific heat of foam is about 1,200 J/(kg·K). How much heat does it take to raise the temperature of 1 kg of foam by 2 K?

_____

_____

got it? ·······························

○ **I get it!** Now I know that the way a material responds to heat depends on _____

_____

○ **I need extra help with** _____

Go to MY SCIENCE Ⓢ **COACH** *online for help with this subject.*

5 Study Guide

Heat flows from _____ objects to _____ objects. The three methods of heat transfer are _____.

LESSON 1 Temperature, Thermal Energy, and Heat

🔑 Temperature is a measure of the average kinetic energy of the particles in an object.

🔑 Thermal energy is the total energy of all the particles in an object.

Vocabulary
- temperature
- Fahrenheit scale
- Celsius scale
- Kelvin scale
- absolute zero
- heat

LESSON 2 The Transfer of Heat

🔑 Heat is transferred from warmer areas to cooler areas by conduction, convection, and radiation.

Vocabulary
- convection
- convection current
- radiation
- conduction

LESSON 3 Thermal Properties

🔑 Some materials conduct heat well, while other materials do not.

🔑 To change the temperature of different objects by the same amount, different amounts of thermal energy are required.

🔑 As the thermal energy of matter increases, its particles usually spread out, causing the substance to expand.

Vocabulary
- conductor
- insulator
- specific heat
- thermal expansion

Review and Assessment

LESSON 1 Temperature, Thermal Energy, and Heat

1. What is the total energy of all the particles in an object called?

   a. chemical energy   b. thermal energy

   c. potential energy   d. mechanical energy

2. The temperature scale used in most of the world is the _____

3. **Apply Concepts** How does heat flow when you place an ice cube in your hand?

   _____

   _____

Use the illustration to answer the questions below.

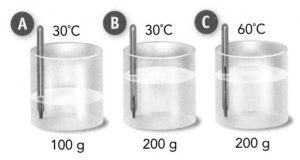

A 30°C	B 30°C	C 60°C
100 g	200 g	200 g

4. **Interpret Data** Compare the average motion of the particles in the three containers. Explain your answer.

   _____

   _____

   _____

   _____

   _____

5. **Draw Conclusions** Compare the total amount of thermal energy in containers A and B. Explain your answer.

   _____

   _____

   _____

   _____

LESSON 2 The Transfer of Heat

6. What is the process by which heat transfers from one particle of matter to another when the particles collide?

   a. conduction   b. convection

   c. expansion   d. radiation

7. A convection current is _____

   _____

   _____

   _____

8. **Classify** Identify each example of heat transfer as conduction, convection, or radiation: opening the windows in a hot room; a lizard basking in the sun; putting ice on a sprained ankle.

   _____

   _____

9. **Infer** How can heat be transferred across empty space? Explain your answer.

   _____

   _____

   _____

10. **Make Judgments** Suppose you try to heat your home using a fireplace in one of the rooms. Would a fan be helpful? Explain.

   _____

   _____

   _____

   _____

11. **Write About It** Explain why a school might ask teachers to keep the windows closed and the shades down during a heat wave.

5 Review and Assessment

Thermal Properties

12. Suppose you want to know the amount of heat needed to raise the temperature of 2 kg of copper by 10°C. What property of the copper do you need to know?

    a. the thermal energy of the copper

    b. the temperature of the copper

    c. the specific heat of copper

    d. the melting point of copper

13. Wool is a good insulator, which means _____

_____

14. Apply Concepts When they are hung, telephone lines are allowed to sag. Explain why.

_____

_____

_____

15. Interpret Diagrams Why are two panes of glass used in the window shown below? (*Hint*: Air is an insulator.)

Glass

Air space

_____

_____

_____

16. math! Iron has a specific heat of 450 J/(kg·K). Design a set of three iron cooking pots. How much heat is required to increase the temperature of each pot by 100 K?

 How does heat flow from one object to another?

17. Suppose you were out camping and the weather turned cold. How would you keep warm? Explain each action you would take. Tell whether conduction, convection, or radiation is involved with each heat transfer.

_____

_____

_____

_____

_____

_____

_____

_____

_____

_____

_____

_____

_____

_____

_____

_____

Standardized Test Prep

Multiple Choice

Circle the letter of the best answer.

1. The temperature of four pies is shown below.

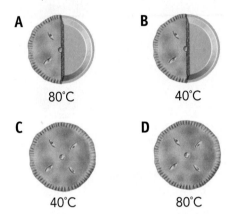

A   80°C   B   40°C

C   40°C   D   80°C

Which statement is true?

A   A and D have the same thermal energy.
B   C and D have the same thermal energy.
C   B has twice the thermal energy as C.
D   D has twice the thermal energy as A.

2. What does a thermometer measure?

A   temperature
B   thermal energy
C   heat
D   specific heat

3. Which statement describes the direction of heat flow?

A   Heat flows between two objects at the same temperature.
B   Thermal energy can only be absorbed by cool objects.
C   Heat flows from a warmer object to a cooler object.
D   Heat flows from a cooler object to a warmer object.

4. The specific heat of iron is 450 J/(kg·K). How much thermal energy must be transferred to 15 kg of iron to raise its temperature by 4.0 K?

A   450 J
B   2,700 J
C   5,400 J
D   27,000 J

5. Which of the following can be classified as a good conductor of thermal energy?

A   air
B   wood
C   silver
D   wool

Constructed Response

Use your knowledge of science to help you answer Question 6. Write your answer on a separate sheet of paper.

6. Using the principles of conduction, convection, and radiation, explain how the water in the pot gets hot.

Aerogel Windows

Close the Window!

Even when they are shut tight, windows can let as much as half of a building's heat out. Scientists at the National Aeronautics and Space Administration (NASA) are working on a new material that may make glass windows a thing of the past.

Aerogel is a nearly transparent solid made from silicon dioxide—the same ingredient found in sand and glass.

Unlike glass, aerogel is 99.8 percent air. This makes it the world's least dense solid. Yet it insulates 39 times better than the best fiberglass insulation.

Aerogel absorbs infrared radiation, stopping most forms of energy transfer, including heat. This should make it an amazing material for windows! Unfortunately, tiny pores scatter some of the visible light, which gives aerogel a blue haze.

NASA is researching ways to make aerogel truly transparent. That could prove to be the future of windows!

▲ Aerogel, the world's least dense solid, is nonflammable and absorbs heat.

Write About It Write an advertisement for aerogel windows or insulation. Be creative! Promote the idea that the government would give homeowners a rebate for installing a cutting-edge energy solution.

THERMAL EXPANSION

Problem

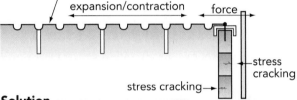

metal roof
expansion/contraction
force
stress cracking
stress cracking

Solution

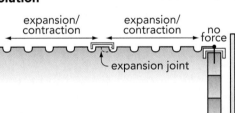

expansion/contraction
expansion/contraction
no force
expansion joint

△ When a metal roof expands from the sun's heat, the expanding metal pushes against the concrete wall. An expansion joint adds space for the metal to expand.

Make Way for Heat

Sometimes when things heat up, it's time to get out. School board officials stopped construction on a Florida school when cement blocks in the building cracked. The school hired an architecture firm to explore the problem. An engineer discovered that thermal expansion was responsible for the damage. But where was the heat coming from?

The school was designed with a metal roofing system. When metal warms up, it expands. Concrete blocks attached to the metal should have been installed with expansion joints. These joints slip sideways as the metal expands. Unfortunately, there was no slip room over one of the entrances to the building. Something had to give—and it was the concrete blocks! Engineers fixed the problem by adding expansion joints to the roof of the building.

Building in a warm climate? Don't forget to account for thermal expansion!

Design It Do some research about thermal expansion and expansion joints. Make sketches of your own design for a building or bridge. Your design should use expansion joints to account for thermal expansion.

◁ Even concrete cracks under pressure from thermal expansion.

WHY ARE THE PEOPLE IN THIS BUILDING SAFE FROM LIGHTNING?

How does an electric circuit work?

Lightning strikes Earth more than 100 times every second. Buildings can be protected from lightning strikes with tall metal poles called lightning rods. When lightning strikes, it is more likely to hit the rod than the building. A lightning strike can flow through the rod and into metal wires that are connected to the ground. This prevents the building from being damaged and anyone inside from being injured.

△ Communicate **How is a lightning bolt like the electricity that runs through power lines? Discuss this with a partner.**

_____

_____

_____

_____

▶ **UNTAMED SCIENCE** Watch the **Untamed Science** video to learn more about electricity.

6 Getting Started

Check Your Understanding

1. **Background** Read the paragraph below and then answer the question.

When you lift up a basketball, you apply a **force** to it. The **energy** you use to lift it gets transferred to the ball as gravitational **potential energy.** The higher you lift the ball, the more energy you use and the more gravitational potential energy the ball gains.

A **force** is a push or pull exerted on an object.

Energy is the ability to do work or cause change.

Potential energy is the stored energy that results from the position or shape of an object.

- What happens to the ball's gravitational potential energy if it is dropped?

> **MY READING WEB** If you had trouble completing the question above, visit **My Reading Web** and type in *Electricity.*

Vocabulary Skill

Latin Word Origins Many science words in English come from Latin. For example, the word *solar*, which means "of the sun," comes from the Latin *sol*, which means "sun."

Latin Word	Meaning of Latin Word	Example
circuitus	going around	circuit, *n.* a complete, unbroken path
currere	to run	current, *n.* a continuous flow
insula	island	insulator, *n.* a material through which charges cannot flow

2. **Quick Check** Choose the word that best completes the sentence.

- An electric _____ is formed by the movement of electric charges from one place to another.

static electricity

static discharge

electric circuit

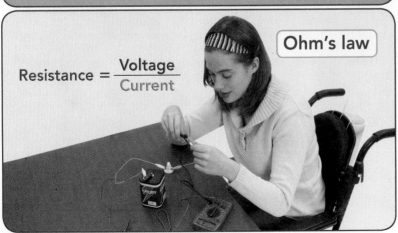

Ohm's law

$$\text{Resistance} = \frac{\text{Voltage}}{\text{Current}}$$

Chapter Preview

LESSON 1
- electric force
- electric field
- static electricity
- conservation of charge
- friction
- conduction
- induction
- polarization
- static discharge

🔁 Relate Cause and Effect
△ Draw Conclusions

LESSON 2
- electric current
- electric circuit
- conductor
- insulator
- voltage
- resistance

🔁 Ask Questions
△ Classify

LESSON 3
- Ohm's law
- series circuit
- parallel circuit

🔁 Compare and Contrast
△ Make Models

LESSON 4
- power
- short circuit
- third prong
- grounded
- fuse
- circuit breaker

🔁 Summarize
△ Calculate

> **VOCAB FLASH CARDS** For extra help with vocabulary, visit **Vocab Flash Cards** and type in *Electricity*.

Electric Charge and Static Electricity

UNLOCK THE BIG

🔑 **How Do Charges Interact?**

🔑 **How Does Charge Build Up?**

my planet Diary

Force Fields

Misconception: Force fields exist only in science fiction stories.

Fact: Force fields are an important part of your everyday life.

You're actually sitting in a force field right now! A force field exists around any object that repels or attracts other objects. A giant gravitational force field surrounds Earth. This field keeps you from floating off into space. Earth's magnetic field makes compass needles point north. You make your own force field every time you get shocked when you reach for a doorknob!

MISCONCEPTIONS

Answer the questions below.

1. A gravitational field keeps you on Earth. What other uses might force fields have?

_____

_____

2. Describe how a different science fiction invention could be rooted in real science.

_____

_____

> PLANET DIARY Go to **Planet Diary** to learn more about force fields.

 Lab zone Do the Inquiry Warm-Up *Can You Move a Can Without Touching It?*

Vocabulary
- electric force • electric field • static electricity
- conservation of charge • friction • conduction
- induction • polarization • static discharge

Skills
- Reading: Relate Cause and Effect
- Inquiry: Draw Conclusions

How Do Charges Interact?

You're already late for school and one of your socks is missing! You finally find it sticking to the back of your blanket. How did that happen? The explanation has to do with electric charges.

Types of Charge Atoms contain charged particles called electrons and protons. If two electrons come close together, they push each other apart. In other words, they repel each other. Two protons behave the same way. If a proton and an electron come close together, they attract one another. Protons attract electrons because the two have opposite electric charges. The charge on a proton is positive (+). The charge on an electron is negative (−).

The two types of electric charges interact in specific ways, as you see in **Figure 1.** 🔑 **Charges that are the same repel each other. Charges that are different attract each other.** The interaction between electric charges is called electricity. The force between charged objects is called **electric force.**

FIGURE 1 ···
Repel or Attract?
✏️ △Draw Conclusions On each sphere, write if it has a positive (+) or a negative (−) charge. Compare your answers with a group. Can you tell for sure which spheres are positively charged and which are negatively charged? What conclusions can you draw?

_____

_____

_____

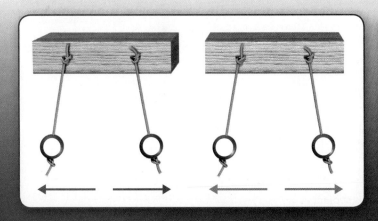

Electric Fields You may have heard of a gravitational field, which is the space around an object (such as a planet) where the object's gravitational force is exerted. Similarly, an electric field extends around a charged object. An **electric field** is a region around a charged object where the object's electric force is exerted on other charged objects. Electric fields and forces get weaker the farther away they are from the charge.

An electric field is invisible. You can use field lines to represent it, as shown in **Figure 2**. A field line shows the force that would be exerted on a positive charge at any point along that line. Positive charges are repelled by positive charges and attracted to negative charges, so field lines point away from positive charges and toward negative charges. Single charges have straight field lines, since a positive charge will be repelled away from or attracted to it in a straight line. When multiple charges are present, each charge exerts a force. These forces combine to make more complicated field lines.

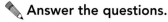

FIGURE 2 ·····················

Electric Fields

Field lines show the direction of the force acting on a positive charge.

✎ **Answer the questions.**

1. **Identify** Identify which charge is positive and which charge is negative.

2. **Interpret Diagrams** The boxes on the electric field are the same size. How many field lines are inside the white box?

_____

3. **Interpret Diagrams** The blue box is closer to the charges. How many field lines are in this box?

_____

4. **Draw Conclusions** What is the relationship between the number of field lines in an area and the strength of the electric force?

_____

_____

_____

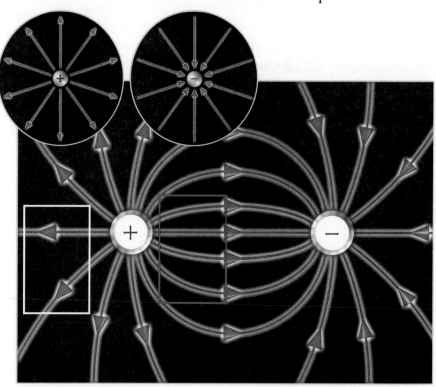

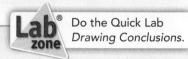

Do the Quick Lab
Drawing Conclusions.

How Does Charge Build Up?

Most objects have no overall charge. An atom usually has as many electrons as it has protons, so each positive charge is balanced by a negative charge. This leaves the atom uncharged, or neutral.

An uncharged object can become charged by gaining or losing electrons. If an object loses electrons, it is left with more protons than electrons. It has an overall positive charge. If an object gains electrons, it will have an overall negative charge. The buildup of charges on an object is called **static electricity.** In static electricity, charges build up on an object, but they do not flow continuously.

FIGURE 3 ····································
Charge Buildup
Rubbing two objects together can produce static electricity.

✎ **Interpret Photos** Circle the phrases that best complete the statements. Follow the directions to draw how the charges are arranged in each photo.

1 The balloon is (positively/ negatively/not) charged. The balloon (attracts/repels/neither attracts nor repels) the girl's hair.

2 Rubbing the balloon allows more electrons to move onto the balloon. The balloon is now (positively/negatively) charged. **Draw what the charges on the balloon look like now.**

3 The (positive/negative) charges in the girl's hair are now attracted to the negative charges on the balloon. **Draw how the charges on the balloon are arranged now.**

161

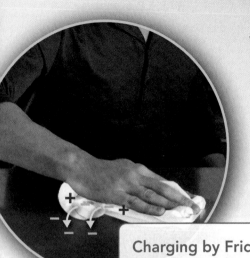

Charging Objects

Charges are neither created nor destroyed. This is a rule known as the law of **conservation of charge.** An object can't become charged by destroying or creating its own electrons. If one object loses electrons, another object must pick them up. 🔑 **There are four methods by which charges can redistribute themselves to build up static electricity: by friction, by conduction, by induction, and by polarization.**

Charging by Friction

When two uncharged objects are rubbed together, some electrons from one object can move onto the other object. The object that gains electrons becomes negatively charged. The object that loses electrons becomes positively charged. Charging by **friction** is the transfer of electrons from one uncharged object to another by rubbing the objects together.

Charging by Conduction

When a charged object touches another object, electrons can be transferred. Charging by **conduction** is the transfer of electrons from one object to another by direct contact. Electrons transfer from the object that has more negative charge to the object that has more positive charge. A positively charged object, like the metal ball, gains electrons when an uncharged person touches it. The girl starts out neutral, but electrons move from her hair, through her arm, to the ball. This leaves her hair positively charged, and the strands repel each other.

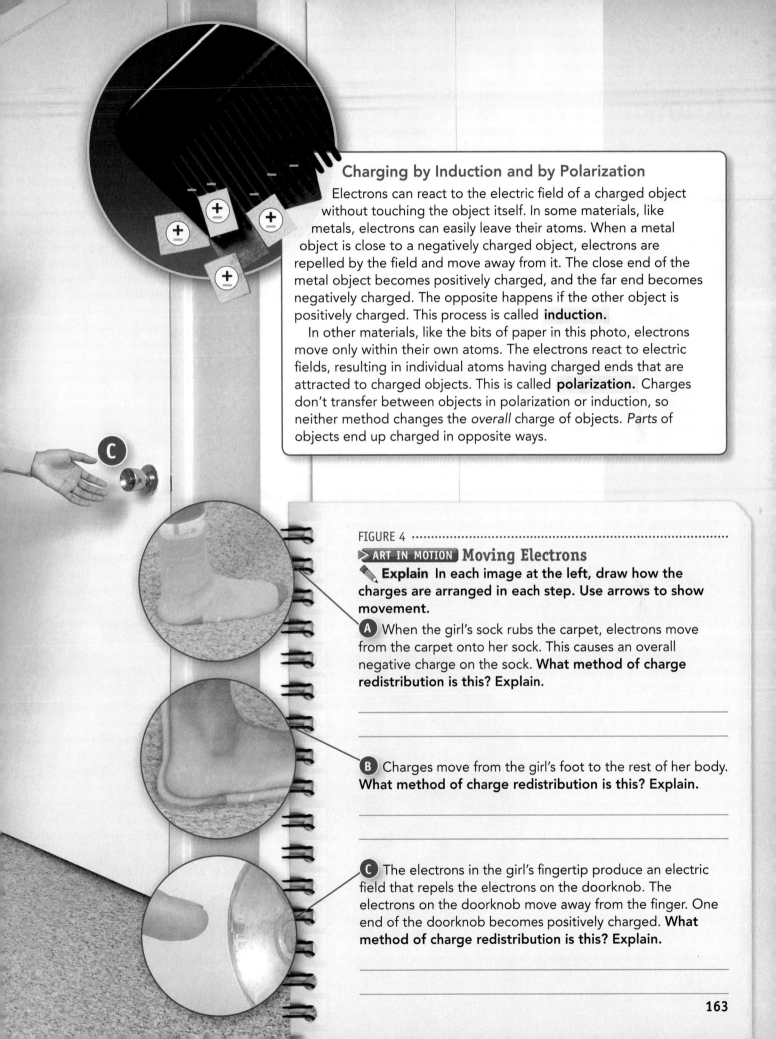

Charging by Induction and by Polarization

Electrons can react to the electric field of a charged object without touching the object itself. In some materials, like metals, electrons can easily leave their atoms. When a metal object is close to a negatively charged object, electrons are repelled by the field and move away from it. The close end of the metal object becomes positively charged, and the far end becomes negatively charged. The opposite happens if the other object is positively charged. This process is called **induction.**

In other materials, like the bits of paper in this photo, electrons move only within their own atoms. The electrons react to electric fields, resulting in individual atoms having charged ends that are attracted to charged objects. This is called **polarization.** Charges don't transfer between objects in polarization or induction, so neither method changes the *overall* charge of objects. *Parts* of objects end up charged in opposite ways.

FIGURE 4 ·······················

> ART IN MOTION **Moving Electrons**

✎ **Explain** In each image at the left, draw how the charges are arranged in each step. Use arrows to show movement.

A When the girl's sock rubs the carpet, electrons move from the carpet onto her sock. This causes an overall negative charge on the sock. **What method of charge redistribution is this? Explain.**

_____

_____

B Charges move from the girl's foot to the rest of her body. **What method of charge redistribution is this? Explain.**

_____

_____

C The electrons in the girl's fingertip produce an electric field that repels the electrons on the doorknob. The electrons on the doorknob move away from the finger. One end of the doorknob becomes positively charged. **What method of charge redistribution is this? Explain.**

_____

_____

163

Machines called Van de Graaff generators can create lightning bolts indoors!

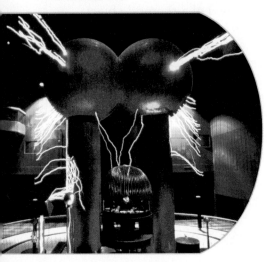

Static Discharge

If your hair becomes charged and sticks up after you remove a sweater, it doesn't stay that way forever. Positively charged objects gradually gain electrons from the air. Negatively charged objects gradually lose electrons to the air. The objects eventually become neutral again. The loss of static electricity as electric charges transfer from one object to another is called **static discharge.**

Static discharge often produces a spark. Moving electrons can heat the air around their path until it glows. The glowing air is the spark you see. The tiny spark you may have felt or seen when near a doorknob is an example of static discharge. Sparks from discharge happen more frequently during winter. This is because objects hold on to charge better in dry air. In humid weather, water collects on the surfaces of objects. The water picks up charge from the objects, so they don't stay charged as long as they would in dry weather.

apply it!

⚠ **Draw Conclusions** Anyone who works with computers has to be aware of static discharge. Even small discharges can damage electrical equipment.

❶ What activities should you avoid to prevent static discharge while working on a computer?

_____

_____

_____

_____

❷ What should the conditions of the room you are in be like?

_____

_____

_____

Lightning bolts are an example of static discharge. During thunderstorms, air swirls violently. Water droplets within the clouds become charged. Electrons move from areas of negative charge to areas of positive charge, producing an intense spark. That spark is lightning.

Some lightning reaches Earth. Negative charges at the bottoms of storm clouds create an electric field. This causes Earth's surface to become positively charged through induction. Electrons jump between the clouds and Earth's surface, producing a giant spark of lightning as they travel through the air.

⟳ Relate Cause and Effect
Pick one example of cause and effect in this section. Underline the cause, and then circle the effect that results.

FIGURE 5 ·································

Static Discharge
Lightning is just a much bigger version of the sparks you feel when you shock yourself on a doorknob.

✎ **Relate Text and Visuals** In the white circles, draw how positive and negative charges are arranged during a lightning strike.

Do the Quick Lab
Sparks Are Flying.

🔑 Assess Your Understanding

1a. Describe What happens to an object's atoms when the object becomes positively charged?

_____

_____

b. [CHALLENGE] Explain how you could use a piece of silk and a glass rod to attract a stream of tap water.

_____

_____

_____

_____

got it? ·································

○ **I get it!** Now I know that the four methods of building up static electricity are _____

_____

_____

○ **I need extra help with** _____

Go to my science 🔒 COACH *online for help with this subject.*

Electric Current

UNLOCK THE BIG

🔑 **How Is Electric Current Made?**

🔑 **How Do Conductors Differ From Insulators?**

🔑 **What Affects Current Flow?**

my plaNeT DiaRY

CAREERS

Be a Superconductor—of Science!

John Vander Sande wants your city to run more efficiently. A company he cofounded is working to replace old power lines with materials that let electric current flow more efficiently. These materials are called superconductors. Superconductors are often found in lab equipment, as shown at the left, but companies like Vander Sande's are finding other uses for them. Vander Sande didn't start his career working with power lines. He began his work in materials science as a professor at the Massachusetts Institute of Technology (MIT). He got into superconducting by chance after hearing about discoveries at a lecture by one of his colleagues. He encourages everyone to stay open to opportunities in science, because they can pop up anywhere at any time.

Answer the question below.

Describe an instance in your life when hearing something by chance led to a new opportunity.

_____

_____

_____

_____

_____

_____

▶ PLANET DIARY Go to **Planet Diary** to learn more about superconductors.

Lab zone Do the Inquiry Warm-Up *How Can Current Be Measured?*

How Is Electric Current Made?

Dozens of sushi dishes ride along a conveyor belt in **Figure 1.** The conveyer belt carries full dishes past customers and carries empty plates back to the kitchen. You might be wondering what a conveyer belt of rice, vegetables, and fish could possibly have to do with electricity. Like the sushi plates, electric charges can be made to move in a confined path.

Vocabulary
- electric current • electric circuit
- conductor • insulator
- voltage • resistance

Skills
- Reading: Ask Questions
- Inquiry: Classify

Flow of Electric Charges Lightning releases a large amount of electrical energy. However, the electric charge from lightning doesn't last long enough to power your radio or your TV. These devices need electric charges that flow continuously. They require electric current.

Recall that static electric charges do not flow continuously. **When electric charges are made to flow through a material, they produce an electric current. Electric current** is the continuous flow of electric charges through a material. The amount of charge that passes through a wire in a given period of time is the rate of electric current. The unit for the rate of current is the ampere, named for André Marie Ampère, an early investigator of electricity. The name of the unit is often shortened to amp or A. The number of amps describes the amount of charge flowing past a given point each second.

FIGURE 1 ·······
Electric Current
The conveyor belt represents a current. If it represented a greater current, more plates would pass by you in the same amount of time. One way for this to occur would be for the belt to go faster.

✎ **Make Models** Suppose the belt couldn't go faster. Draw a different way a greater current could be represented.

FIGURE 2 ·····························

Circuits

Just like charges in a wire, people can move around in circuits. One possible jogging circuit is outlined in this photo.

✎ **Interpret Photos** Trace another possible circuit. What could break this circuit?

_____

_____

_____

_____

Current in a Circuit The electric currents that power your computer and music player need very specific paths to work. In order to maintain an electric current, charges must be able to flow continuously in a loop. A complete, unbroken path that charges can flow through is called an **electric circuit.**

Someone jogging along the roads in **Figure 2** is moving like a charge in an electric circuit. If the road forms a complete loop, the jogger can move in a continuous path. However, the jogger cannot continue if any section of the road is closed. Similarly, if an electric circuit is complete, charges can flow continuously. If an electric circuit is broken, charges will not flow.

Electric circuits are all around you. All electrical devices, from toasters to televisions, contain electric circuits.

Lab ® Do the Quick Lab
zone *Producing Electric Current.*

🔑 Assess Your Understanding

1a. Review What is the unit of current?

_____

b. Predict What could break the circuit between your home and an electric power plant?

_____

got it?

○ I get it! Now I know that electric current is

made of _____

_____

○ I need extra help with _____

Go to **my science** 🅢 **coach** *online for help with this subject.*

How Do Conductors Differ From Insulators?

You can safely touch the rubber coating on an appliance cord. If you touched the wire inside, you'd get shocked. That's because charges can flow more easily through some materials than others.

A **conductor** is a material through which charge can flow easily. Electrons can move freely, allowing conductors to be charged by induction. Metals, such as copper, are good conductors. This is why current-carrying wires are usually made out of metal.

Wires are surrounded by insulators. **Insulators** are materials, such as rubber, that do not allow charges to flow. However, electrons can move around within their own atoms, allowing for polarization. They can also be stripped off when charging by friction.

The difference between conductors and insulators comes from how strongly electrons are attached to atoms. 🔑 **The atoms in conductors have loosely bound electrons that can move freely. Electrons in insulators cannot move freely among atoms.**

🔄 **Ask Questions** Current, conductors, and insulators all show up in your daily life. Write down a question about one of these topics that you would like answered.

_____

_____

_____

apply it!

All objects are made up of conductors or insulators, not just the ones you usually see in electronic devices.

❶ Identify The gloves that electricians wear when working on power lines should be made out of (insulating/conducting) materials.

❷ Classify Circle the conductors in these photos. Be careful—only parts of some items are conductors!

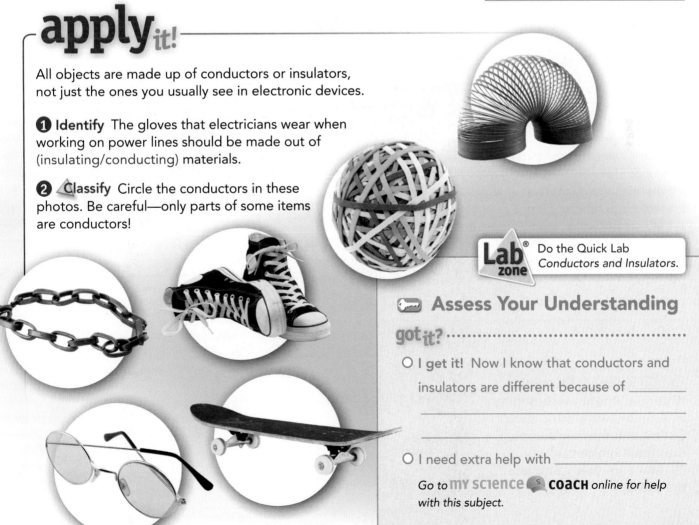

Lab zone Do the Quick Lab *Conductors and Insulators.*

🔑 **Assess Your Understanding**

got it? ......

○ **I get it!** Now I know that conductors and insulators are different because of _____

_____

○ **I need extra help with** _____

Go to my science ⓢ coach *online for help with this subject.*

169

What Affects Current Flow?

Suppose you are on a water slide at an amusement park. You climb the steps, sit down, and whoosh! The water current carries you down the slide. Electric charges flow in much the same way water moves down the slide.  **Current flow is affected by the energy of the charges and the properties of the objects that the charges flow through.**

Water Currents

A completely horizontal water slide wouldn't be much fun. A water slide that was only a few centimeters tall wouldn't be much better. Water slides are exciting because of gravitational potential energy. (Remember that gravitational potential energy is the energy an object has because of its height above the ground.) As the water falls down the slide, its potential energy is converted into kinetic energy. The water speeds up, since speed increases as kinetic energy increases. The higher the slide, the more potential energy the water starts with and the faster it will end up moving. At the bottom of the slide, the water has no potential energy. It has all been converted to kinetic energy. The water gains potential energy as it is pumped back to the top, starting the ride again.

✏️ **How could the current through a water slide be interrupted?**

_____

_____

Electric Currents

Electric currents flow through wires like water through pipes. Charges flow because of differences in electric potential energy. Potential energy from an energy source (like a battery) gets converted into different forms of energy. If a circuit contains a light bulb, its potential energy is converted into light and heat. The charges flow back to the energy source and the process restarts.

✏️ **Slides convert gravitational potential energy into kinetic energy. What do circuits convert electric potential energy into?**

_____

FIGURE 3 ·······································

▶ INTERACTIVE ART **Currents**
Water currents have many things in common with electric currents. The table at the right summarizes these similarities.

✏️ **Make Models** Complete the table.

	Water Current	Electric Current
Current is made up of moving	water	charges
Potential energy is converted into	_____	heat, light
The energy source for the circuit is a	_____	battery

Voltage

The *V* on a battery stands for volts, which is the unit of voltage. **Voltage** is the difference in electric potential energy *per charge* between two points in a circuit. (Electric potential energy per charge is also called electric potential.) This energy difference causes charges to flow. Because the voltage of a battery is related to energy per charge, it doesn't tell you how much total energy the battery supplies. A car battery and eight watch batteries both supply 12 volts, but eight watch batteries can't run a car. Each charge has the same amount of energy, but the car battery can provide that energy to many more charges. This results in a higher *total* energy. You can compare voltage to gravitational potential energy *per kilogram*. **Figure 4** shows the difference between total energy and energy per kilogram.

① Mass: 50 kg
Height: 20 m
Energy/kg: 200 J/kg
Total Energy:
_____
_____

FIGURE 4 ⋯⋯⋯⋯⋯⋯⋯⋯⋯⋯

Voltage

The total electric potential energy a charge has depends on voltage, just as the gravitational potential energy a person has depends on his or her height above the ground. Total gravitational potential energy is the energy per kilogram times the number of kilograms, and total electric potential energy is the energy per charge times the number of charges.

✎ **Interpret Diagrams Answer the questions.**

1. In the boxes, calculate the amount of gravitational potential energy each person has.

2. Which two people represent batteries with the same voltage?

_____

3. Draw boxes around the two people who represent batteries that supply the same total amount of energy.

4. Gravitational potential energy per kilogram decreases as you go down the slide. This is like decreasing (voltage/total potential energy).

② Mass: 100 kg
Height: 10 m
Energy/kg: 100 J/kg
Total Energy:
_____
_____

③ Mass: 50 kg
Height: 10 m
Energy/kg: 100 J/kg
Total Energy:
_____
_____

Pump

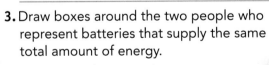
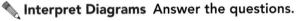

171

FIGURE 5 ·····················

Dimensions and Resistance

The length and diameter of a straw determine how difficult it is to drink through it. Similarly, the length and diameter of a wire determine how difficult it is for charge to flow through it.

✎ **Interpret Photos** Which of the straws in the photo would be the hardest to drink with? Explain. Is this straw like a wire with high or low resistance?

_____

_____

_____

_____

_____

Resistance The amount of current in a circuit depends on more than voltage. Current also depends on the resistance of the circuit. **Resistance** is the measure of how difficult it is for charges to flow through an object. The greater the resistance, the less current there is for a given voltage. The unit of measure of resistance is the ohm (Ω).

The four factors that determine the resistance of an object are diameter, length, material, and temperature. Objects with different characteristics have different resistances. If more than one path is available, more current will flow through the path that has the lower resistance.

Diameter

Milk flows more easily through a wide straw than it does through a narrow straw. Current flows more easily through a wide wire than through a narrow wire.

✎ **How does a wire's diameter affect its electrical resistance? Explain.**

_____

_____

_____

_____

Length

You may have noticed that it is easier to drink milk through a short straw than through a long straw. Similarly, short wires have less resistance than long wires.

✎ **How does an object's length affect its electrical resistance?**

_____

_____

_____

_____

FIGURE 6 ···
Materials and Resistance

When power lines fall down during storms, the workers repairing them must be careful to avoid electric shocks.

✎ **Solve Problems** What should workers wear while doing the job? What should they avoid wearing?

_____

_____

_____

_____

················· ✎ ·············
Word Origins *Resistance* comes from the word *resist*, which comes from the Latin word *resistere*. What do you think *resistere* means?

○ to be opposed to

○ to run

○ to speed up

Temperature

The electrical resistance of most materials increases as temperature increases. As the temperature of most materials decreases, resistance decreases as well.

✎ **Why would it be useful to keep power lines cool in the summer?**

_____

_____

_____

_____

Material

Some materials have electrons that are tightly held to their atoms. They have a high resistance because it is difficult for charges to move. Other materials have electrons that are loosely held to their atoms. They have a low resistance because charges can move through them easily.

✎ **Do conductors or insulators have a lower resistance? Explain.**

_____

_____

_____

_____

Lab zone ® Do the Quick Lab *Modeling Potential Difference.*

🔑 Assess Your Understanding

2a. List List the four factors that determine the resistance of an object.

_____

_____

b. CHALLENGE Battery A supplies 500 charges. Each charge has 2 J of energy. Battery B supplies 50 charges, each of which has 4 J of energy. Which battery supplies more total energy? Which has a higher voltage?

_____

_____

got it? ··

○ **I get it!** Now I know that current is affected by _____

○ **I need extra help with** _____

Go to **my science** ⓢ **coach** *online for help with this subject.*

Electric Circuits

🔑 **What Did Ohm Discover?**

🔑 **What Is a Circuit Made Of?**

my planet Diary

Lights Out

One winter night, a string of bright lights adorning a store window catches your eye. As you look, one bulb suddenly goes out, yet the others stay on! How can that be?

Normally, when a light bulb burns out, it breaks the flow of current through a circuit. But many holiday lights are on circuits that provide more than one possible path for the electric current to follow. This type of circuit provides a path for the current to flow even if one component goes bad. So if one light bulb burns out, the rest of the lights remain lit.

FUN FACTS

Communicate Discuss these questions with a partner and then answer them below.

1. What other devices have you used that can keep working even if one part stops working?

_____

_____

_____

2. When could it be useful to have a device turn off completely if one part breaks?

_____

_____

_____

▷ **PLANET DIARY** Go to **Planet Diary** to learn more about circuits.

Lab zone® Do the Inquiry Warm-Up
Do the Lights Keep Shining?

Vocabulary	Skills
• Ohm's law • series circuit • parallel circuit	⤳ Reading: Compare and Contrast △ Inquiry: Make Models

What Did Ohm Discover?

In the 1800s, Georg Ohm performed many experiments on electrical resistance. **Ohm found that the current, voltage, and resistance in a circuit are always related in the same way.**

Ohm's Observations Ohm set up a circuit with a voltage between two points on a conductor. He measured the resistance of the conductor and the current between those points. Then he changed the voltage and took new measurements.

Ohm found that if the factors that affect resistance are held constant, the resistance of most conductors does not depend on the voltage across them. Changing the voltage in a circuit changes the current but does not change the resistance. Ohm concluded that conductors and most other devices have a constant resistance regardless of the applied voltage.

FIGURE 1 ···

> VIRTUAL LAB **Circuit Relationships**

The work Ohm did on circuits in the 1800s still applies to almost all electric circuits today. The mathematical relationship he found between the components in a circuit holds true for circuits in everyday devices such as cell phones.

✎ **Interpret Data** Suppose you use various cell phone parts to perform experiments similar to Ohm's. You come up with the following data table. Use the data to predict the relationship that Ohm found.

Voltage (V)	Current (A)	Resistance (Ω)
6.0	2.0	3.0
6.0	1.5	4.0
6.0	1.0	6.0
4.2	2.0	2.1
4.2	0.7	6.0
4.2	1.4	3.0

_____

_____

_____

175

Ohm's Law Ohm created a law that describes how voltage, current, and resistance are related. **Ohm's law** says that resistance in a circuit is equal to voltage divided by current. This relationship can be represented by an equation.

$$\text{Resistance} = \frac{\text{Voltage}}{\text{Current}}$$

The units are ohms (Ω) = volts (V) ÷ amps (A). One ohm is equal to one volt per amp. You can rearrange Ohm's law to solve for voltage when you know current and resistance.

$$\text{Voltage} = \text{Current} \times \text{Resistance}$$

You can use the formula to see how changes in resistance, voltage, and current are related. For example, what happens to current if voltage is doubled without changing the resistance? For a constant resistance, if voltage is doubled, current doubles as well.

do the math!

1 Calculate A multimeter is a device that can measure the current in a circuit. Use the reading on the multimeter and the battery to find the voltage and current in this circuit. Calculate the resistance of the bulb.

_____

2 Calculate Batteries gradually lose voltage. A circuit contains 2 ohms of resistance and an old 9-volt battery. Four amps of current run through the circuit. What is the actual voltage?

_____

3 Predict Suppose you tripled the voltage in a circuit but kept the resistance constant. The current in the circuit would be (triple/the same as/a third of) the original current.

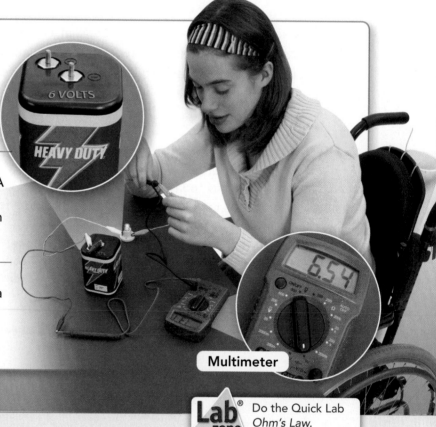

Multimeter

Lab zone® Do the Quick Lab
Ohm's Law.

🔑 **Assess Your Understanding**

got it? •

○ **I get it!** Now I know that Ohm's Law _____

_____

○ **I need extra help with** _____

Go to **MY SCIENCE** 🔵 ˢ **COACH** online for help with this subject.

What Is a Circuit Made Of?

Objects that use electricity contain circuits. 🔑 **All electric circuits have these basic features: devices that run on electrical energy, sources of electrical energy, and conducting wires.**

- Batteries and power plants are examples of energy sources. They supply the voltage that causes current to flow. When the energy source is a battery, current flows from the positive end to the negative end.
- Energy is always conserved in a circuit. Electrical energy doesn't get used up. It gets transformed into other forms of energy, such as heat, light, mechanical, and sound energy. Appliances such as toasters transform electrical energy. These devices resist current, so they are represented in a circuit as resistors.
- Electric circuits are connected by conducting wires. The conducting wires complete the path of the current. They allow charges to flow from the energy source to the device that runs on electric current and back to the energy source.
- A switch is often included to control the current. Opening a switch breaks the circuit, which shuts off the device.

All the parts of a circuit are shown in **Figure 2.** Each part in the photograph is represented in the diagram by a simple symbol.

FIGURE 2 ·····························

Circuit Diagrams

A symbol in a circuit diagram represents a part of the circuit.

✏️ **Make Models** Draw the circuit diagram for a circuit with two resistors, two batteries, and a switch.

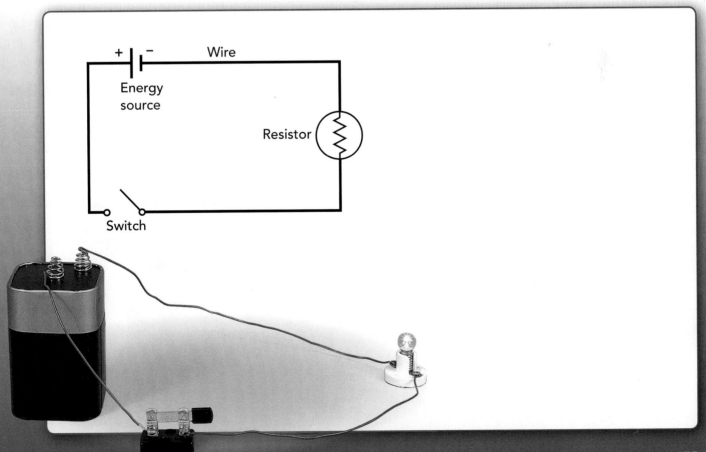

Compare and Contrast On these two pages, underline differences between series and parallel circuits. Below, list their similarities.

_____

_____

_____

_____

_____

Series Circuits

If all the parts of an electric circuit are connected one after another along one path, the circuit is called a **series circuit.** A series circuit has only one path for the current to take.

A series circuit is very simple to design and build, but it has some disadvantages. What happens if a light bulb in a series circuit burns out? A burned-out bulb is a break in the circuit, and there is no other path for the current to take. So if one light goes out, the other lights go out as well.

Another disadvantage of a series circuit is that the light bulbs in the circuit become dimmer as more bulbs are added. Think about what happens to the overall resistance of a series circuit as you add more bulbs. The resistance increases. Remember that for a constant voltage, if resistance increases, current decreases. If you add light bulbs to a series circuit without changing the voltage, the current decreases. The bulbs burn less brightly.

FIGURE 3

Series Circuits

The number of bulbs in a series circuit affects each bulb's brightness. Remember that voltage = current × resistance.

Answer the questions below.

1. **Make Models** Draw the circuit diagram for the circuit in the photo.

2. **Relate Cause and Effect** If the voltage of the battery were doubled, what would happen to the current through each of the bulbs? How would this affect the brightness of the bulbs?

_____

_____

_____

_____

3. **Predict** If the voltage of the battery were doubled **and** three more bulbs were added, what would happen to the current and the brightness of the bulbs?

_____

_____

_____

_____

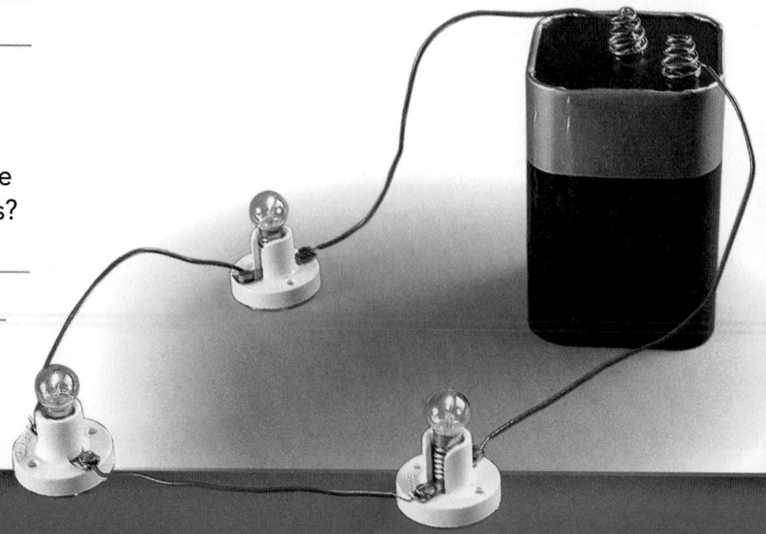

Parallel Circuits In a **parallel circuit,** different parts of the circuit are on separate branches. There are several paths for current to take. Each bulb is connected by a separate path from the battery and back to the battery.

What happens if a light burns out in a parallel circuit? If there is a break in one branch, charges can still move through the other branches. So if one bulb goes out, the others remain lit. Switches can be added to each branch to turn lights on and off without affecting the other branches.

What happens to the resistance of a parallel circuit when you add a branch? The overall resistance actually *decreases*. As new branches are added to a parallel circuit, the electric current has more paths to follow, so the overall resistance decreases. Remember that for a given voltage, if resistance decreases, current increases. The additional current travels along each new branch without affecting the original branches. So as you add branches to a parallel circuit, the brightness of the light bulbs does not change.

FIGURE 4 ·······················
Parallel Circuits
A floor lamp with multiple bulbs can be represented with the same circuit diagram as the circuit at the left. You can turn each bulb on and off individually.

✎ **Make Models On the circuit diagram, draw where the switches must be for a lamp like this. If the lamp is lit as it is in the photo below, trace the path(s) in the circuit through which current flows.**

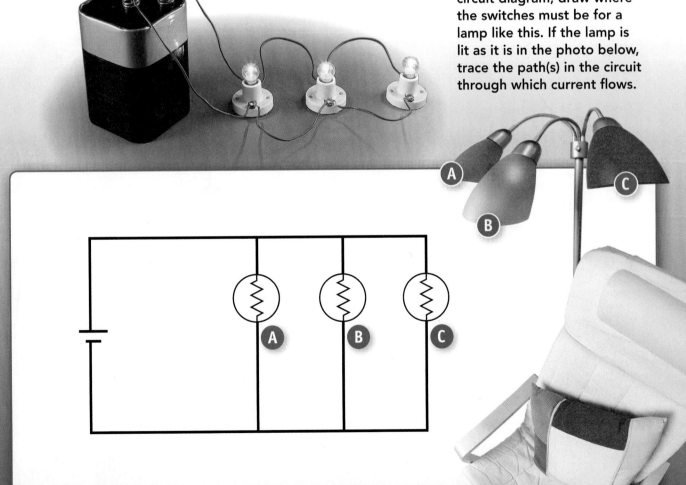

179

How is my house WIRED?

How does an electric circuit work?

FIGURE 5 ....

▶ INTERACTIVE ART Your home is full of electrical devices. When you turn one device on or off, it does not affect other appliances. This means that your home contains a (series/parallel) circuit. Since the devices in your home are part of complete circuits, each device must have a wire running into it and one running out of it.

✎ Mark each circuit element with its symbol (resistor, switch, or energy source). Draw in the appropriate connecting wires. Then answer the questions on the notepaper on the next page.

Key

☰	Wires
⊸∘	Switch
⌇	Resistor
⊣⊢	Energy source

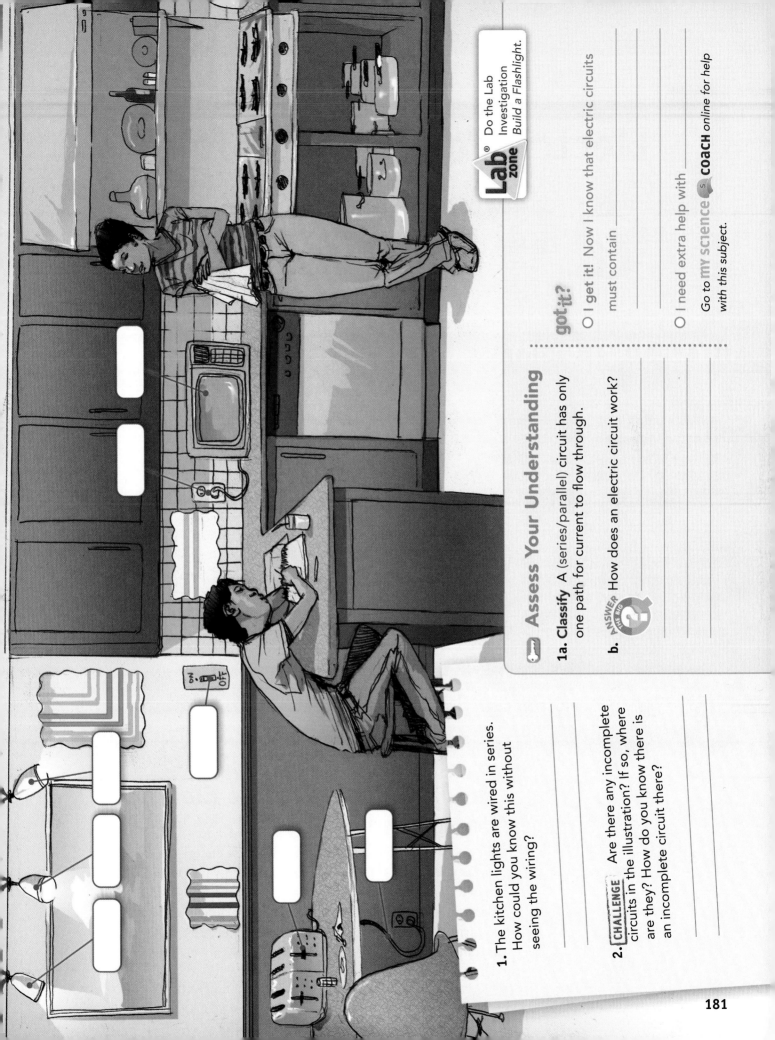

1. The kitchen lights are wired in series. How could you know this without seeing the wiring?

2. **CHALLENGE** Are there any incomplete circuits in the illustration? If so, where are they? How do you know there is an incomplete circuit there?

Assess Your Understanding

1a. Classify A (series/parallel) circuit has only one path for current to flow through.

b. *ANSWER THE BIG* How does an electric circuit work?

got it?

○ I get it! Now I know that electric circuits must contain _____

○ I need extra help with _____

Go to **MY SCIENCE COACH** online for help with this subject.

Lab zone® Do the Lab Investigation *Build a Flashlight.*

181

Electric Power and Safety

🔑 **How Do You Calculate Electric Power and Energy?**

🔑 **How Can Electric Shocks Be Prevented?**

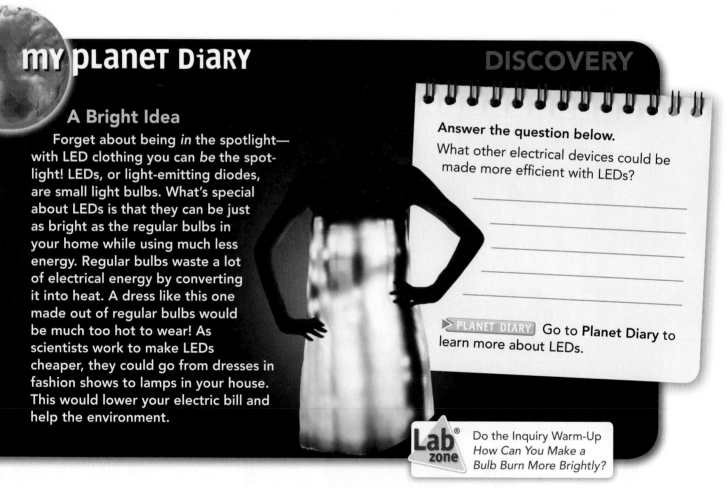

my planet Diary

DISCOVERY

A Bright Idea

Forget about being *in* the spotlight—with LED clothing you can *be* the spotlight! LEDs, or light-emitting diodes, are small light bulbs. What's special about LEDs is that they can be just as bright as the regular bulbs in your home while using much less energy. Regular bulbs waste a lot of electrical energy by converting it into heat. A dress like this one made out of regular bulbs would be much too hot to wear! As scientists work to make LEDs cheaper, they could go from dresses in fashion shows to lamps in your house. This would lower your electric bill and help the environment.

Answer the question below.

What other electrical devices could be made more efficient with LEDs?

_____

_____

_____

_____

_____

▶ PLANET DIARY Go to **Planet Diary** to learn more about LEDs.

Lab ® Do the Inquiry Warm-Up
zone *How Can You Make a Bulb Burn More Brightly?*

How Do You Calculate Electric Power and Energy?

All electrical appliances transform electrical energy into other forms. Hair dryers transform electrical energy into thermal energy to dry your hair. An amplifier that a guitar player uses transforms electrical energy into sound. A washing machine transforms electrical energy into mechanical energy. The rate at which energy is transformed from one form to another is known as **power**. The unit of power is the watt (W).

Vocabulary
- power • short circuit
- third prong • grounded
- fuse • circuit breaker

Skills
- Reading: Summarize
- Inquiry: Calculate

Power Ratings You are already familiar with different amounts of electric power. The power rating of a bright light bulb, for example, might be 100 W. The power rating of a dimmer bulb might be 60 W. The brighter bulb transforms (or uses) electrical energy at a faster rate than the dimmer bulb.

Calculating Power The power of a light bulb or appliance depends on two factors: voltage and current.
🔑 **Power is calculated by multiplying voltage by current.**

$$\text{Power} = \text{Voltage} \times \text{Current}$$

The units are watts (W) = volts (V) × amperes (A). The equation can also be rearranged to let you solve for current if you know power and voltage.

$$\text{Current} = \frac{\text{Power}}{\text{Voltage}}$$

Summarize Summarize what you have learned from these two pages.

_____

_____

_____

_____

_____

_____

_____

_____

do the math! ─ TECH & DESIGN ─

Many appliances around your home are labeled with their power ratings. In the United States, standard wall outlets supply 120 volts.

⚠ **Calculate** Determine the current running through each of these appliances. (The toaster has been done for you.)

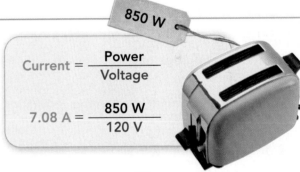

850 W

$$\text{Current} = \frac{\text{Power}}{\text{Voltage}}$$

$$7.08\ A = \frac{850\ W}{120\ V}$$

4000 W

_____ = _____

85 W

_____ = _____

300 W

_____ = _____

Paying for Electrical Energy

The electric bill that comes to your home charges for the month's energy use, not power. Power tells you how much energy an appliance uses in a certain amount of time. **The total amount of energy used is equal to the power of the appliance multiplied by the amount of time the appliance is used.**

$$\text{Energy} = \text{Power} \times \text{Time}$$

Electric power is usually measured in thousands of watts, or kilowatts (kW). To go from watts to kilowatts, you divide by 1,000. Time is measured in hours. A common unit of electrical energy is the kilowatt-hour (kWh).

$$\text{Kilowatt-hours} = \text{Kilowatts} \times \text{Hours}$$

A refrigerator averages a power of 0.075 kW (75 W). Knowing that, you can calculate how much energy it will use in one month (about 720 hours).

$$\text{Energy} = 0.075 \text{ kW} \times 720 \text{ hours}$$

$$\text{Energy} = 54 \text{ kWh}$$

FIGURE 1 ·······························

> REAL-WORLD INQUIRY

Electrical Energy

There are devices that let you measure the energy usage of electronic devices.

✎ **Apply Concepts** Pick an appliance from the previous page. Use the notebook to answer the questions.

1. What would the monitor display if the appliance you picked was plugged in for three hours?

2. [CHALLENGE] Calculate the power rating for the appliance that is plugged into the meter at the left. Assume that it has been running for three hours.

Lab® zone — Do the Quick Lab *Calculating Electric Power and Energy Use.*

⚷ Assess Your Understanding

1a. Review The power of an appliance can be found by multiplying _____ by _____

b. Calculate How much energy does an 850 W toaster consume if it is used for 1.5 hours over the course of a month?

_____

_____

got it?

○ **I get it!** Now I know that electric power and energy depend on _____

_____

○ **I need extra help with** _____

Go to MY SCIENCE ⓢ COACH online for help with this subject.

How Can Electric Shocks Be Prevented?

A **short circuit** is a connection that allows current to take the path of least resistance. Touching a frayed wired causes a short circuit, since current can flow through the person rather than through the wire. Since the new path has less resistance, the current can be very high. Many bodily functions, such as heartbeat, breathing, and muscle movement, are controlled by electrical signals. Because of this, electric shocks can be fatal.

 **Shocks can be prevented with devices that redirect current or break circuits.** Ground wires connect the circuits in a building directly to Earth, giving charges an alternate path in the event of a short circuit. The **third prong** you may have seen on electrical plugs connects the metal parts of appliances to the building's ground wire. Any circuit connected to Earth in this way is **grounded.**

The circuits in your home also contain devices that prevent circuits from overheating, since overheated circuits can result in fires. **Fuses** are devices that melt if they get too hot. This breaks the circuit. **Circuit breakers** are switches that will bend away from circuits as they heat up. Unlike fuses, which break when they are triggered, circuit breakers can be reset.

FIGURE 2 ···

Fuses

Fuses are often found in appliances such as coffee makers. A fuse will melt and break, cutting off the circuit, before the appliance can get so hot that it catches fire.

✎ **Infer** What other electronic devices may contain fuses? Explain your reasoning.

_____

_____

_____

Lab zone® Do the Quick Lab *Electric Shock and Short Circuit Safety.*

 Assess Your Understanding

got it? ··

○ **I get it!** Now I know that electric safety devices _____

_____

_____

○ **I need extra help with** _____

Go to **my science** ● **coach** *online for help with this subject.*

185

The basic features of an electric circuit are _____

_____

_____

LESSON 1 Electric Charge and Static Electricity

🔑 Charges that are the same repel each other. Charges that are different attract each other.

🔑 There are four methods by which charges can redistribute themselves to build up static electricity: by friction, by conduction, by induction, and by polarization.

Vocabulary
- electric force   • electric field
- static electricity   • conservation of charge
- friction   • conduction
- induction   • polarization   • static discharge

LESSON 2 Electric Current

🔑 When electric charges are made to flow through a material, they produce an electric current.

🔑 The atoms in conductors have loosely bound electrons that can move freely. Electrons in insulators cannot move freely among atoms.

🔑 Current flow is affected by the energy of the charges and the properties of the objects that the charges flow through.

Vocabulary
- electric current   • electric circuit
- conductor   • insulator   • voltage   • resistance

LESSON 3 Electric Circuits

🔑 Ohm found that the current, voltage, and resistance in a circuit are always related in the same way.

🔑 All electric circuits have the same basic features: devices that are run by electrical energy, sources of electrical energy, and conducting wires.

Vocabulary
- Ohm's law   • series circuit   • parallel circuit

LESSON 4 Electric Power and Safety

🔑 Power is calculated by multiplying voltage by current.

🔑 The total amount of energy used is equal to the power of the appliance multiplied by the amount of time the appliance is used.

🔑 Shocks can be prevented with devices that redirect current or break circuits.

Vocabulary
- power   • short circuit   • third prong
- grounded   • fuse   • circuit breaker

Review and Assessment

LESSON 1 Electric Charge and Static Electricity

1. What type of charge transfer occurs when two objects are rubbed together?

  a. friction   **b.** induction

  c. conduction   **d.** polarization

2. The transfer of electrons from a cloud to the ground during a lightning strike is an example of _____

3. Apply Concepts Draw the electric field for a single positive charge. Be sure to show which way the field lines point.

4. Relate Cause and Effect Explain what happens to the electrons in a metal object when it is held near a negatively charged object. What happens to the overall charge of the metal object?

_____

_____

_____

_____

_____

_____

5. Write About It A park needs a sign to tell visitors what to do during a thunderstorm. Write a paragraph that explains why standing under a tall tree during a thunderstorm is dangerous.

LESSON 2 Electric Current

6. Which of these objects is an insulator?

  a. gold ring   **b.** copper coin

  c. glass rod   **d.** steel fork

7. An electric current is _____

_____

8. Classify The appliances in your home can be made of several different materials. What kinds of materials are the wires made of? What kinds of materials surround the wire for safety?

_____

9. Infer Copper wires carry electric current from power plants to users. How is the resistance of these power lines likely to vary during the year in an area that has very hot summers? Explain.

_____

_____

_____

10. Make Models Water will not flow down a flat slide because there is no potential energy difference between the two ends. How could this situation be represented in an electric circuit? Explain your reasoning.

_____

_____

_____

LESSON 3 Electric Circuits

11. Lisa built an electric circuit. When she added a second light bulb, the first bulb became dimmer. What type of circuit did Lisa build?

   a. series   **b.** parallel

   c. open   **d.** short

12. According to Ohm's law, the resistance in a circuit can be determined by _____

_____

Use the diagram below to answer Questions 13 and 14.

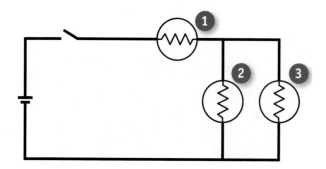

13. Predict Will any of the bulbs light if you open the switch? Explain.

_____

_____

14. Control Variables Which bulbs would continue to shine if Bulb 1 broke? Which would shine if Bulb 2 broke instead? Explain.

_____

_____

_____

_____

15. math! Most homes contain 120-V outlets. Suppose you have lamps with resistances of 120 Ω, 144 Ω, and 240 Ω. Predict which one will draw the most current. Check your prediction by calculating the current that runs through each lamp.

LESSON 4 Electric Power and Safety

16. What unit is used to measure electric power?

   a. ampere (A)   **b.** volt (V)

   c. watt (W)   **d.** ohm (Ω)

17. An appliance's total electrical energy consumption is calculated by _____

_____

18. Infer If you touch an electric wire and get a shock, what can you infer about the resistance of your body compared to the resistance of the circuit?

_____

_____

19. Calculate A device draws 40 A of current and has a 12-V battery. What is its power?

_____

APPLY THE BIG **?** How does an electric circuit work?

....

20. Identify the parts that make up the circuit in a laptop computer. Describe what happens inside the circuit when the computer is on.

_____

_____

_____

_____

_____

_____

_____

_____

_____

_____

_____

Standardized Test Prep

Multiple Choice

Circle the letter of the best answer.

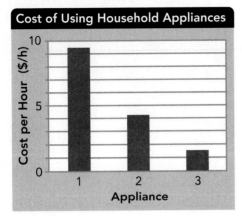

Cost of Using Household Appliances

Cost per Hour ($/h) vs. Appliance

1. Which of the following is a valid interpretation of the graph?

    A   The voltage is highest in Appliance 1.

    B   Appliance 1 uses the most power.

    C   During one month, a family pays more to run Appliance 1 than Appliance 2.

    D   Appliance 1 draws the least current.

2. Your alarm clock has a voltage of 120 V and a resistance of 1200 Ω. What current does the alarm clock draw?

    A   0.10 A

    B   10.0 A

    C   12.0 A

    D   100 A

3. You want to build a device that can conduct current but will be safe if touched by a person. Which of the following pairs of materials could you use?

    A   glass to conduct and rubber to insulate

    B   copper to conduct and silver to insulate

    C   sand to conduct and plastic to insulate

    D   silver to conduct and plastic to insulate

4. How does a fuse prevent electrical fires?

    A   by providing a path for excess charges to get to the ground

    B   by melting if the current gets too high

    C   by reducing the voltage supplied to electrical devices

    D   by storing potential energy for later use

5. What happens when an object is rubbed against another object to charge by friction?

    A   Electrons are transferred from one object to another.

    B   Electrons in one of the objects disappear.

    C   Electrons in one object suddenly become negatively charged.

    D   Electrons are created by the friction between the objects.

Constructed Response

Use your knowledge of science to help you answer Question 6. Write your answer on a separate sheet of paper.

6. A lightning bolt can have a voltage of over 100 million volts. Explain why lightning cannot power your cell phone but a 6-volt battery can. Then explain what would happen if a 100-million-volt battery was plugged into a cell phone. Use Ohm's law in your answer.

SOMETHING for NOTHING

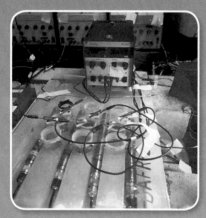

This complicated device can supposedly harness free energy.

The race is on to find a new, cheap energy source. Any online search for "free energy" will find a lot of Web sites. These sites promise clean, free electricity if you buy or invest in their devices.

But can they back up their promises? Many sites suggest that the power companies have conspired against the people who have discovered and invented these free-energy devices. One site even claims that there is a fourth law of motion. This fourth law is an extension of Newton's Third Law of Motion. If every action has an equal and opposite reaction, the site claims, then that reaction can power the original action.

Debate It Some free-energy devices claim to be able to generate electricity using a perpetual motion machine. Some claim to harness latent heat from the air. Some claim to use magnets. Research how energy is generated, and evaluate these claims. Debate as a class whether it is possible to have truly free energy.

Does free electricity really exist? Some people say yes.

In 1913, Nikola Tesla patented a turbine that ran off of steam. Many people have tried to find a way to use Tesla's engine to generate free electricty.

Going GREEN

Every time you turn on a light, you are using energy. We know this, but we don't always think about where the energy comes from. In most cases, that energy has come from fossil fuels, extracted from the ground, refined, and burned for their energy, in a process that causes a lot of pollution. Some scientists and government policymakers are exploring green (environmentally friendly) sources of energy.

According to the U.S. Environmental Protection Agency (EPA), green energy comes from technologies that don't produce waste products that will harm the environment. This includes resources like solar power and wind power, as well as geothermal energy from hot springs under the Earth's crust.

Reduced air pollution is just one of many benefits of green energy. Green energy also lowers greenhouse gas emissions and can cost less for consumers—like your family! Going green also creates jobs. Having many different sources makes the energy grid more stable. If one source stops working, we will still be able to get energy from other sources. What's not to love? Unfortunately, green energy technologies are expensive to develop.

▲ The flow of water is a renewable resource. But hydroelectric dams can damage habitats by changing the course of rivers.

Debate It Research the benefits and costs of developing green energy technologies. Organize a classroom debate about the costs and benefits of green energy. Be prepared to argue both sides of the issue.

HOW CAN THIS TRAIN MOVE WITHOUT TOUCHING THE TRACK?

How are electricity and magnetism related?

This type of train is called a maglev, or magnetic levitation train, and operates at speeds of 430 km/h (about twice as fast as a conventional train). It does not have a traditional engine, which means it does not give off any pollutants. Instead, the maglev train uses electricity in the track to power magnets that propel the train forward and levitation magnets to keep the train floating about 10 mm above the track.

Draw Conclusions How can this train move without touching the track?

_____

_____

_____

_____

> UNTAMED SCIENCE Watch the **Untamed Science** video to learn more about magnetism and electromagnetism.

Magnetism and Electromagnetism

Getting Started

Check Your Understanding

1. **Background** Read the paragraph below and then answer the question.

While Chung works, his computer shuts down. Both the street and his house are dark, so he knows there is no electricity. A fallen tree has snapped an electric wire. The wire was the conductor that brought him power. Chung reaches for the light switch, but then remembers that no electric current will flow when he turns it on.

> **Electricity** is a form of energy sometimes created by the movement of charged particles.
>
> A material through which charges can easily flow is a **conductor.**
>
> **Electric current** is the continuous flow of electric charges through a material.

- How can electricity be restored to Chung's house?

_____

_____

> **MY READING WEB** If you had trouble completing the question above, visit **My Reading Web** and type in *Magnetism and Electromagnetism.*

Vocabulary Skill

Use Context to Determine Meaning Science books often use unfamiliar words. Look for context clues in surrounding words and phrases to figure out the meaning of a new word. In the paragraph below, look for clues to the meaning of *magnetic force.*

The attraction or repulsion between magnetic poles is **magnetic force.** A force is a push or pull that can cause an object to change its motion. A magnetic force is produced when magnetic poles interact.

Example	Magnetic force
Definition	*n.* attraction or repulsion between magnetic poles
Explanation	Force is a push or pull.
Other Information	Magnetic force is produced when magnetic poles interact.

2. **Quick Check** In the paragraph above, circle the explanation of the word *force.*

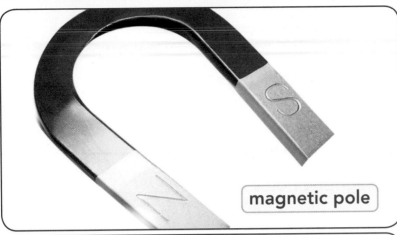

magnetic pole

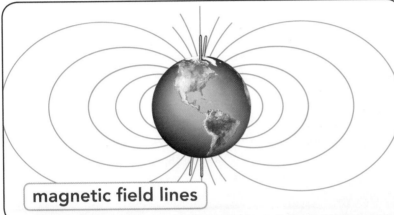

magnetic field lines

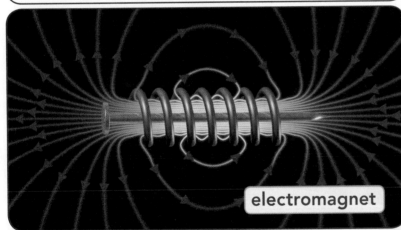

electromagnet

generator

Chapter Preview

LESSON 1
- magnet
- magnetism
- magnetic pole
- magnetic force
- ↻ Summarize
- △ Infer

LESSON 2
- magnetic field
- magnetic field lines
- compass
- magnetic declination
- ↻ Identify the Main Idea
- △ Observe

LESSON 3
- electromagnetism
- solenoid
- electromagnet
- ↻ Relate Cause and Effect
- △ Predict

LESSON 4
- galvanometer
- electric motor
- ↻ Sequence
- △ Graph

LESSON 5
- electromagnetic induction
- direct current
- alternating current
- generator
- transformer
- ↻ Ask Questions
- △ Make Models

> **VOCAB FLASH CARDS** For extra help with vocabulary, visit **Vocab Flash Cards** and type in *Magnetism and Electromagnetism.*

What Is Magnetism?

UNLOCK
THE BIG
?

🔑 **What Are the Properties of Magnets?**

🔑 **How Do Magnetic Poles Interact?**

MY PLANET DIARY

FUN FACTS

Crocodile Sense

Crocodiles are threatened animals. So, if they are not protected, they may become endangered and then disappear altogether. However, in Florida, many crocodiles live where people do, so they threaten people's safety.

To keep both people and crocodiles safe, biologists tried to move crocodiles away from people. But there was a problem. Crocodiles use Earth's magnetic field to help them navigate. Whenever they relocated a crocodile, it eventually returned, if it was not killed on the way back. But then the biologists heard that scientists in Mexico had taped a magnet to each side of a crocodile's head before relocating it. They thought that the magnets would inter-fere with the crocodile's ability to use Earth's magnetic field to find its way back. Biologists here did the same thing. So far, it has been successful.

Communicate Discuss the following questions with a partner. Write your answers below.

Why do you think it is important to relocate crocodiles?

_____

_____

_____

_____

_____

_____

▶ PLANET DIARY Go to **Planet Diary** to learn more about magnetism.

Lab® zone
Do the Inquiry Warm-Up *Natural Magnets.*

What Are the Properties of Magnets?

Imagine that you're in Shanghai, China, zooming along in a maglev train propelled by magnets. Your 30-kilometer trip from the airport to the city station takes less than eight minutes. The same trip in a taxi would take about an hour.

Vocabulary
- magnet
- magnetism
- magnetic pole
- magnetic force

Skills
- Reading: Summarize
- Inquiry: Infer

Magnets When you think of magnets, you might think about the objects that hold notes to your refrigerator. But magnets can be large, like the one in Figure 1. They can be small like those on your refrigerator, in your wallet, on your kitchen cabinets, or on security tags at a store. A **magnet** is any material that attracts iron and materials that contain iron.

Discovering Magnets Magnets have many modern uses, but they are not new. The ancient Greeks discovered that a rock called magnetite attracted materials containing iron. The rocks also attracted or repelled other magnetic rocks. The attraction or repulsion of magnetic materials is called **magnetism.**

Magnets have the same properties as magnetite rocks. 🔑 Magnets attract iron and materials that contain iron. Magnets attract or repel other magnets. In addition, one end of a magnet will always point north when allowed to swing freely.

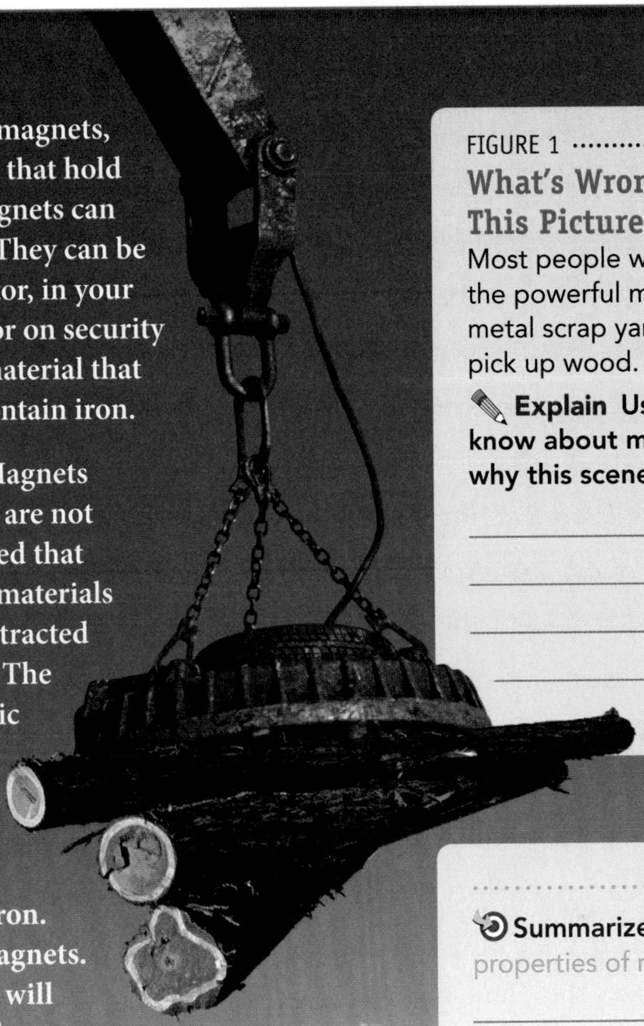

FIGURE 1 ·······················

What's Wrong With This Picture?
Most people would not expect the powerful magnet used at a metal scrap yard to be able to pick up wood.

✏️ **Explain** Use what you know about magnets to explain why this scene is impossible.

_____

_____

_____

_____

_____

·················· ✏️ ··········

🔄 **Summarize** Summarize the properties of magnetite.

_____

_____

_____

_____

Lab zone ® Do the Lab Investigation *Detecting Fake Coins.*

🔑 Assess Your Understanding

got it? ···

○ I get it! Now I know that three properties of magnets are that magnets _____

_____

_____

○ I need extra help with _____

Go to MY SCIENCE ⓢ COACH online for help with this subject.

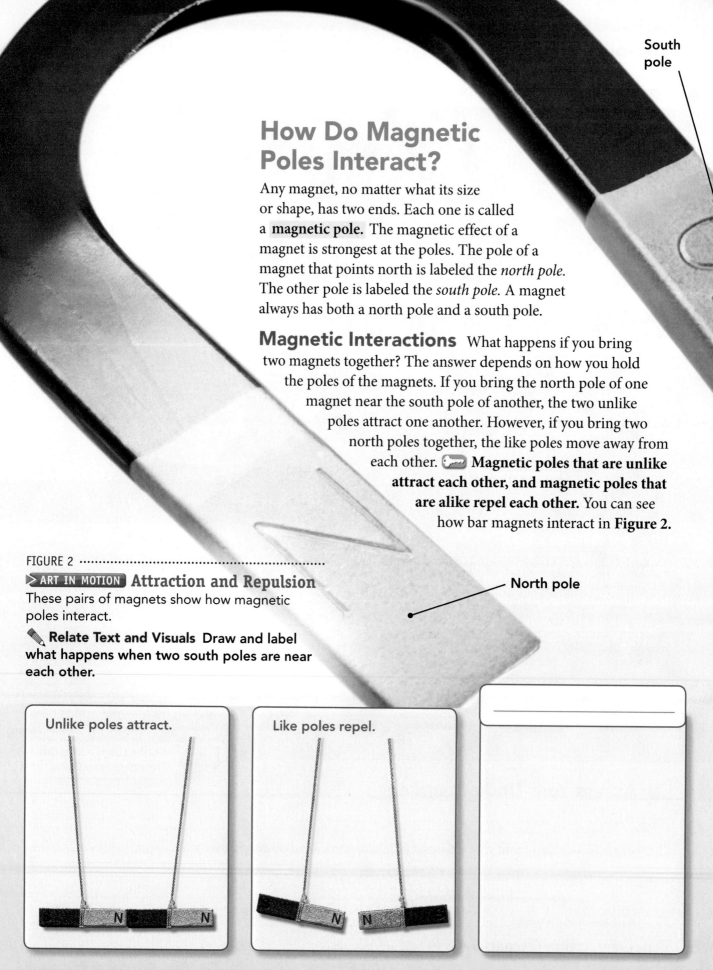

South pole

How Do Magnetic Poles Interact?

Any magnet, no matter what its size or shape, has two ends. Each one is called a **magnetic pole.** The magnetic effect of a magnet is strongest at the poles. The pole of a magnet that points north is labeled the *north pole.* The other pole is labeled the *south pole.* A magnet always has both a north pole and a south pole.

Magnetic Interactions What happens if you bring two magnets together? The answer depends on how you hold the poles of the magnets. If you bring the north pole of one magnet near the south pole of another, the two unlike poles attract one another. However, if you bring two north poles together, the like poles move away from each other. 🔑 **Magnetic poles that are unlike attract each other, and magnetic poles that are alike repel each other.** You can see how bar magnets interact in **Figure 2.**

FIGURE 2 ·······································

▶ ART IN MOTION **Attraction and Repulsion**
These pairs of magnets show how magnetic poles interact.

✏ **Relate Text and Visuals** Draw and label what happens when two south poles are near each other.

North pole

Unlike poles attract.

N N N

Like poles repel.

N N

Magnetic Force The attraction or repulsion between magnetic poles is **magnetic force.** A force is a push or a pull that can cause an object to move. A magnetic force is produced when magnetic poles come near each other and interact. Any material that exerts a magnetic force is a magnet.

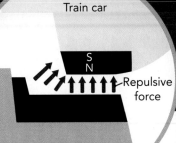

Train car

Repulsive force

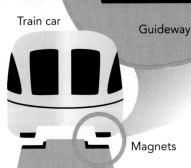

Train car

Guideway

apply it!

The maglev train you read about earlier depends on magnetic force to float above the guideway, or track. The magnetic force is produced by magnets in the bottom of the train and in the guideway.

Magnets

Guideway

1 **Infer** For the train to float, which pole of the guideway's magnet should face the north pole of the train car's magnet?

_____

2 **CHALLENGE** List some advantages of the fact that the train does not touch the guideway.

_____

_____

Lab zone Do the Quick Lab *Magnetic Poles.*

🔑 Assess Your Understanding

1a. Identify What areas of a magnet have the strongest magnetic effect?

_____

_____

_____

b. Relate Cause and Effect How can two magnets demonstrate magnetic force?

_____

_____

_____

got it? ∙∙∙

○ **I get it!** Now I know that magnetic poles that are unlike _____

and magnetic poles that are alike _____

○ **I need extra help with** _____

Go to MY SCIENCE 🔵 COACH *online for help with this subject.*

2 Magnetic Fields

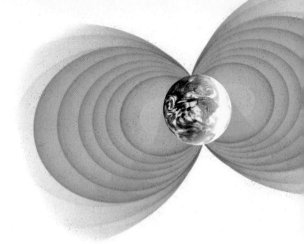

🔑 **What Is a Magnetic Field's Shape?**

🔑 **What Is Earth's Magnetic Field Like?**

UNLOCK
THE BIG
❓

my planet DiaRY

Cow Magnets

You probably know that cows eat grass. Did you know that they also eat metal? When cows graze, they may ingest metal objects that contain iron such as nails, wires, and old cans. If the metal is sharp, it could pierce the cow's stomach, causing infection, illness, or even death.

To ensure that their cows are safe, farmers have their cows swallow a magnet. Once inside the cow's stomach, the magnet attracts the iron in the metal that the cow eats. This keeps the metal from moving around and possibly puncturing other organs. One magnet can protect a cow for life.

FUN FACTS

Read the following questions. Write your answers below.

1. Why is it dangerous for a cow to eat metal?

_____

_____

_____

_____

2. As a farmer, what else could you do to keep metal objects from harming the cows?

_____

_____

> PLANET DIARY Go to **Planet Diary** to learn more about magnetic fields.

Lab® zone

Do the Inquiry Warm-Up *Predict the Field.*

Vocabulary
- magnetic field • magnetic field lines
- compass • magnetic declination

Skills
- Reading: Identify the Main Idea
- Inquiry: Observe

What Is a Magnetic Field's Shape?

You know that a magnetic force is strongest at the poles of a magnet. But magnetic force is not limited to the poles. It is exerted all around a magnet. The area of magnetic force around a magnet is known as its **magnetic field.** Because of magnetic fields, magnets can interact without even touching.

Representing Magnetic Field Lines Figure 1 shows the magnetic field of a bar magnet. The **magnetic field lines** are shown in purple. Magnetic field lines are lines that map out the invisible magnetic field around a magnet. **Magnetic field lines spread out from one pole, curve around the magnet, and return to the other pole.** The lines form complete loops from pole to pole and never cross. Arrowheads indicate the direction of the magnetic field lines. They always leave the north pole and enter the south pole. The closer together the lines are, the stronger the field. Magnetic field lines are closest together at the poles.

FIGURE 1 ⋯⋯⋯⋯⋯⋯⋯⋯⋯⋯
Magnetic Field Lines
Magnetic fields are invisible, but you can represent a field using magnetic field lines.

✏ **Complete the tasks below.**

1. **Relate Text and Visuals** In the boxes, identify where the magnetic field is strong and where it is weak.

2. **CHALLENGE** Forces that affect objects without touching them are called *field* forces. Is gravity a field force? Explain.

_____

_____

_____

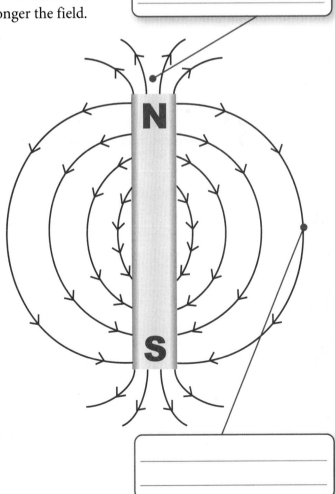

201

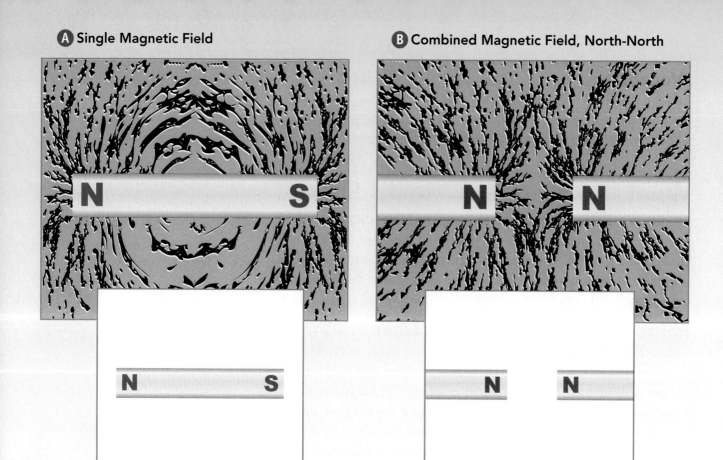

A Single Magnetic Field

B Combined Magnetic Field, North-North

FIGURE 2 ···

▶ INTERACTIVE ART **Magnetic Fields**
Different magnetic pole arrangements will produce different magnetic fields.

✎ **Make Models** In the box below each diagram, draw the corresponding magnetic field lines with arrowheads to show direction.

A Single Magnetic Field Although you cannot see a magnetic field, you can see its effects. **Figure 2A** shows iron filings sprinkled on a sheet of clear plastic that covers one magnet. The magnetic forces of the magnet act on the iron filings and align them along the invisible magnetic field lines. The result is that the iron filings form a pattern similar to magnetic field lines.

Combined Magnetic Fields When the magnetic fields of two or more magnets overlap, the result is a combined field. **Figures 2B** and **2C** show the effects of magnetic force on iron filings when the poles of two bar magnets are brought near each other. Compare the pattern of a north-north pole arrangement and a north-south pole arrangement. The fields from two like poles repel each other. But the fields from unlike poles attract each other, forming a strong field between the magnets.

C Combined Magnetic Field, North-South

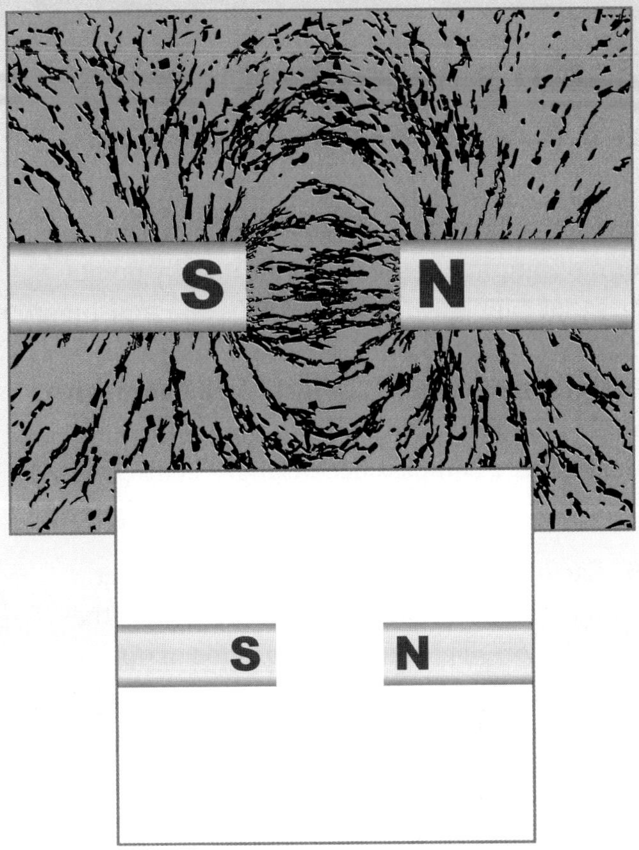

apply it!

When magnets come together, you can feel magnetic forces.

❶ **Observe** You hold two refrigerator magnets and push them toward each other. What will you observe that lets you know that the fields of the magnets are interacting?

_____

_____

_____

❷ **Develop Hypotheses** Why might a magnet that sticks to your refrigerator be unable to pick up a faraway paper clip?

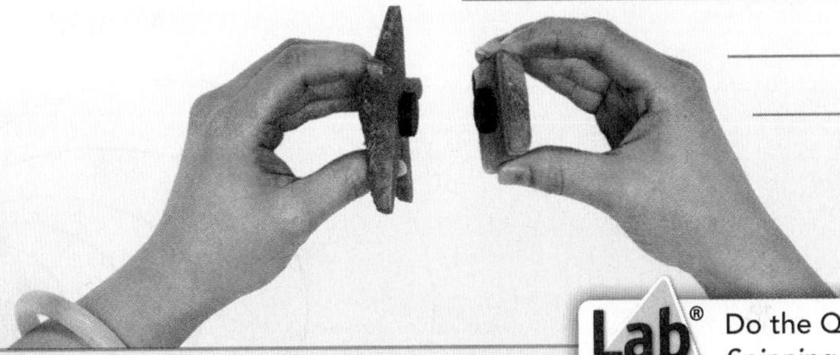

_____

_____

_____

_____

_____

Lab zone Do the Quick Lab *Spinning in Circles.*

Assess Your Understanding

1a. Define What is a magnetic field?

_____

_____

_____

_____

b. Describe Describe the magnetic field of a south-south pole arrangement.

_____

_____

_____

_____

got it? ....

○ **I get it!** Now I know that a magnetic field's shape is _____

_____

_____

○ **I need extra help with** _____

Go to MY SCIENCE ⓢ COACH *online for help with this subject.*

What Is Earth's Magnetic Field Like?

People have used compasses as tools for navigation for centuries. A **compass** is a device that has a magnet on a needle that spins freely. It is used for navigation because its needle usually points north. But why does that happen? In the late 1500s an Englishman, Sir William Gilbert, proved that a compass behaves as it does because Earth acts as a giant magnet. **Just like a bar magnet, Earth has a magnetic field around it and two magnetic poles.** So, the poles of a magnetized compass needle align themselves with Earth's magnetic field. See Earth's magnetic field in **Figure 3**.

Earth's Core Earth's core is a large sphere of metal that occupies Earth's center. The core is divided into two parts—the outer core and the inner core. The outer core is made of hot swirling liquid iron. The motion of this iron creates a magnetic field similar to the magnetic field of a bar magnet.

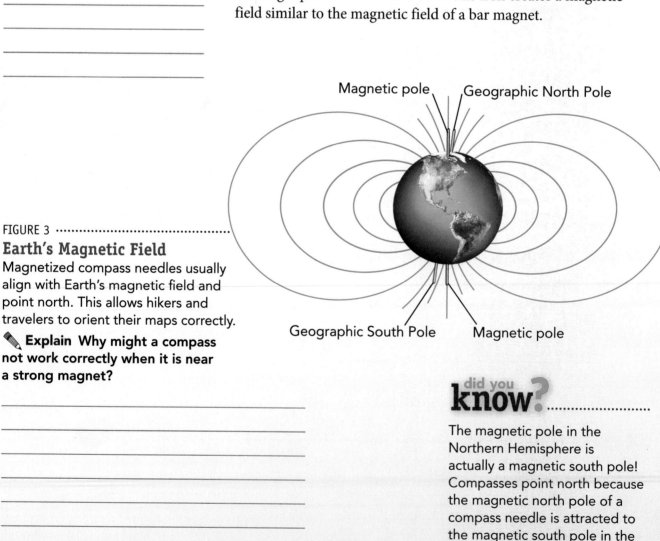

FIGURE 3

Earth's Magnetic Field
Magnetized compass needles usually align with Earth's magnetic field and point north. This allows hikers and travelers to orient their maps correctly.

✎ **Explain Why might a compass not work correctly when it is near a strong magnet?**

_____

_____

_____

_____

_____

_____

⟳ **Identify the Main Idea**
What is the main idea in the Earth's Core section?

_____

_____

_____

_____

_____

did you know?

The magnetic pole in the Northern Hemisphere is actually a magnetic south pole! Compasses point north because the magnetic north pole of a compass needle is attracted to the magnetic south pole in the Northern Hemisphere.

Earth's Magnetic Poles

Earth's Magnetic Poles You know that Earth has geographic poles. But Earth also has magnetic poles that are located on Earth's surface where the magnetic force is strongest. As you just saw in **Figure 3,** the magnetic poles are not in the same place as the geographic poles. Suppose you could draw a line between you and the geographic North Pole. Then imagine a second line drawn between you and the magnetic pole in the Northern Hemisphere. The angle between these two lines is the angle between geographic north and the north to which a compass needle points. This angle is known as **magnetic declination.**

The magnetic declination of a location changes. Earth's magnetic poles do not stay in one place as the geographic poles do.

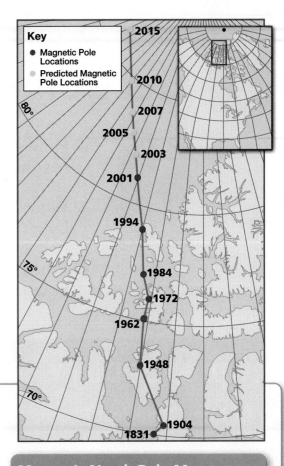

Key
● Magnetic Pole Locations
○ Predicted Magnetic Pole Locations

2015
2010
2007
2005
2003
2001
1994
1984
1972
1962
1948
1904
1831

80°
75°
70°

do the math!

The last expedition to directly observe the pole's location was in May 2001. The map shows estimated positions after 2001.

❶ Calculate What is the total distance the pole traveled from 1948 to 2001?

_____

_____

_____

❷ Interpret Data What was the average speed of the pole's movement from 1948 to 2001?

_____

_____

Magnetic North Pole Movement	
Year of Reading	Distance Moved Since Previous Reading (km)
1948	420
1962	150
1972	120
1984	120
1994	180
2001	287

Lab® zone Do the Quick Lab *Earth's Magnetic Field.*

🔑 Assess Your Understanding

got it? ....

○ **I get it!** Now I know that Earth has a magnetic field _____

○ I need extra help with _____

Go to my science ⓢ coach *online for help with this subject.*

Electromagnetic Force

UNLOCK THE BIG ?

🔑 **How Are Electric Currents and Magnetic Fields Related?**

🔑 **What Is a Magnetic Field Produced by a Current Like?**

🔑 **What Are the Characteristics of Solenoids and Electromagnets?**

MY PLANET DiARY

FUN FACTS

More Than Just Plastic

How do plastic cards with stripes, such as your library card, work? The black stripe on the back of the card is made up of tiny magnetic particles. Information can be recorded on the stripe. When a card is swiped through a card-reading machine, the cardholder's information is relayed from the card to a computer or sent to a place for verification.

If the card is placed near magnetic material, the arrangement of the magnetic particles on the stripe can get rearranged. Once this happens, the card becomes useless because it no longer holds the cardholder's information. If you are ever given a credit card to use, make sure you keep it away from magnets or else you may leave the store empty-handed!

Communicate Discuss the question with a partner. Then write your answer below.

List types of cards that have a magnetic stripe.

_____

_____

_____

_____

_____

_____

> PLANET DIARY Go to **Planet Diary** to learn more about electromagnetic force.

Lab zone® Do the Inquiry Warm-Up *Electromagnetism.*

Vocabulary
- electromagnetism
- solenoid
- electromagnet

Skills
- Reading: Relate Cause and Effect
- Inquiry: Predict

How Are Electric Currents and Magnetic Fields Related?

You know that a magnet has a magnetic field. But did you know that an electric current produces a magnetic field? In 1820, the Danish scientist Hans Christian Oersted (UR STED) accidentally discovered this fact. He was teaching a class at the University of Copenhagen. During his lecture he produced a current in a wire just like the current in a battery-powered flashlight. When he brought a compass near the wire, he observed that the compass needle changed direction.

Oersted's Experiment Oersted could have assumed that something was wrong with his equipment, but instead he decided to investigate further. So he set up several compasses around a wire. With no current in the wire, all of the compass needles pointed north. When he produced a current in the wire, he observed that the compass needles pointed in different directions to form a circle. Oersted concluded that the current had produced a magnetic field around the wire. Oersted's results showed that magnetism and electricity are related.

Cause	Effect
There is no current in the wire.	_____ _____ _____ _____
_____ _____ _____ _____	The compass needles pointed in different directions to form a circle.

✏️
↻ Relate Cause and Effect
Use the information about Oersted's experiment to complete the chart.

Electric Current and Magnetism

Oersted's experiment showed that wherever there is electricity, there is magnetism. **An electric current produces a magnetic field.** This relationship between electricity and magnetism is called **electromagnetism.** Although you cannot see electromagnetism directly, you can see its effect. That is, a compass needle moves when it is in a magnetic field produced by an electric current, as you can see in **Figure 1.**

FIGURE 1 ·······························
Moving Compass Needles
These photographs show you how an electric current produces a magnetic field.

✎ **Interpret Photos** In the boxes, explain what is happening to the compass needles when the current in the wire is turned on or off.

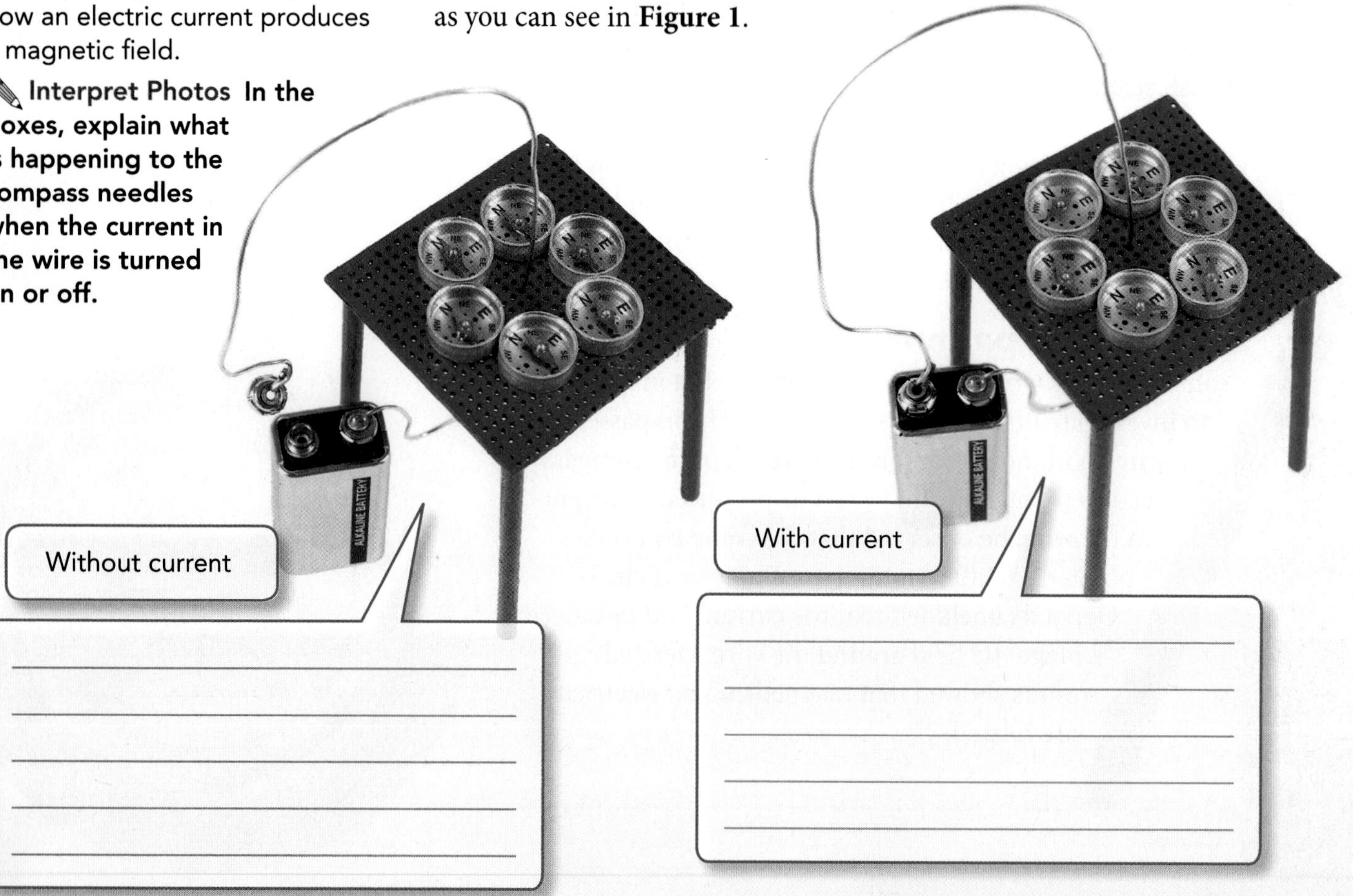

Without current

With current

Do the Quick Lab *Electric Current and Magnetism.*

Assess Your Understanding

1a. Explain What did Oersted conclude?

_____

_____

_____

b. Relate Cause and Effect How does a current affect a compass?

_____

_____

_____

got it?

○ **I get it!** Now I know that an electric current produces a _____

○ **I need extra help with** _____

Go to MY SCIENCE COACH online for help with this subject.

What Is a Magnetic Field Produced by a Current Like?

🔑 **The magnetic field produced by a current has a strength and a direction. The field can be turned on or off, have its direction reversed, or have its strength changed.** To turn a magnetic field produced by a current on or off, you turn the current on or off. To change the direction of the magnetic field, you reverse the direction of the current.

There are two ways to change the strength of a magnetic field. First, you can increase the amount of current in the wire. Second, you can make a loop or coil in the wire. The magnetic field around the wire forms a circle. When you make a loop in a wire, the magnetic field lines bunch close together inside the loop. This strengthens the magnetic field. Every additional loop strengthens the magnetic field even more. **Figure 2** shows three different ways to change the characteristics of a magnetic field.

FIGURE 2 ···

Change Magnetic Field Characteristics

✏️ **Interpret Diagrams** Write the ways used to change the magnetic fields in diagrams A and B. In diagram C, draw a picture to show a third way to change magnetic fields and describe it.

C

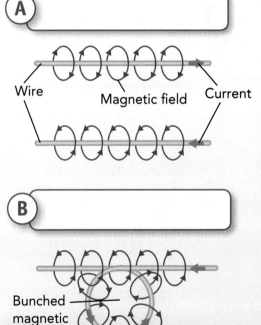

A

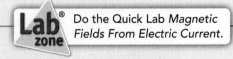

Wire   Magnetic field   Current

B

Bunched magnetic field

Lab ® Do the Quick Lab *Magnetic* zone *Fields From Electric Current.*

🔑 **Assess Your Understanding**

got it? ···

O **I get it!** Now I know that the magnetic field produced by a current can be changed by _____

_____

O **I need extra help with** _____

Go to my science 🔵 coach online for help with this subject.

What Are the Characteristics of Solenoids and Electromagnets?

You know that you can strengthen the magnetic field around a wire with a current by coiling the wire. 🔋 **Both solenoids and electromagnets use electric current and coiled wires to produce strong magnetic fields.**

Solenoids By running current through a wire which is wound into many loops, you strengthen the magnetic field in the center of the coil as shown in **Figure 3**. A coil of wire with a current is called a **solenoid.** The two ends of a solenoid act like the poles of a magnet. However, the north and south poles change when the direction of the current changes.

Electromagnets If you place a material with strong magnetic properties inside a solenoid, the strength of the magnetic field increases. This is because the material, called a ferromagnetic material, becomes a magnet. A solenoid with a ferromagnetic core is called an **electromagnet.** Both the current in the wire and the magnetized core produce the magnetic field of an electromagnet. Therefore, the overall magnetic field of an electromagnet is much stronger than that of a solenoid. An electromagnet is turned on and off by turning the current on and off.

FIGURE 3 ···

▶ REAL-WORLD INQUIRY **A Solenoid and an Electromagnet**
An electromagnet is a solenoid with a ferromagnetic core.

✏️ Interpret Diagrams **Explain how the diagram shows you that the magnetic field of the electromagnet is stronger than that of the solenoid on its own.**

_____

_____

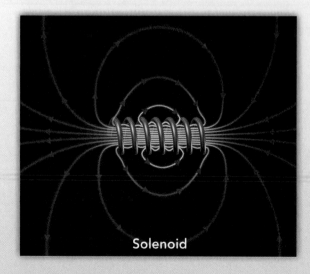
Solenoid

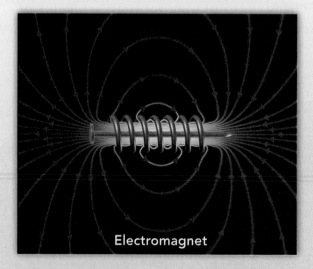
Electromagnet

Regulating Strength You can increase the strength of an electromagnet in four ways. First, you can increase the current in the solenoid. Second, you can add more loops of wire to the solenoid. Third, you can wind the coils of the solenoid closer together. Finally, you can use a material that is more magnetic than iron for the core. Alnico is such a material.

Using Electromagnets Electromagnets are very common. They are used in electric motors, earphones, and many other everyday objects. Electromagnets are even used in junkyards to lift old cars and other heavy steel objects.

Vocabulary Use Context to Determine Meaning Underline clues in the text that help you determine the meaning of *alnico*.

apply it!

An electromagnet makes a doorbell ring. A pushed button closes the circuit and turns on the electromagnet. Current flows through the electromagnet, producing a strong magnetic field.

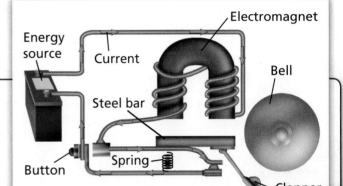

Energy source · Current · Electromagnet · Steel bar · Bell · Button · Spring · Clapper

❶ **Predict** What effect will the magnetic field have on the steel bar? The clapper?

_____

_____

_____

❷ **CHALLENGE** What turns off the electromagnet?

_____

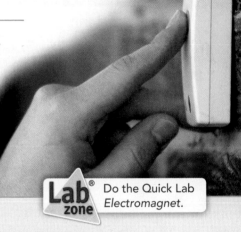

Lab zone Do the Quick Lab *Electromagnet.*

🔑 Assess Your Understanding

2a. Define What is a solenoid?

_____

_____

b. Apply Concepts What are four ways to make an electromagnet stronger?

_____

_____

_____

got it?

○ **I get it!** Now I know that both solenoids and electromagnets _____

_____

_____

_____

○ **I need extra help with** _____

Go to my science COACH online for help with this subject.

Electricity, Magnetism, and Motion

UNLOCK THE BIG ?

🔑 How Is Electrical Energy Transformed Into Mechanical Energy?

🔑 How Does a Galvanometer Work?

🔑 What Does an Electric Motor Do?

mY PLaNeT DiaRY

DISCOVERY

Miniature Motor

In 1960, scientist and California Institute of Technology (Caltech) professor Richard Feynman publicly offered a prize of $1,000 to the first person to build an electric motor no larger than 0.3969 cubic millimeters. A Caltech graduate named William McLellan accepted the challenge. He used a toothpick, microscope slides, fine hairs from a paintbrush, and wires only 1/80th of a millimeter wide to build the world's smallest motor. McLellan showed his tiny motor to Feynman and collected the $1,000 prize. Scientists today have found many uses for tiny motors in products such as high-definition televisions, cars, and ink-jet printers.

A tiny motor capable of producing high-resolution, DVD-quality images.

Communicate Work with a partner to answer the question.

What might be some other uses of tiny motors?

_____

_____

_____

_____

_____

_____

▶ PLANET DIARY Go to **Planet Diary** to learn more about electric motors.

 Lab zone Do the Inquiry Warm-Up *How Are Electricity, Magnets, and Motion Related?*

How Is Electrical Energy Transformed Into Mechanical Energy?

What do trains, fans, microwave ovens, and clocks have in common? The answer is that these objects, along with many other everyday objects, use electricity. In addition, all these objects move or have moving parts. How does electricity produce motion?

Vocabulary
- galvanometer
- electric motor

Skills
↻ Reading: Sequence
△ Inquiry: Graph

Energy and Motion As you know, magnetic force can produce motion. For example, magnets move together or apart when they are close. You also know that an electric current in a wire produces a magnetic field. So, a magnet can move a wire with a current, just as it would move another magnet. The direction of movement depends on the direction of the current. See **Figure 1.**

The ability to move an object over a distance is called energy. The energy associated with electric currents is called electrical energy. The energy an object has due to its movement or position is called mechanical energy.

Energy Transformation Energy can be transformed from one form into another. ⌐ **When a wire with a current is placed in a magnetic field, electrical energy is transformed into mechanical energy.** This transformation happens when the magnetic field produced by the current causes the wire to move.

FIGURE 1 ·····················
Producing Motion
A wire with a current can be moved by a magnet.

✏ **Complete the tasks.**

1. **Identify** What affects the direction of the wire's movement?

_____

_____

2. **Classify** In each box, write down the type of energy that is being pointed out.

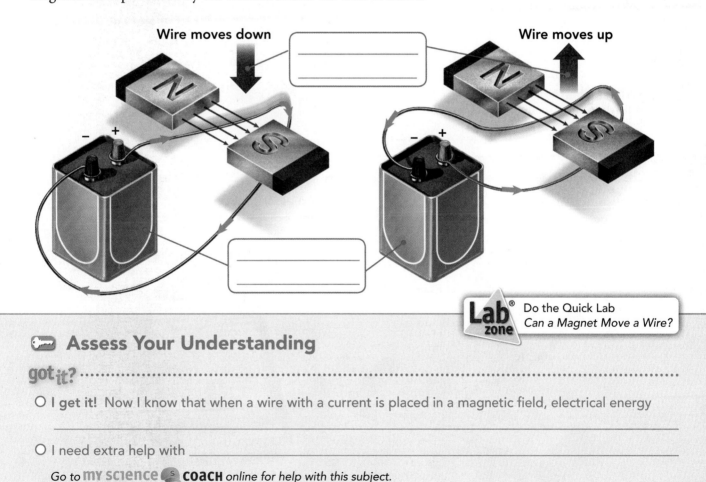

Wire moves down

Wire moves up

⚠ **Lab** zone Do the Quick Lab *Can a Magnet Move a Wire?*

⌐ Assess Your Understanding

got it? ···

○ **I get it!** Now I know that when a wire with a current is placed in a magnetic field, electrical energy

_____

○ **I need extra help with** _____

Go to **my science** ⓢ **COACH** *online for help with this subject.*

How Does a Galvanometer Work?

You have learned that a straight wire with a current moves when it is placed in a magnetic field. But what happens if you place a loop of wire with a current in a magnetic field? Look at **Figure 2.** The current in one side of the loop flows in the opposite direction than the current in the other side of the loop. The direction of the current determines the direction in which the wire moves. Therefore, the sides of the loop move in opposite directions. Once each side has moved as far up or down as it can go, it will stop moving. As a result, the loop can rotate only a half turn.

Inside a Galvanometer The rotation of a wire loop in a magnetic field is the basis of a galvanometer. A **galvanometer** is a device that measures small currents. 🔑 **An electric current turns the pointer of a galvanometer.** In a galvanometer, an electromagnet is suspended between opposite poles of two permanent magnets. The electromagnet's coil is attached to a pointer, as you can see in **Figure 2.** When a current is in the electromagnet's coil, it produces a magnetic field. This field interacts with the permanent magnet's field, causing the coil and the pointer to rotate. The distance the loops and the pointer rotate depends on the amount of current in the wire.

✏️ **Sequence** In the second paragraph on this page, underline and number the steps that explain how a galvanometer works.

FIGURE 2 ··

How a Galvanometer Works

✏️ **Answer the questions about a galvanometer.**

1. **Predict** What would happen if the current flowed in the opposite direction?

_____

_____

2. **Interpret Diagrams** Where does the needle point when there is no current?

_____

A Because the current on each side of the wire loop flows in different directions, one side of the loop moves down as the other side moves up. This causes the loop to rotate.

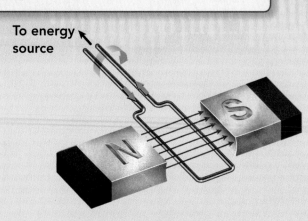

To energy source

B An electromagnet turns the pointer to indicate the amount of current present.

Uses of Galvanometers

A galvanometer has a scale that is marked to show how much the pointer turns for a known current. You can use the galvanometer to measure an unknown current. Galvanometers are useful in everyday life. For example, electricians use them in their work. Some cars use them as fuel gauges. Galvanometers are also used in lie detectors to measure how much current a person's skin conducts. People who are stressed sweat more. Water conducts electricity. Therefore, their moist skin conducts more electric current.

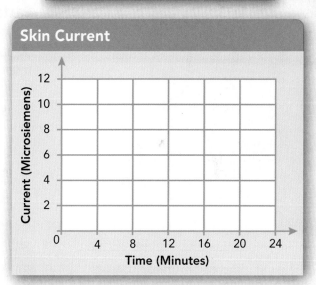

do the math!

This data from a galvanometer show the current conducted by a person's skin. The current is measured in microsiemens, a unit used to measure small amounts of electricity.

Minutes	0	4	8	12	16	20
Microsiemens	5	7	3	1	8	10

1 **Graph** Use the data in the table to plot points on the graph.

2 **CHALLENGE** What would a point at (24, 12) tell you about the person?

_____

_____

_____

_____

_____

_____

Skin Current

Graph with Y-axis labeled "Current (Microsiemens)" marked 2, 4, 6, 8, 10, 12 and X-axis labeled "Time (Minutes)" marked 4, 8, 12, 16, 20, 24

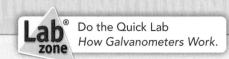 Do the Quick Lab
How Galvanometers Work.

🔑 Assess Your Understanding

1a. Review What does a galvanometer measure?

_____

b. Relate Cause and Effect What causes the pointer to move in a galvanometer?

_____

_____

got it?

○ **I get it!** Now I know that a galvanometer works by using _____

_____

○ **I need extra help with** _____

Go to my science ⁵ coach *online for help with this subject.*

What Does an Electric Motor Do?

Have you ever wondered how a remote-controlled car moves? A remote-controlled car's wheels are turned by a rod, or axle, which is connected to an electric motor. An **electric motor** is a device that uses an electric current to turn an axle. 🔑 **An electric motor transforms electrical energy into mechanical energy.**

Look at **Figure 3** to read about the parts of a motor.

If current only flowed in one direction through the armature, the armature could only rotate a half a turn. However, the brushes and commutator enable the current in the armature to change direction. Current always flows from the positive to the negative terminal of a battery. The current in the armature is reversed each time the commutator moves to a different brush. This causes the side of the armature that just moved up to move down. The side that just moved down will move up. The armature rotates continuously. See **Figure 4.**

FIGURE 3 ···

Parts of a Motor

A simple electric motor contains four parts.

✎ **Observe Which part of an electric motor must be attached directly to the energy source?**

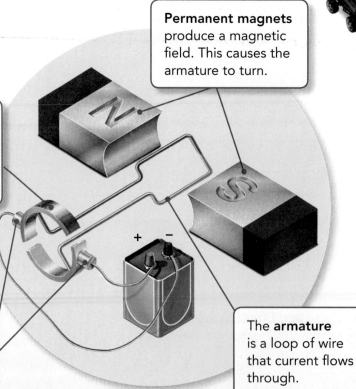

Permanent magnets produce a magnetic field. This causes the armature to turn.

The **commutator** consists of two semicircular pieces of metal. It conducts current from the brushes to the armature.

Brushes conduct current to the rest of the commutator. They do not move.

The **armature** is a loop of wire that current flows through.

FIGURE 4 ·····

▶ **INTERACTIVE ART** **How a Motor Works**

The magnetic field around the armature interacts with the field of the permanent magnet, allowing the armature to turn continuously. The direction of the current determines which way the armature turns.

✎ **Infer** Based on the direction the armature is turning in each diagram, draw arrows showing the direction of the current.

The current is in opposite directions on each side of the armature causing one side to move up while the other side moves down.

The commutator rotates with the armature. The direction of current reverses with each half turn so the armature spins continuously.

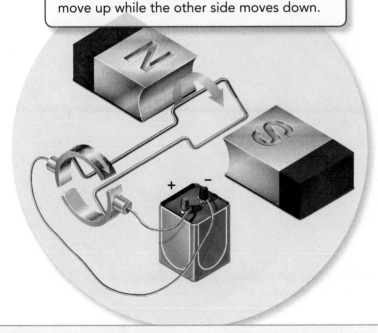

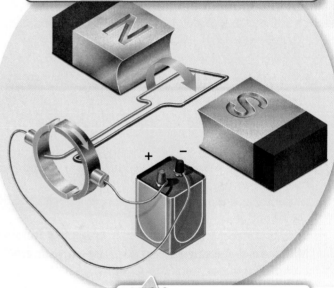

Lab zone — Do the Quick Lab *Parts of an Electric Motor.*

🔑 **Assess Your Understanding**

2a. Define What is an electric motor?

_____

_____

_____

b. Summarize What makes the armature turn continuously?

_____

_____

got it?

○ **I get it!** Now I know that an electric motor transforms _____

_____

_____

○ **I need extra help with** _____

Go to **my science** 💬 **COACH** *online for help with this subject.*

Electricity From Magnetism

🔑 **How Can an Electric Current Be Produced in a Conductor?**

🔑 **How Does a Generator Work?**

🔑 **What Does a Transformer Do?**

my planeT DiaRY

MRI Technologist

Does working in the medical field interest you? Are you good at operating devices? Do you have a knack for soothing anxious people? If you answered yes, you should think about becoming an Magnetic Resonance Imaging (MRI) technologist.

When a patient is put into an MRI machine, radio waves and magnetic fields are used to create images of the patient's internal structures. The doctors use these detailed pictures to determine what is wrong with the patient. The MRI technologist's responsibilities include operating the MRI machine, comforting nervous patients, and maintaining patient confidentiality. You can become an MRI technologist by completing a bachelor's degree program, an associate's degree program, or a certificate program.

Read the following question. Write your answer below.

What do you think might happen to the MRI image if you wore metal jewelry while in the MRI machine? Why?

_____

_____

_____

_____

▶ PLANET DIARY Go to **Planet Diary** to learn more about electricity from magnetism.

Lab zone Do the Inquiry Warm-Up
Electric Current Without a Battery.

Vocabulary

- electromagnetic induction • direct current
- alternating current • generator • transformer

Skills

- Reading: Ask Questions
- Inquiry: Make Models

How Can an Electric Current Be Produced in a Conductor?

An electric motor uses electrical energy to produce motion. Can motion produce electrical energy? In 1831, scientists discovered that moving a wire in a magnetic field can cause an electric current. This current allows electrical energy to be supplied to homes, schools, and businesses all over the world.

To understand how electrical energy is supplied by your electric company, you need to know how current is produced. A magnet can make, or induce, current in a conductor, such as a wire, as long as there is motion. 🔑 **An electric current is induced in a conductor when the conductor moves through a magnetic field.** Generating electric current from the motion of a conductor through a magnetic field is called **electromagnetic induction.** Current that is generated in this way is called induced current.

✎ **Ask Questions** Read the paragraph. Then write two questions that you still have about producing electric current.

_____

_____

_____

_____

_____

_____

_____

_____

_____

_____

Induction of Electric Current

Induction of Electric Current Michael Faraday and Joseph Henry each found that motion in a magnetic field will induce a current. Either the conductor can move through the magnetic field, or the magnet can move. In **Figure 1,** a conductor, the coil of wire, is connected to a galvanometer, forming a closed circuit. If the coil and the magnet do not move, the galvanometer's pointer does not move. However, when either the wire coil or the magnet moves, the galvanometer registers a current. Moving the coil or the magnet induces the current without any voltage source. The direction of an induced current depends on the direction that the coil or magnet moves. When the motion is reversed, the direction of the current also reverses.

FIGURE 1 ·······················

Motion Produces a Current

Electric current is induced in a wire whenever the magnetic field around it is changing. The field changes when either the magnet or the wire moves.

✎ **Complete the tasks.**

1. **Describe** Under each diagram, label the direction of the current using *clockwise* or *counterclockwise*.

2. **CHALLENGE** Make a general statement that relates the motion of the circuit (up or down) to the direction of the current (clockwise or counterclockwise).

_____
_____
_____
_____
_____
_____
_____
_____
_____

Moving Coil

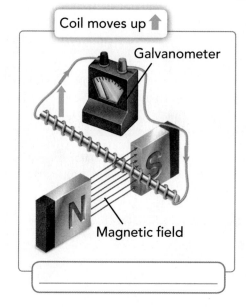

Coil moves up ⬆

Galvanometer

Magnetic field

_____

Coil moves down ⬇

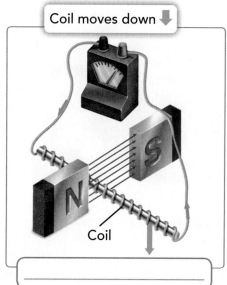

Coil

_____

Moving Magnet

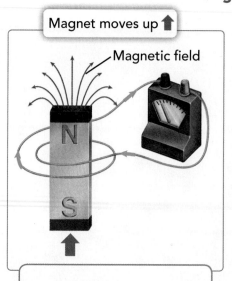

Magnet moves up ⬆

Magnetic field

_____

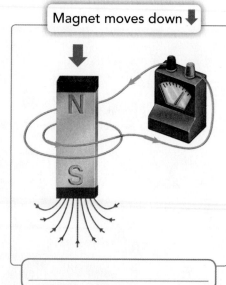

Magnet moves down ⬇

_____

Alternating and Direct Current A current with charges that flow in one direction is called **direct current,** or DC. A battery produces direct current when a battery is placed in a circuit and charges flow in one direction. They move from one end of the battery, around the circuit, and into the other end of the battery.

If a wire in a magnetic field changes direction repeatedly, the induced current also keeps changing direction. A constantly reversing current is called **alternating current,** or AC. You could induce alternating current by moving either the coil or the magnet up and down repeatedly in the **Figure 1** circuit.

Alternating current has a major advantage over direct current. An AC voltage can be easily raised or lowered. This means that a high voltage can be used to send electrical energy over great distances. Then the voltage can be reduced to a safer level for everyday use. The electric current in the circuits in homes, schools, and other buildings is alternating current. Look at **Figure 2** to learn about how electricity has changed over time.

1880

1860

1882
Direct Current
Thomas Edison opens a generating plant in New York City. It serves an area of about 2.6 square kilometers.

1888
Alternating Current
Nikola Tesla receives patents for a system of distributing alternating current.

Today
Direct and Alternating Current
An electric car runs on direct current from its battery. However, alternating current is needed to charge the battery.

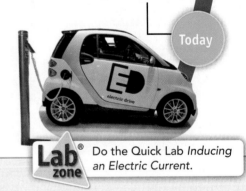

Today

FIGURE 2 ....
The History of Electricity
The work of several scientists brought electricity from the laboratory into everyday use.

✎ **Draw Conclusions** Why do you think we use alternating current today?

_____

_____

Lab ® Do the Quick Lab *Inducing*
zone *an Electric Current.*

🔑 **Assess Your Understanding**

1a. Describe What is one way to induce an electric current?

_____

_____

b. Classify Give an example of an electronic appliance that runs on AC and one that runs on DC.

_____

_____

got_it? ....

○ **I get it!** Now I know that electric current is induced when _____

_____

○ I need extra help with _____

Go to my science ⓢ **coach** *online for help with this subject.*

How Does a Generator Work?

An electric **generator** is a device that transforms mechanical energy into electrical energy. 🗝 **A generator uses motion in a magnetic field to produce current.**

In **Figure 3,** you can see how an AC generator works. Turn the crank, and the armature rotates in the magnetic field. As the armature rotates, one side of it moves up as the other moves down. This motion induces a current in the armature. Slip rings turn with the armature. The turning slip rings allow current to flow into the brushes. When the brushes are connected to a circuit, the generator can be used as an energy source.

The electric company uses giant generators to produce most of the electrical energy you use each day. Huge turbines turn the armatures of the generators. Turbines are circular devices with many blades. They spin when water, steam, or hot gas flows through them. This turns the armatures, which generates electric current.

FIGURE 3 ·······

> INTERACTIVE ART **How a Generator Works**

In a generator, an armature rotates in a magnetic field to induce a current.

✎ **Describe** Write what each part of the generator does in the boxes.

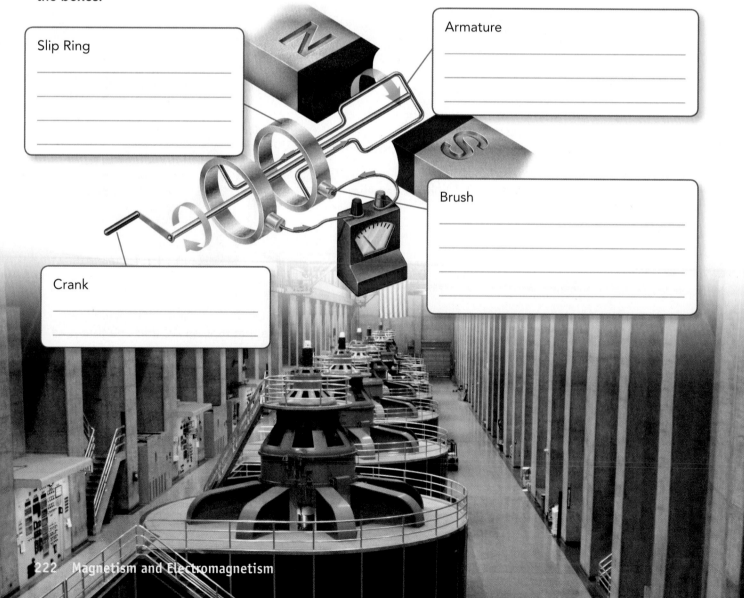

Slip Ring

Armature

Brush

Crank

EXPLORE THE BIG **?**

How are electricity and magnetism related?

FIGURE 4 ···
Wind-up cell phone chargers are small generators that let you charge your cell phone anywhere.

✎ **Analyze Models and Systems** Complete the tasks below.

When I turn the crank of the wind-up cell phone charger, or generator, I turn an armature in a(n) _____.
This generates a(n) _____ in the wire, which powers the phone.

If you connect the output wires of the charger to a battery, _____ will flow through the armature, producing a _____. The permanent magnet in the charger will then cause the armature to _____. Draw what you will observe that lets you know this is happening.

 Lab zone ® Do the Quick Lab *How Generators Work.*

🔑 Assess Your Understanding

2a. Review What is one way to induce an electric current?

_____

_____

_____

b. ANSWER THE BIG **?** How are electricity and magnetism related?

_____

_____

_____

_____

got it? ···

○ **I get it!** Now I know an electric current is induced when _____

_____

○ **I need extra help with** _____

Go to **my science ⑤ coach** online for help with this subject.

What Does a Transformer Do?

The electrical energy generated by electric companies is transmitted over long distances at very high voltages. However, in your home, electrical energy is used at much lower voltages. Transformers change the voltage so you can use electricity.

🔑 **A transformer is a device that increases or decreases voltage.** A **transformer** consists of two separate coils of insulated wire wrapped around an iron core. The primary coil is connected to a circuit with a voltage source and alternating current. The secondary coil is connected to a separate circuit that does not contain a voltage source. The changing current in the primary coil produces a changing magnetic field. This changing magnetic field induces a current in the secondary coil.

The change in voltage from the primary coil to the secondary coil depends on the number of loops in each coil. In step-up transformers, as shown in **Figure 5,** the primary coil has fewer loops than the secondary coil. Step-up transformers increase voltage. In step-down transformers, the primary coil has more loops. Voltage is reduced. The greater the difference between the number of primary and secondary coils in a transformer, the more the voltage will change. The relationship is a ratio.

$$\frac{\text{voltage}_{\text{primary}}}{\text{voltage}_{\text{secondary}}} = \frac{\text{coils}_{\text{primary}}}{\text{coils}_{\text{secondary}}}$$

$$\frac{120\text{ v}}{6\text{ v}} = 20$$

In this transformer, the voltage in the primary coil is twenty times higher than the voltage in the secondary coil. This means there are twenty times as many loops in the primary coil as there are in the secondary coil. If the primary coil has forty loops, then the secondary coil has two.

FIGURE 5 ·······························

Transformers

A step-up transformer, like the one shown below, is used to help transmit electricity from generating plants. Step-down transformers are used in power cords for some small electronics.

✏️ **Make Models** Draw wire loops to show both the primary and secondary coils of this step-down transformer.

This kind of plug contains a step-down transformer.

Step-Up Transformer

Primary coil   Secondary coil

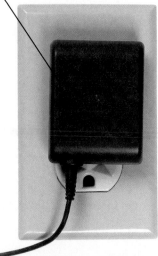

Step-Down Transformer

do the math!

Transforming Electricity

The illustration shows how transformers change voltage between the generating plant and your home. For each transformer in the illustration below, state whether it is a step-up or step-down transformer.

In the boxes, calculate the ratio of loops in the primary coil to loops in the secondary coil.

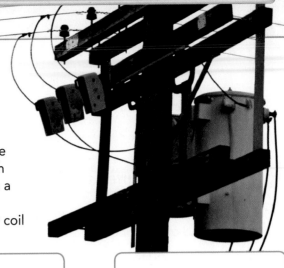

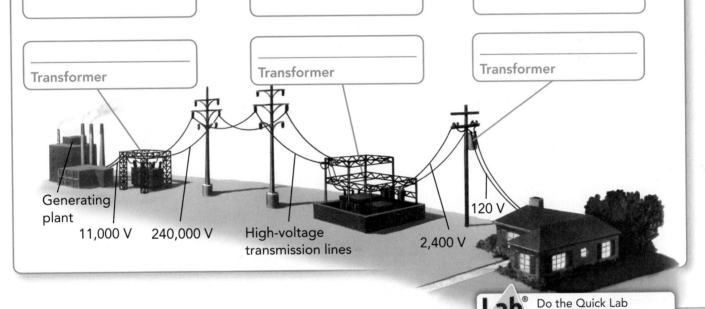

Transformer

Transformer

Transformer

Generating plant

11,000 V   240,000 V

High-voltage transmission lines

2,400 V

120 V

Lab zone ® | Do the Quick Lab *How Transformers Work.*

🔑 Assess Your Understanding

3a. Identify Which coil has more loops in a step-down transformer?

_____

_____

b. Infer Why do some appliances have step-down transformers built in?

_____

_____

_____

got it? ·

○ **I get it!** Now I know a transformer is a device used to _____

_____

○ **I need extra help with** _____

Go to my science s coach *online for help with this subject.*

Study Guide

_____ in a wire produces a _____
and movement of a wire through a _____
produces _____.

LESSON 1 What Is Magnetism?

🔑 Magnets attract iron and materials that contain iron. Magnets attract or repel other magnets. In addition, one end of a magnet will always point north when allowed to swing freely.

🔑 Magnetic poles that are unlike attract each other, and magnetic poles that are alike repel each other.

Vocabulary
- magnet
- magnetism
- magnetic pole
- magnetic force

LESSON 2 Magnetic Fields

🔑 Magnetic field lines spread out from one pole, curve around the magnet, and return to the other pole.

🔑 Like a bar magnet, Earth has a magnetic field around it and two magnetic poles.

Vocabulary
- magnetic field
- magnetic field lines
- compass
- magnetic declination

LESSON 3 Electromagnetic Force

🔑 An electric current produces a magnetic field.

🔑 The magnetic field produced by a current can be turned on or off, reverse direction, or change its strength.

🔑 Both solenoids and electromagnets use electric current and coiled wires to produce strong magnetic fields.

Vocabulary
- electromagnetism   • solenoid   • electromagnet

LESSON 4 Electricity, Magnetism, and Motion

🔑 By placing a wire with a current in a magnetic field, electrical energy can be transformed into mechanical energy.

🔑 An electric current turns the pointer of a galvanometer.

🔑 An electric motor transforms electrical energy into mechanical energy.

Vocabulary
- galvanometer   • electric motor

LESSON 5 Electricity From Magnetism

🔑 An electric current is induced in a conductor when the conductor moves through a magnetic field.

🔑 A generator uses motion in a magnetic field to produce current.

🔑 A transformer is a device that increases or decreases voltage.

Vocabulary
- electromagnetic induction   • direct current
- alternating current   • generator   • transformer

Review and Assessment

LESSON 1 What Is Magnetism?

1. A magnet is attracted to a soup can because the can has

 a. a south pole. b. a north pole.

 c. a magnetic field. d. iron in it.

2. Any magnet, no matter its shape, has two ends, and each one is called a _____

3. **Predict** What will happen to a bar magnet suspended from a string when it swings freely?

_____

_____

_____

4. **Interpret Diagrams** In the diagram, what do the arrows represent? Explain your answer.

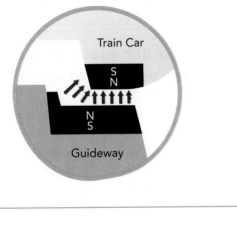

_____

_____

_____

_____

5. **Design Experiments** If two magnets' poles are not labeled, how can you tell which poles are the same and which are different?

_____

_____

_____

LESSON 2 Magnetic Fields

6. A compass works because its magnetic needle

 a. points east. b. spins freely.

 c. points west. d. repels magnets.

7. _____ map out the magnetic field around a magnet.

8. **Make Models** How is Earth like a magnet?

_____

_____

_____

9. **Draw Conclusions** Look at the diagram below. Is the left magnetic pole a north or south pole? Explain your answer.

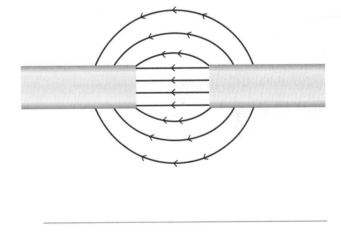

_____

_____

_____

10. **Write About It** Imagine that you are the early inventor of the compass. Write an advertisement for your product that tells explorers how a compass works.

227

Electromagnetic Force

11. The relationship between electricity and magnetism is called

   a. electrical energy.   **b.** induced current.

   c. electromagnetism. **d.** ferromagnetism.

12. A coil of wire with a current is called

  a _____

13. Relate Cause and Effect You have a magnetic field produced by a current. What would you do to change the direction and increase the strength of the field?

_____

_____

_____

_____

_____

_____

Electricity, Magnetism, and Motion

14. Electrical energy is transformed into mechanical energy in a

   a. motor.   **b.** solenoid.

   c. transformer.   **d.** electromagnet.

15. A galvanometer is a device that

  measures _____

16. Compare and Contrast How is a motor similar to a galvanometer? How is it different?

_____

_____

_____

_____

_____

_____

Electricity From Magnetism

17. A device that changes the voltage of alternating current is a

   a. transformer.   **b.** motor.

   c. generator.   **d.** galvanometer.

18. Generating a current by moving a conductor in a magnetic field is _____

_____

19. [**Write About It**] You are a television news reporter covering the opening of a new dam that will help to generate electrical energy. Write a short news story describing how the dam transforms mechanical energy from the motion of the water into electrical energy.

APPLY THE BIG ? **How are electricity and magnetism related?**

20. A crane in a junkyard may have an electromagnet to lift heavy metal objects. Explain how electricity and magnetism work in an electromagnet so that a crane can lift heavy metal objects.

_____

_____

_____

_____

_____

_____

_____

_____

_____

Standardized Test Prep

Multiple Choice

Circle the letter of the best answer.

The graph below shows how a solenoid's loops affect its magnetic field strength. Use the graph to answer Question 1.

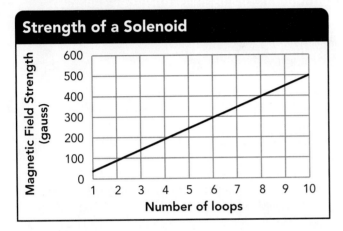

Strength of a Solenoid

1. Predict the strength of a 12-loop solenoid.

   A   300 gauss   B   600 gauss

   C   700 gauss   D   1200 gauss

2. You can increase a step-up transformer's voltage with

   A   a power source connected to the primary coil.

   B   a source connected to the secondary coil.

   C   increasing the number of loops in the primary coil.

   D   increasing the number of loops in the secondary coil.

3. To measure the current induced by moving a wire through a magnetic field, which piece of equipment would a scientist need?

   A   a galvanometer

   B   a transformer

   C   an insulated wire

   D   an LED

4. What happens when a magnet moves through a coil of wire?

   A   The magnet loses magnetism.

   B   A current is induced in the wire.

   C   A current is induced in the magnet.

   D   Electrical energy is transformed into mechanical energy.

5. How could you modify a solenoid to produce a stronger magnetic field?

   A   Remove loops from the solenoid.

   B   Convert the solenoid to an electromagnet by adding a ferromagnetic core.

   C   Wind the loops farther apart.

   D   Decrease the current in the solenoid.

Constructed Response

Use the diagram below and your knowledge of science to help you answer Question 6. Write your answer on a separate sheet of paper.

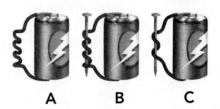

A   B   C

6. Three electromagnets are illustrated in the diagram above. Will the electromagnet labeled A or B produce a stronger magnetic field? Will the electromagnet B or C produce a stronger field? Explain your answers.

MAGNETIC PICTURES

Now, instead of using X-rays, doctors use magnets to look in detail at systems inside the body. ▼

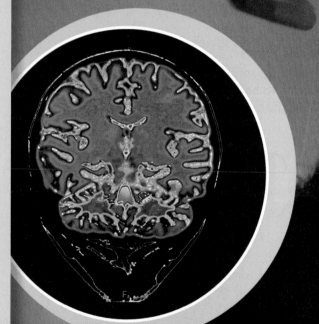

▲ This MRI of a healthy brain shows both hemispheres in bright pink and the cerebellum in green.

Doctors can look inside your body to detect infection, bleeding, or tumors in the brain—without surgery or high-energy radiation that can damage tissues. They can get very detailed views of ligaments, tendons, and muscles that reveal injuries. They can find breast cancers that mammograms miss, and they can map areas of low blood flow after a heart attack. How do they do this? They use Magnetic Resonance Imaging (MRI).

MRI machines use powerful electromagnets, radio waves, and computers to take pictures of the inside of bodies. This process works because human bodies contain so much water. First, the large magnet in the MRI machine aligns the hydrogen atoms in the water molecules within the field. Then, the machine emits a radio frequency pulse that spins all of the hydrogen atoms the same way. The hydrogen atoms release energy in the form of a radio signal as they return to their normal positions, and computers can turn that signal into pictures. Healthy tissues respond differently to the magnet than unhealthy or damaged tissues.

Research It MRI scanning rooms have strict rules about what is allowed inside because metal objects can become deadly. Research the safety concerns for MRI use on humans. Then write a safety brochure to share your findings.

A SHOCKING MESSAGE!

In the 1830s, before the telephone had been invented, people were experimenting with ways to communicate across long distances. Samuel Morse and Alfred Vail discovered that it was possible to use an electromagnet to send a signal through cheap wire.

The electromagnet is part of an electric circuit. On one end of the wire is a telegraph switch. Closing the switch completes the circuit, sending an electric current through the wire. Opening the switch stops the current. On the other end of the wire is a telegraph with an electromagnet, a metal key, and a metal plate. As the electric current flows through the electromagnet, a magnetic field forms.

The metal key is then attracted to the metal plate. The sender can close and open the switch quickly, making a short clicking sound called a "dot" on the other end. Or, the sender can hold the switch closed and create a longer sound, called a "dash." Leaving the switch open for a moment comes across as a "space," or a break in the sounds.

This pattern of dots, dashes, and spaces became a new tool for communicating without using voices—Morse code. Telegraph operators could spell out words and phrases. Three dots, followed by three dashes, followed by three dots, for example, is the Morse code signal for SOS, or help!

Signal It Work with a partner to find resources that will help you construct your own electromagnetic telegraph machine! Predict which materials will best conduct a signal, and then verify your predictions by building a model.

Safety Symbols

These symbols warn of possible dangers in the laboratory and remind you to work carefully.

 Safety Goggles Wear safety goggles to protect your eyes in any activity involving chemicals, flames or heating, or glassware.

 Lab Apron Wear a laboratory apron to protect your skin and clothing from damage.

 Breakage Handle breakable materials, such as glassware, with care. Do not touch broken glassware.

 Heat-Resistant Gloves Use an oven mitt or other hand protection when handling hot materials such as hot plates or hot glassware.

 Plastic Gloves Wear disposable plastic gloves when working with harmful chemicals and organisms. Keep your hands away from your face, and dispose of the gloves according to your teacher's instructions.

 Heating Use a clamp or tongs to pick up hot glassware. Do not touch hot objects with your bare hands.

 Flames Before you work with flames, tie back loose hair and clothing. Follow instructions from your teacher about lighting and extinguishing flames.

 No Flames When using flammable materials, make sure there are no flames, sparks, or other exposed heat sources present.

 Corrosive Chemical Avoid getting acid or other corrosive chemicals on your skin or clothing or in your eyes. Do not inhale the vapors. Wash your hands after the activity.

 Poison Do not let any poisonous chemical come into contact with your skin, and do not inhale its vapors. Wash your hands when you are finished with the activity.

 Fumes Work in a well-ventilated area when harmful vapors may be involved. Avoid inhaling vapors directly. Only test an odor when directed to do so by your teacher, and use a wafting motion to direct the vapor toward your nose.

 Sharp Object Scissors, scalpels, knives, needles, pins, and tacks can cut your skin. Always direct a sharp edge or point away from yourself and others.

 Animal Safety Treat live or preserved animals or animal parts with care to avoid harming the animals or yourself. Wash your hands when you are finished with the activity.

 Plant Safety Handle plants only as directed by your teacher. If you are allergic to certain plants, tell your teacher; do not do an activity involving those plants. Avoid touching harmful plants such as poison ivy. Wash your hands when you are finished with the activity.

 Electric Shock To avoid electric shock, never use electrical equipment around water, or when the equipment is wet or your hands are wet. Be sure cords are untangled and cannot trip anyone. Unplug equipment not in use.

 Physical Safety When an experiment involves physical activity, avoid injuring yourself or others. Alert your teacher if there is any reason you should not participate.

 Disposal Dispose of chemicals and other laboratory materials safely. Follow the instructions from your teacher.

 Hand Washing Wash your hands thoroughly when finished with an activity. Use soap and warm water. Rinse well.

 General Safety Awareness When this symbol appears, follow the instructions provided. When you are asked to develop your own procedure in a lab, have your teacher approve your plan before you go further.

Using a Laboratory Balance

The laboratory balance is an important tool in scientific investigations. You can use a balance to determine the masses of materials that you study or experiment with in the laboratory.

Different kinds of balances are used in the laboratory. One kind of balance is the triple-beam balance. The balance that you may use in your science class is probably similar to the balance illustrated in this Appendix. **To use the balance properly, you should learn the name, location, and function of each part of the balance you are using. What kind of balance do you have in your science class?**

The Triple-Beam Balance

The triple-beam balance is a single-pan balance with three beams calibrated in grams. The back, or 100-gram, beam is divided into ten units of 10 grams each. The middle, or 500-gram, beam is divided into five units of 100 grams each. The front, or 10-gram, beam is divided into ten units of 1 gram each. Each of the units on the front beam is further divided into units of 0.1 gram. What is the largest mass you could find with a triple-beam balance?

The following procedure can be used to find the mass of an object with a triple-beam balance:
1. Place the object on the pan.
2. Move the rider on the middle beam notch by notch until the horizontal pointer on the right drops below zero. Move the rider back one notch.
3. Move the rider on the back beam notch by notch until the pointer again drops below zero. Move the rider back one notch.
4. Slowly slide the rider along the front beam until the pointer stops at the zero point.
5. The mass of the object is equal to the sum of the readings on the three beams.

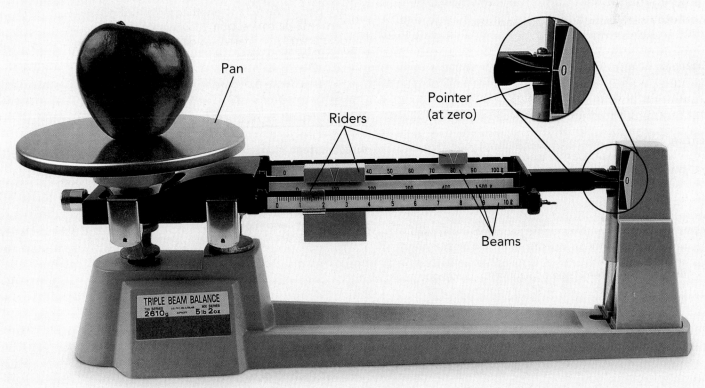

Pan

Riders

Pointer (at zero)

Beams

TRIPLE BEAM BALANCE
2610 g   5 lb 2 oz

GLOSSARY

A

absolute zero The temperature at which no more energy can be removed from matter. (137)
cero absoluto Temperatura a cuyo punto ya no se puede extraer energía de la materia.

acceleration The rate at which velocity changes. (16)
aceleración Ritmo al que cambia la velocidad.

alternating current Current consisting of charges that move back and forth in a circuit. (221)
corriente alterna Corriente de cargas eléctricas que se mueven hacia delante y hacia atrás en un circuito.

average speed The overall rate of speed at which an object moves; calculated by dividing the total distance an object travels by the total time. (10)
velocidad media Índice de velocidad general de un objeto en movimiento; se calcula dividiendo la distancia total recorrida por el tiempo total empleado.

C

Celsius scale The temperature scale on which water freezes at 0°C and boils at 100°C. (137)
escala Celsius Escala de temperatura en la que el punto de congelación del agua es 0°C y el punto de ebullición es 100°C.

centripetal force A force that causes an object to move in a circle. (59)
fuerza centrípeta Fuerza que hace que un objeto se mueva circularmente.

chemical energy A form of potential energy that is stored in chemical bonds between atoms. (119)
energía química Forma de energía potencial almacenada en los enlaces químicos de los átomos.

circuit breaker A reusable safety switch that breaks the circuit when the current becomes too high. (185)
interruptor de circuito Interruptor de seguridad reutilizable que corta un circuito cuando la corriente es demasiado alta.

compass A device with a magnetized needle that can spin freely; a compass needle always points north. (204)
brújula Instrumento con una aguja imantada que puede girar libremente; la aguja siempre apunta hacia el norte.

compound machine A device that combines two or more simple machines. (96)
máquina compuesta Dispositivo que combina dos o más máquinas simples.

conduction 1. The transfer of thermal energy from one particle of matter to another. (141) 2. A method of charging an object by allowing electrons to flow from one object to another object through direct contact. (162)
conducción 1. Transferencia de energía térmica de una partícula de materia a otra. 2. Método de transferencia de electricidad que consiste en permitir que los electrones fluyan por contacto directo de un cuerpo a otro.

conductor 1. A material that conducts heat well. (145) 2. A material that allows electric charges to flow. (169)
conductor 1. Material que puede conducir bien el calor. 2. Material que no permite fácilmente que las cargas eléctricas fluyan.

conservation of charge The law that states that charges are neither created nor destroyed. (162)
conservación de carga eléctrica Ley que establece que las cargas no se crean ni se destruyen.

convection The transfer of thermal energy by the movement of a fluid. (141)
convección Transferencia de energía térmica por el movimiento de un líquido.

convection current The movement of a fluid, caused by differences in temperature, that transfers heat from one part of the fluid to another. (141)
corriente de convección Movimiento de un líquido ocasionado por diferencias de temperatura y que transfiere calor de un área del líquido a otra.

D

direct current Current consisting of charges that flow in only one direction in a circuit. (221)
corriente directa Corriente de cargas eléctricas que fluyen en una sola dirección en un circuito.

distance The length of the path between two points. (7)
distancia Medida del espacio entre dos puntos.

efficiency The percentage of the input work that is converted to output work. (82)
eficiencia Porcentaje del trabajo aportado que se convierte en trabajo producido.

elastic potential energy The energy of stretched or compressed objects. (113)
energía elástica potencial Energía de los cuerpos estirados o comprimidos.

electric circuit A complete, unbroken path through which electric charges can flow. (168)
circuito eléctrico Trayecto completo y continuo a través del cual pueden fluir las cargas eléctricas.

electric current The continuous flow of electric charges through a material. (167)
corriente eléctrica Flujo continuo de cargas eléctricas a través de un material.

electric field The region around a charged object where the object's electric force is exerted on other charged objects. (160)
campo eléctrico Región alrededor de un objeto cargado, donde su fuerza eléctrica interactúa con otros objetos cargados eléctricamente.

electric force The force between charged objects. (159)
fuerza eléctrica Fuerza entre cuerpos cargados eléctricamente.

electric motor A device that transforms electrical energy to mechanical energy. (216)
motor eléctrico Instrumento que convierte la energía eléctrica en energía mecánica.

electrical energy The energy of electric charges. (118, 213)
energía eléctrica Energía de las cargas eléctricas.

electromagnet A magnet created by wrapping a coil of wire with a current around a ferromagnetic core. (210)
electroimán Imán creado al enrollar una espiral de alambre con corriente alrededor de un núcleo ferromagnético.

electromagnetic energy The energy of light and other forms of radiation, which travels through space as waves. (119)
energía electromagnética Energía de la luz y otras formas de radiación, que viaja a través del espacio en forma de ondas.

electromagnetic induction The process of generating an electric current from the motion of a conductor through a magnetic field. (219)
inducción electromagnética Proceso por el cual se genera una corriente eléctrica a partir del movimiento de un conductor a través de un campo magnético.

electromagnetic wave 1. A wave made up of a combination of a changing electric field and a changing magnetic field. 2. A wave that transfers electric and magnetic energy through the vacuum of space. (69)
onda electromagnética 1. Onda formada por la combinación de un campo eléctrico cambiante y un campo magnético cambiante. 2. Onda que transfiere energía eléctrica y magnética a través del vacío del espacio.

electromagnetism The relationship between electricity and magnetism. (208)
electromagnetismo Relación entre la electricidad y el magnetismo.

energy The ability to do work or cause change. (108, 213)
energía Capacidad para realizar un trabajo o producir cambios.

energy transformation A change from one form of energy to another; also called an energy conversion. (120)
transformación de la energía Cambio de una forma de energía a otra; también se le llama conversión de energía.

Fahrenheit scale The temperature scale on which water freezes at 32°F and boils at 212°F. (137)
escala Fahrenheit Escala de temperatura en la que el punto de congelación del agua es 32°F y el punto de ebullición es 212°F.

fluid friction Friction that occurs as an object moves through a fluid. (39)
fricción de fluido Fricción que ocurre cuando un cuerpo se mueve a través de un fluido.

force A push or pull exerted on an object. (33)
fuerza Empuje o atracción que se ejerce sobre un cuerpo.

free fall The motion of a falling object when the only force acting on it is gravity. (57)
caída libre Movimiento de un objeto que cae cuando la única fuerza que actúa sobre éste es la gravedad.

friction 1. The force that two surfaces exert on each other when they rub against each other. (37) **2.** The transfer of electrons from one uncharged object to another uncharged object by rubbing. (162)
fricción 1. Fuerza que dos superficies ejercen una sobre la otra al frotarse. **2.** Transferencia de electrones al frotarse un cuerpo no cargado con otro cuerpo no cargado.

fulcrum The fixed point around which a lever pivots. (88)
fulcro Punto fijo en torno al cual gira una palanca.

fuse A safety device with a thin metal strip that will melt if too much current passes through a circuit. (185)
fusible Elemento de seguridad que tiene una tira metálica delgada que se derrite si una corriente demasiado fuerte pasa por un circuito.

G

---

galvanometer A device that uses an electromagnet to detect small amounts of current. (214)
galvanómetro Instrumento que usa un electroimán para detectar la intensidad de una pequeña corriente.

generator A device that transforms mechanical energy into electrical energy. (222)
generador eléctrico Instrumento que convierte la energía mecánica en energía eléctrica.

gravitational potential energy Potential energy that depends on the height of an object. (112)
energía gravitatoria potencial Energía potencial que depende de la altura de un cuerpo.

gravity The attractive force between objects; the force that moves objects downhill. (41)
gravedad Fuerza que atrae a los cuerpos entre sí; fuerza que mueve un cuerpo cuesta abajo.

grounded Allowing charges to flow directly from the circuit into the building's ground wire and then into Earth in the event of a short circuit. (185)
conectado a tierra Permitir que las cargas eléctricas fluyan directamente del circuito al cable a tierra del edificio y luego a la Tierra en caso de un cortocircuito.

H

---

heat The transfer of thermal energy from a warmer object to a cooler object. (139)
calor Transferencia de energía térmica de un cuerpo más cálido a uno menos cálido.

I

---

inclined plane A simple machine that is a flat, sloped surface. (85)
plano inclinado Máquina simple que consiste en una superficie plana con pendiente.

induction A method of redistributing the charge on an object by means of the electric field of another object; the objects have no direct contact. (163)
inducción Método de redistribuir la carga de un cuerpo haciendo uso del campo eléctrico de otro; los cuerpos no están en contacto directo.

inertia The tendency of an object to resist a change in motion. (45)
inercia Tendencia de un objeto a resistir un cambio en su movimiento.

input force The force exerted on a machine. (77)
fuerza aplicada Fuerza que se ejerce sobre una máquina.

instantaneous speed The speed of an object at one instant of time. (11)
velocidad instantánea Velocidad de un objeto en un instante del tiempo.

insulator 1. A material that does not conduct heat well. (145) **2.** A material that does not easily allow electric charges to flow. (169)
aislante 1. Material que no conduce bien el calor. **2.** Material que no permite fácilmente que las cargas eléctricas fluyan.

International System of Units (SI) A system of measurement based on multiples of ten and on established measures of mass, length, and time. (7)
Sistema Internacional de Unidades Sistema de medidas basado en los múltiplos de diez y en las medidas establecidas de masa, longitud y tiempo.

J

joule A unit of work equal to one newton-meter. (73)
julio Unidad de trabajo equivalente a un newton-metro.

K

Kelvin scale The temperature scale on which zero is the temperature at which no more energy can be removed from matter. (137)
escala Kelvin Escala de temperatura en la cual el cero es la temperatura a cuyo punto no se puede extraer más energía de la materia.

kinetic energy Energy that an object has due to its motion. (110)
energía cinética Energía que tiene un cuerpo debido a su movimiento.

L

law of conservation of energy The rule that energy cannot be created or destroyed. (124)
ley de conservación de la energía Regla que dice que la energía no se puede crear ni destruir.

law of conservation of momentum The rule that in the absence of outside forces the total momentum of objects that interact does not change. (54)
principio de la conservación del momento Regla que establece que, en ausencia de fuerzas externas, la cantidad de movimiento total de los cuerpos que se relacionan no cambia.

lever A simple machine that consists of a rigid bar that pivots about a fixed point. (88)
palanca Máquina simple que consiste en una barra rígida que gira en torno a un punto fijo.

M

machine A device that changes the amount of force exerted, the distance over which a force is exerted, or the direction in which force is exerted. (77)
máquina Dispositivo que altera la cantidad de fuerza ejercida, la distancia sobre que se ejerce la fuerza, o la dirección en la que se ejerce la fuerza.

magnet Any material that attracts iron and materials that contain iron. (197)
imán Material que atrae hierro o materiales que contienen el hierro.

magnetic declination The angle between geographic north and the north to which a compass needle points. (205)
declinación magnética Ángulo (en una ubicación particular) entre el norte geográfico y el polo magnético ubicado en el hemisferio norte de la Tierra.

magnetic field The region around a magnet where the magnetic force is exerted. (201)
campo magnético Área alrededor de un imán donde actúa la fuerza magnética.

magnetic field lines Lines that map out the magnetic field around a magnet. (201)
líneas del campo magnético Líneas que representan el campo magnético alrededor de un imán.

magnetic force A force produced when magnetic poles interact. (199)
fuerza magnética Fuerza que se produce cuando hay actividad entre los polos magnéticos.

magnetic pole The ends of a magnetic object, where the magnetic force is strongest. (198)
polo magnético Extremo de un cuerpo magnético, donde la fuerza magnética es mayor.

magnetism The force of attraction or repulsion of magnetic materials. (197)
magnetismo Poder de atracción o repulsión de los materiales magnéticos.

mass The amount of matter in an object. (43)
masa Cantidad de materia que hay en un cuerpo.

mechanical advantage The number of times a machine increases a force exerted on it. (80)
ventaja mecánica Número de veces que una máquina amplifica la fuerza que se ejerce sobre ella.

mechanical energy Kinetic or potential energy associated with the motion or position of an object. (114, 213)
energía mecánica Energía cinética o potencial asociada con el movimiento o la posición de un cuerpo.

momentum The product of an object's mass and velocity. (53)
momento Producto de la masa de un cuerpo multiplicada por su velocidad.

motion The state in which one object's distance from another is changing. (4)
movimiento Estado en el que la distancia entre un cuerpo y otro va cambiando.

N

net force The overall force on an object when all the individual forces acting on it are added together. (34)
fuerza neta Fuerza total que se ejerce sobre un cuerpo cuando se suman las fuerzas individuales que actúan sobre él.

newton A unit of measure that equals the force required to accelerate 1 kilogram of mass at 1 meter per second per second. (33)
newton Unidad de medida equivalente a la fuerza necesaria para acelerar 1 kilogramo de masa a 1 metro por segundo cada segundo.

nuclear energy The potential energy stored in the nucleus of an atom. (117)
energía nuclear Energía potencial almacenada en el núcleo de un átomo.

O

Ohm's law The law that states that resistance in a circuit is equal to voltage divided by current. (176)
ley de Ohm Regla que establece que la resistencia en un circuito es equivalente al voltaje dividido por la corriente.

output force The force exerted on an object by a machine. (77)
fuerza desarrollada Fuerza que una máquina ejerce sobre un cuerpo.

P

parallel circuit An electric circuit in which different parts of the circuit are on separate branches. (179)
circuito paralelo Circuito eléctrico en el que las distintas partes del circuito se encuentran en ramas separadas.

polarization The process through which electrons are attracted to or repelled by an external electric field, causing the electrons to move within their own atoms. (163)
polarización Proceso por el cual un campo eléctrico externo atrae o repele a los electrones y hace que éstos se muevan dentro de su átomo.

potential energy The energy an object has because of its position; also the internal stored energy of an object, such as energy stored in chemical bonds. (112)
energía potencial Energía que tiene un cuerpo por su posición; también es la energía interna almacenada en un cuerpo, como la energía almacenada en los enlaces químicos.

power The rate at which one form of energy is transformed into another. (182)
potencia Rapidez de la conversión de una forma de energía en otra.

pulley A simple machine that consists of a grooved wheel with a rope or cable wrapped around it. (93)
polea Máquina simple que consiste en una rueda con un surco en el que yace una cuerda o cable.

R

radiation The transfer of energy through space by electromagnetic waves. (141)
radiación Transferencia de energía a través del espacio por ondas electromagnéticas.

reference point A place or object used for comparison to determine if an object is in motion. (5)
punto de referencia Lugar u objeto usado como medio de comparación para determinar si un objeto está en movimiento.

resistance The measurement of how difficult it is for charges to flow through an object. (172)
resistencia Medida de la dificultad de una carga eléctrica para fluir por un cuerpo.

rolling friction Friction that occurs when an object rolls over a surface. (39)
fricción de rodamiento Fricción que ocurre cuando un cuerpo rueda sobre una superficie.

S

satellite Any object that orbits around another object in space. (58)
satélite Cualquier cuerpo que orbita alrededor de otro cuerpo en el espacio.

screw A simple machine that is an inclined plane wrapped around a central cylinder to form a spiral. (87)
tornillo Máquina simple que consiste en un plano inclinado enrollado alrededor de un cilindro central para formar una espiral.

series circuit An electric circuit in which all parts are connected one after another along one path. (178)
circuito en serie Circuito eléctrico en el que todas las partes se conectan una tras otra en una trayectoria.

short circuit A connection that allows current to take the path of least resistance. (185)
cortocircuito Conexión que permite que la corriente siga el camino de menor resistencia.

simple machine The most basic device for making work easier, these are the smaller building blocks for complex machines. (85)
máquina simple Aparatos sencillos que facilitan el trabajo; son los componentes de las máquinas compuestas.

sliding friction Friction that occurs when one solid surface slides over another. (38)
fricción de deslizamiento Fricción que ocurre cuando una superficie sólida se desliza sobre otra.

slope The steepness of a graph line; the ratio of the vertical change (the rise) to the horizontal change (the run). (14)
pendiente Inclinación de una gráfica lineal; la razón del cambio vertical (el ascenso) al cambio horizontal (el avance).

solenoid A coil of wire with a current. (210)
solenoide Bobina de alambre con una corriente.

specific heat The amount of heat required to raise the temperature of 1 kilogram of a material by 1 kelvin, which is equivalent to 1°C. (146)
calor específico Cantidad de calor que se requiere para elevar la temperatura de 1 kilogramo de un material en 1°C.

speed The distance an object travels per unit of time. (9)
rapidez Distancia que viaja un objeto por unidad de tiempo.

static discharge The loss of static electricity as electric charges transfer from one object to another. (164)
descarga estática Pérdida de la electricidad estática cuando las cargas eléctricas se transfieren de un cuerpo a otro.

static electricity A buildup of charges on an object. (161)
electricidad estática Acumulación de cargas eléctricas en un cuerpo.

static friction Friction that acts between objects that are not moving. (38)
fricción estática Fricción que actúa sobre los cuerpos que no están en movimiento.

T

temperature The measure of the average kinetic energy of the particles of a substance. (136)
temperatura Medida de la energía cinética promedio de las partículas de una sustancia.

thermal energy The total energy of all the particles of an object. (118)
energía térmica Energía total de las partículas de un cuerpo.

thermal expansion The expansion of matter when it is heated. (147)
expansión térmica Expansión de la materia cuando se calienta.

third prong The round prong of a plug that connects any metal pieces in an appliance to the safety grounding wire of a building. (185)
tercera terminal Terminal redondeado de un enchufe que conecta cualquier pieza de metal de un artefacto con el cable a tierra de un edificio.

transformer A device that increases or decreases voltage, which often consists of two separate coils of insulated wire wrapped around an iron core. (224)
transformador Aparato que aumenta o disminuye el voltaje, que consiste de dos bobinas de alambre aislado y devanado sobre un núcleo de hierro.

V

velocity Speed in a given direction. (12)
velocidad Rapidez en una dirección dada.

voltage The difference in electrical potential energy per charge between two places in a circuit. (171)
voltaje Diferencia en el potencial eléctrico que hay entre dos áreas de un circuito.

W

watt The unit of power when one joule of work is done in one second. (75)
vatio Unidad de potencia equivalente a un julio por segundo.

wedge A simple machine that is an inclined plane that moves. (86)
cuña Máquina simple que consiste de un plano inclinado que se mueve.

weight A measure of the force of gravity acting on an object. (43)
peso Medida de la fuerza de gravedad que actúa sobre un cuerpo.

wheel and axle A simple machine that consists of two attached circular or cylindrical objects that rotate about a common axis, each one with a different radius. (95)
rueda y eje Máquina simple que consiste en dos objetos circulares o cilíndricos unidos, de diferente radio, que giran en torno a un eje común.

work Force exerted on an object that causes it to move. (70)
trabajo Fuerza que se ejerce sobre un cuerpo para moverlo.

Staff Credits

The people who made up the *Interactive Science* team—representing composition services, core design digital and multimedia production services, digital product development, editorial, editorial services, manufacturing, and production—are listed below.

Jan Van Aarsen, Samah Abadir, Ernie Albanese, Bridget Binstock, Suzanne Biron, MJ Black, Nancy Bolsover, Stacy Boyd, Jim Brady, Katherine Bryant, Michael Burstein, Pradeep Byram, Jessica Chase, Jonathan Cheney, Arthur Ciccone, Allison Cook-Bellistri, Rebecca Cottingham, AnnMarie Coyne, Bob Craton, Chris Deliee, Paul Delsignore, Michael Di Maria, Diane Dougherty, Kristen Ellis, Theresa Eugenio, Amanda Ferguson, Jorgensen Fernandez, Kathryn Fobert, Julia Gecha, Mark Geyer, Steve Gobbell, Paula Gogan-Porter, Jeffrey Gong, Sandra Graff, Adam Groffman, Lynette Haggard, Christian Henry, Karen Holtzman, Susan Hutchinson, Sharon Inglis, Marian Jones, Sumy Joy, Sheila Kanitsch, Courtenay Kelley, Chris Kennedy, Toby Klang, Greg Lam, Russ Lappa, Margaret LaRaia, Ben Leveillee, Thea Limpus, Dotti Marshall, Kathy Martin, Robyn Matzke, John McClure, Mary Beth McDaniel, Krista McDonald, Tim McDonald, Rich McMahon, Cara McNally, Melinda Medina, Angelina Mendez, Maria Milczarek, Claudi Mimo, Mike Napieralski, Deborah Nicholls, Dave Nichols, William Oppenheimer, Jodi O'Rourke, Ameer Padshah, Lorie Park, Celio Pedrosa, Jonathan Penyack, Linda Zust Reddy, Jennifer Reichlin, Stephen Rider, Charlene Rimsa, Stephanie Rogers, Marcy Rose, Rashid Ross, Anne Rowsey, Logan Schmidt, Amanda Seldera, Laurel Smith, Nancy Smith, Ted Smykal, Emily Soltanoff, Cindy Strowman, Dee Sunday, Barry Tomack, Patricia Valencia, Ana Sofia Villaveces, Stephanie Wallace, Christine Whitney, Brad Wiatr, Heidi Wilson, Heather Wright, Rachel Youdelman

Photography

All uncredited photos copyright © 2011 Pearson Education.

Front Cover
Soccer player, Mike Powell/Allsport Concepts/Getty Images; **grass,** Ilker Canikligil/Shutterstock; **ball,** Carsten Reisinger/Shutterstock

Back Cover
Carsten Reisinger/Shutterstock

Front Matter
Page vi, Liane Cary/age Fotostock; **vii,** Brian Snyder/Reuters; **viii,** Roland Weihrauch/AFP/Getty Images; **ix,** Max Rossi/Reuters; **x,** Nutscode/T Service/Photo Researchers, Inc.; **xi,** Nick Suydam/Alamy; **xii,** Construction Photography/Corbis; **xiii all,** iStockphoto.com; **xv laptop,** iStockphoto.com; **xvii girl,** JupiterImages/Getty Images; **xx laptop,** iStockphoto.com; **xxii soccer players,** Randy Siner/AP Images; **xxiii,** Darryl Leniuk/Getty Images.

Chapter 1
Pages xxii–1 spread, Liane Cary/age Fotostock; **3 t,** Ingram Publishing/SuperStock; **3 m1,** Daniel Roland/AP Images; **3 m2,** Medford Taylor/National Geographic Stock; **3 b,** Randy Siner/AP Images; **4 bkgrnd,** Paul & Lindamarie Ambrose/Getty Images; **4 inset,** *Portrait of Nicolaus Copernicus* (16th century).

Pomeranian School. Oil on canvas. Nicolaus Copernicus Museum, Frombork, Poland/Lauros/Giraudon/The Bridgeman Art Library International; **5 r,** Louie Psihoyos/Science Faction; **6 inset,** Ingram Publishing/SuperStock; **6 bkgrnd,** Image 100/Corbis; **7 spider,** Thepalmer/iStockphoto.com; **8 bl,** Jillian Bauer/Newhouse News Service/Landov; **8 br,** Bill Ridder/The Paris News/AP Images; **8 disco ball,** Liz O. Baylen/Washington Times/Zuma Press; **9,** John Walton/PA Photos/Landov; **10 t,** Adam Pretty/AP Images; **10 b,** Daniel Roland/AP Images; **10 map,** Adrian Hillman/iStockphoto.com; **11,** Andres Stapff/Reuters/Landov; **12,** Medford Taylor/National Geographic Stock; **13,** Google Earth Pro; **14,** Iconica/Smith Collection/Getty Images; **16,** Kim Taylor/Minden Pictures; **17 t,** David Young-Wolff/PhotoEdit, Inc.; **17 br,** Randy Siner/AP Images; **17 bl,** The Laramie Boomerang/Barbara J. Perenic/AP Images; **19,** John Foxx/Stockbyte/Getty Images; **20,** Gerhard Zwerger-Schoner/Photolibrary New York; **22 t,** Thepalmer/iStockphoto.com; **22 m,** Andres Stapff/Reuters/Landov; **22 b,** David Young-Wolff/PhotoEdit.

Interchapter Feature
Page 26 bkgrnd, Sam Morris/AP Photo; **26 inset,** Neil Munns/AP Images; **27 bkgrnd,** Ralph Crane/Time & Life Pictures/Getty Images.

Chapter 2
Pages 28–29 spread, Max Rossi/Reuters; **31 t,** Mark Humphrey/AP Images; **31 m2,** Darryl Leniuk/Getty Images; **31 b,** David Wall/Lonely Planet Images/Zuma Press; **32,** ColorBlind LLC/Blend Images/Photolibrary New York; **33,** Mark Humphrey/AP Images; **36,** Space Island Group; **37 bkgrnd,** Kate Thompson/National Geographic Stock; **37 l,** Elena Elisseeva/Shutterstock; **37 m1,** Ian Wilson/Shutterstock; **37 m2,** Jeff Whyte/iStockphoto.com; **37 r,** Ron Sachs/CNP/Newscom; **37 inset l,** KMITU/iStockphoto.com; **37 inset r,** Lijuan Guo/iStockphoto.com; **37 inset m,** Brian Palmer/iStockphoto.com; **40 marbles,** Dorling Kindersley; **40 sandpaper,** Steve Gorton/Dorling Kindersley; **40 oil,** Dorling Kindersley; **40 foil,** Clive Streeter/Dorling Kindersley; **40–41,** Darryl Leniuk/Getty Images; **43,** JPL/NASA; **44,** The Picture Desk/Art Archive; **44–45,** David Wall/Lonely Planet Images/Zuma Press; **46,** David Trood/Getty Images; **47,** Andrea Raso/Lapresse/Zuma Press; **48 r,** UPI/drr.net; **48 l,** Mark J. Terrill/AP Images; **49 b,** Kim Kyung Hoon/Reuters; **49 t,** Steve Helber/AP Images; **52,** Crista Jeremiason/Santa Rosa Press-Democrat; **53,** Peter Blackwell/npl/Minden Pictures; **56,** Alaska Stock Images/National Geographic Stock; **57,** Copyright © 1995 Richard Megna/Fundamental Photographs; **58,** NASA; **59,** UberFoto/Alamy; **60,** Mark J. Terrill/AP Images; **63,** Andrea Raso/Lapresse/Zuma Press.

Interchapter Feature
Page 64 bkgrnd, Rick Fischer/Masterfile; **64 inset,** Car Culture/Corbis; **65 b,** Harry Taylor/Dorling Kindersley; **65 t,** Colin Cuthbert/Photo Researchers, Inc.

Chapter 3
Pages 66–67 spread, Roland Weihrauch/AFP/Getty Images; **69 t,** Javier Pierini/Getty Images; **69 m2,** Huntstock/Photolibrary New York; **69 b,** Yiorgos Karahalis/Reuters; **70,** John Stillwell/AP Images; **72,** Laurie Noble/Digital Vision/

this is your book

you can write in it